Georgetown University:

Origin

and Early Years

JOHN M. DALEY, S.J.

GEORGETOWN UNIVERSITY PRESS

Washington, D.C., 1957

TO MY MOTHER

AND IN MEMORY

OF MY FATHER

It is good to see that among the scholarly studies in American Catholic history which are now appearing with ever greater frequency, there is a growing number of college and university histories. Biographies are necessary; so, too, are chronicles of parishes, dioceses, religious orders, of ecclesiastical movements and organizations. But the histories of institutes of higher learning, by reason of their national and even international cultural influence, are particularly indispensable.

Georgetown University enjoys a primacy of honor among the Catholic colleges and universities of the United States. Established in 1789 as the "Academy at George Town, Patowmack River, Maryland," and opened on November 22, 1791, it thus became the first Catholic college in our country. The founder, the Most Reverend John Carroll, first bishop and archbishop of Baltimore and "Father of the American Church," even declared that he rested upon this school all his "hope of permanency and success to our H. Religion in the United States." If the college, through circumstances beyond his control, developed along lines somewhat different from those he had anticipated, it certainly came to fulfill—probably more than fulfill—the substance of his dream. For after the re-establishment of the Society of Jesus in America, Georgetown, entrusted to the Fathers of the Society, not only grew apace, but became parent or protoparent of most of the Jesuit schools, colleges, and seminaries in this country. Surely an institution so venerable and so influential deserves to be the subject of a scholarly history.

Father John M. Daley, S.J., has done a good turn to the University which he serves and to American Church history in general by writing *Georgetown University: Origin and Early Years*. Like most of our American Catholic institutions, Georgetown was founded without an endowment. Inevitably, therefore, her beginnings were marked by years of desperate struggle for survival; and her historian must deal with many administrative details and problems of personnel.

But Father Daley is no mere cataloguer of financial statements, faculty lists, and curricula. He tries always to analyze the character of those in charge of the college, and to re-create their personalities by bringing out their individual traits. As for the early students, although he does not have extensive alumni diaries and correspondence to draw upon, he is nevertheless able to give a representative account of their life, in and out of the classroom.

There are some delightful glimpses of this hardy existence: The 5:00 A.M. ablutions at the quadrangle pump, and dryings at the roller-towels hung between the adjacent locust trees; the lining up according to height in Old North, for the daily parade to dinner in Old South. The long hours spent over the classics: English, Latin, Greek, French; and the long hours devoted to compositions, grandiloquent, perhaps, but *correct!*

The joys of the topmost scholars, rewarded with banquet and holiday; the chagrin of the sluggards, publicly denounced from the Black List, and sentenced to "spend an hour each day . . . at the clock;" the May devotions inaugurated by the Sodality; the debates promoted by the Philodemic and the Philonomosian Societies; the long walks and jaunts into town and country which, despite the vigilance of the prefects, were not without incident; the visits of prominent people, like Washington and Lafayette; the handball games, and the fencing and boxing matches; and now and then, for variety, a minor riot. But I must not go into further detail, lest I spoil the treat which lies in store for the reader.

As one follows Father Daley's good-humored account of the life and times of the earliest men (and boys) of Georgetown (and notes with satisfaction the gentle correctives he administers to a few immemorial legends), one cannot escape the general impression that Georgetown owes not only her origin but her very pattern to Archbishop Carroll. Carroll was always so proper and circumspect that it is rather difficult to savor his personality in the pages of his formal biographies. In the founding of Georgetown, however, we are able to see him at closer hand, more intimately; and the view we get is a revealing one. He emerges as a man of unique foresight and discernment, but of genuine humanity; patient yet truly enthusiastic; always aware that he is setting precedents and always cautious that these be good precedents. An "ardent friend of American liberty" and far more appreciative of the American mentality than even some of his closest confreres, he sees that in this Academy, as in the nation at large, the accidentals of piety and practice must be adapted to the way of thinking of the new nation. It is not without significance that the least successful of the early Georgetown faculty were precisely those who understood least well the point of view of the American boy.

Students and alumni of Georgetown College and University will be particularly grateful to Father Daley for this devoted and competent story of the formative years of Alma Mater. Students of Catholic education and American Catholic history will join them in welcoming the book. Readers one and all will hope that the author or another will quickly add further volumes to this initial volume, continuing the history of Georgetown through the still richer after-years. Those who know Georgetown are proud of her. They would be prouder still if they were more fully acquainted with her fine traditions, with the fine traditions of the school which the Father of the American Church opened so long ago, to "Students of every religious profession," for the "Cultivation of Virtue and literary Improvement," high above the Potomac "on one of the most lovely situations that imagination can frame."

ROBERT F. McNAMARA
Georgetown College, '32.

St. Bernard's Seminary

The founding of any college can never be a matter of purely personal interest or isolated concern. By the very nature of its work and purpose, its dedication to the search for truth and the training of youth to the continuance of that unending search, a college exercises an influence on present and future generations transcending ephemeral considerations of numerical size, elegance of campus and facilities, and even, to a certain degree, eminence and prestige of its faculties. Even reduced to its minimal essentials—"Mark Hopkins on one end of a log and a student on the other"—a college is a phenomenon of social significance and interest.

By consequence, the story of any such foundation is a subject worthy of and demanding the efforts of the historian. Particularly is this true if the history is to attempt a documented recounting and appraisal, rather than to collect the anecdotes and legends. The history, in a word, cannot be confined to the campus alone; but it must take into account also the horizontal plane of the social milieu into which the college is born, as well as the vertical plane of antecedent events, and of succeeding development. The problem facing the chronicler, then, is not only one of accuracy and factual reporting, but in addition the problem of selection of those details which directly or indirectly contributed to the initiation of the college, helped or impeded its development, and illustrate its spirit and peculiar "flavor."

Such details individuate a story otherwise very likely to degenerate into a conventional, not to say stereotyped, pattern. Practically all stories of early days of college life and growth are pretty much standardized: the idea and ideal germinating in the mind of a man or a small group of men; the small and struggling attempts at getting under way; the early difficulties sometimes threatening the very existence of the institution; the quaint customs and regulations inviting hilarious, if not odious, comparison with more modern counterparts; and so forth. The pattern is easily recognizable in innumerable college histories, more especially in those which may lay some modest claim to "antiquity," in the sense of having their roots laid in the pioneering or colonial days of our country.

Many of the above-mentioned details inevitably appear in this present history of the beginnings and first half-century of Georgetown University. They are all part of the story. But beyond these surface manifestations, there is a deeper significance to the founding of Georgetown, which not only individualizes her story, but presents the chronicler with an advantage and with a disadvantage.

The advantage, of course, is that in telling a unique story, he has the sure knowledge that he will not be telling a twice-told tale. The disadvantage is, that in setting the story in its proper scene, he has to recount on occasion facts which are unpleasant and sometimes painful to recall, but none the less historical. They, too, are part of the story.

For, prescinding for the moment from the contribution Georgetown University has made to the last hundred and sixty-eight years, the special significance of her founding lies in the fact that it was a concrete and living exemplification of a principle which is a part of our American way of life, enshrined in our Constitution, namely, the principle of religious freedom, not as a forced or grudging concession, but as a fundamental right, guaranteed by the basic law of the land.

It is this fact which gives the story of Georgetown its special significance. She is the first institution of Catholic higher education in the United States, and as such she is symbolic of the American constitutional principle of religious freedom, with whose birth her own coincides. Previous attempts at such foundations, outlined briefly in the text, were abortive and came to naught, because of the existent colonial laws, dependent on the penal code of the mother country, subjecting the Catholic people of the country to disenfranchisement and disability. Suffice it in this regard to instance only the legislation of October 20, 1654, following the Puritan ascendancy in Maryland, and the acts of the Maryland Legislature of 1704 and of 1756. These are instances of the spirit of intolerance and persecution which we would prefer to forget, but which must have at least some passing mention, in the fulfillment of the canons of impersonal historical truth, and in properly placing the founding of Georgetown in its historical perspective.

The spirit of religious freedom which accompanied the achievement of civil liberty was a notable part of the social atmosphere current in the time of Georgetown's foundation, and the same spirit is reflected in principles and actions of Georgetown's founders, and stated specifically in the preliminary prospectus of 1786.

But to tell the whole story of Georgetown, the historian has to look also, as has been said, at the vertical plane of history, to discover another interesting and significant facet of background and antecedent. This phase must take into account the fortunes of the Society of Jesus, of which all but a few of the founders and early administration and clerical faculty had been members. Chief among these, of course was the founder himself, John Carroll, whose life and career are intimately entwined in the affairs of Georgetown for more than half the period covered in this volume. Equally entwined in its affairs is the history of the Society of Jesus.

Technically, Georgetown was not founded by the Jesuits; for, since the issuance of the Brief *Dominus ac Redemptor*, wrung from Pope Clement XIV on August 16, 1773, by the implacable enemies of the Society in Spain, France and Portugal, the Society was non-existent, save for a tiny remnant in White Russia. And there would be no Jesuits again until 1805, when the surviving members in America were permitted by Pope Pius VII to re-affiliate with this group in Russia, a step towards the complete and universal restoration of the Society of Jesus in 1814. Nevertheless, Georgetown was founded by men who had been trained and fashioned in the Society, and who, though living as diocesan priests and missionaries, retained the spirit, the ideals and motivations of their early training. A major part of the funds for the beginning and early support of the college came from the colonial estates and properties held in trust for the disbanded Society. It was but natural, then, that in their new undertaking Carroll and his associates should follow the principles and the methods of the Society of Jesus, which had proved so successful for two hundred years on the continent of Europe. Thus it is quite true to say that from the beginning, as it is today, Georgetown was a Jesuit institution.

It is a temptation for the historian, himself a member of the Society of Jesus, to dwell on the events of those years between 1773 and 1814, to recall the perseverance and fortitude of the men who dutifully stayed at their appointed tasks, though their hearts were stricken with grief at the dissolution of their beloved Society. But that story has been told and re-told elsewhere; hence only those details of it have been included here which are pertinent to the story of Georgetown's founding. Certainly, one of the primary motivations for the institution of Georgetown was the necessity of replenishing the dwindling number of clergy to take care of a growing population. Not that Georgetown was founded specifically as a seminary—that would come later, with the founding of St. Mary's in Baltimore

—but that vocations to the priesthood could be germinated and fostered only in a Catholic educational atmosphere. In his account of the state of Catholicism in the United States made to the Congregation for the Propagation of the Faith on March 1, 1785 John Carroll, then vicar apostolic, reported that there were approximately twenty-one priests, to care for some twenty thousand Catholics, scattered over a wide area of the eastern seaboard. Many of these were aged and enfeebled by years of hardship and labor. These must be replaced by younger and more vigorous recruits, if the Church were to survive and to progress in America. Further, the Church in America, released from its dependence on ecclesiastical authority in England, must erect its own organization and conduct its own affairs. There must be a succession of native-born priests to carry on these works; and to provide the seedground for vocations, there must be a school.

But for the laity, too, there had to be a beginning of Catholic education, if the faith was to be preserved and enhanced, and the Church to take her proper place in the educational life and influence of the new and growing nation. Certainly, the development of American Catholic higher education has been remarkable since that November day in 1791, when the first Catholic College opened its doors to its first student. Today, there are in the United States some 254 Catholic colleges and universities, with an enrollment of a quarter of a million students.

It is a part of the Georgetown heritage, a source of her just pride and gratitude, as well as of her continuing inspiration, that she was chosen, in the providence of God, to be in the vanguard of this mighty procession. It is her joy that through her efforts more than one presently flourishing sister college was brought into being. And though, in the century and a half and more of her existence, she has been surpassed in numbers and size by others, she yields to none in her unremitting dedication and devotion to the cause for which she was founded; she keeps alive and fresh before her the vision and the zeal of her founder, John Carroll. And not least does she glory in, and find renewed inspiration from, the title bestowed upon her by the late Pope Pius XI, renewed by the present Holy Father, of "Alma Mater of all Catholic colleges in the United States."

The task of acknowledging kind and generous assistance is a pleasant but difficult one. Memory is almost bound to prove faulty. At the outset, then, I wish to say "Thank you" to all those whose identification must, unfortunately, be self made.

To the Reverend William C. Repetti, S.J. of Georgetown University; the Reverend Edward A. Ryan, S.J. of Woodstock College; the Reverend Henry Browne, formerly the archivist of the Catholic University of America; the Reverend Thomas McAvoy, C.S.C. of the Catholic Archives of America, Notre Dame University; the Reverend Joseph C. Teschitel, S.J., archivist of the Society of Jesus, Rome; Brother Joseph Ramspacher, S.J. of the office of the Provincial of the Maryland Province of the Society of Jesus; and to the Very Reverend John Duggan, the Reverend Paul Love, Miss Elizabeth Bradley and Miss Emma Rollman of the chancery office of the Archdiocese of Baltimore I am sincerely grateful. I am likewise indebted to the staff of Georgetown University Library for many time saving helps. For their encouraging and urging the writing I shall always be grateful to Reverend Hunter Guthrie, S.J. and Reverend Edward B. Bunn, S.J., presidents of Georgetown University. For his kindness in writing the preface I am indebted to the Reverend Robert McNamara. A word of thanks must be added to the Alumni of Georgetown University. Their generosity to the Annual Alumni Fund made possible a publication grant. The work, indeed, would not have been finished were it not for the Reverend Joseph T. Durkin, S.J., and the Reverend Stephen Winters, S.J. "Thank you" then seems small.

JOHN M. DALEY, S.J.

Georgetown University

GEORGETOWN UNIVERSITY

CONTENTS

The Gates of Georgetown

CHAPTER I

Earlier Jesuit
Schools in Maryland

Georgetown was not the first Jesuit school in Maryland. Earlier chroniclers of the university's history have on occasion pointed to March 25, 1634, as the day when Georgetown began. On that day Father Andrew White, S.J., with his companions, Father John Altham and Brother Thomas Gervase, had arrived in Maryland with the first settlers. The party had sailed from Southampton in the *Ark* and the *Dove* in late November, 1633. Although no lineal connection may be found between the earlier schools and the founding of Georgetown, one would be guilty of failing to look over the shoulder of the present, were he not to glimpse, at least, these earlier foundations.

Provision for the education of youth did not loom large in the measures of Cecil and George Calvert for the successful administration of their colony.[1] The meager beginnings of things educational undertaken by the Jesuits, had to be supported by the home front in England, and by the lands obtained by the priests as settlers, since "the matter of religious worship or the propagation of the faith did not enter into the accounts

---

[1] Leo Joseph McCormick, *Church-State Relationships in Education in Maryland* (Washington: Catholic University Press, 1942), p. 2.

of liabilities which the proprietary considered to be his. Nor did education."[2]

Much of the teaching done by the early Jesuits had to be limited to small groups and families. One can hardly imagine that this was pleasing to the Society's teachers, trained in the Society's methods and schools in Europe, and imbued with the realization of the high place that education held in their work for the salvation of souls. The general of the Society, Father Mutius Vitelleschi, wrote on September 15, 1640, to Father John Brooks, superior of the mission: "The hope held out of a college I am happy to entertain and when it shall have matured, I will not be backward in extending my approval."[3] No detailed information of the furthering of this plan is available, and it could well be, as some have thought, that "college" only in the sense of a central house of the mission is here referred to. Ten years later, however, the then general, Very Reverend Father Francis Piccolomini, wrote to Father Philip Fisher: "I do not doubt that the school opened by the Father, your companion, will be worth the pains."[4]

On the western shore of the Chesapeake Bay, near Britton Bay and overlooking the distant Potomac, stood Newtown Manor which would come into the possession of the Society of Jesus in 1668. Here sometime after 1653, a school was opened under the direction of Ralph Crouch. Crouch, a very zealous man, is referred to in many accounts, sometimes as a Jesuit priest, other times as a Jesuit scholastic,[5] but more often as Brother Ralph Crouch. He was, in fact, a layman when he came to America.

---

[2] Thomas Hughes, *History of the Society of Jesus in North America, Text,* (New York: Longmans, Green and Co., 1907), Vol. 1, p. 264.

[3] *Ibid.,* p. 346, and *Documents,* Vol. 1, Part I, p. 25.

[4] *Ibid., Documents,* Vol. 1, Part I, p. 39. Philip Fisher was the alias used by Father Thomas Copley, S.J. See Rev. Wm. P. Treacy, *Old Catholic Maryland and its Early Jesuit Missionaries* (Swedesboro, N.J.: privately published, 1889).

[5] McCormick, *op. cit.,* p. 5.

He had been for some time in the novitiate of the Society of Jesus at Watten, but for some reason left the novitiate, and about 1640, came to assist the Jesuit fathers in the Maryland mission. For approximately twenty years he labored, instructing the children in catechism, assisting the fathers and teaching humanities first at St. Mary's city and later in the school at Newtown. In 1659, having returned to Europe, Ralph Crouch was readmitted into the Jesuit novitiate at Watten, and died at Liége on November 18, 1679.[6]

As a necessary source of income for his school, Crouch had established his claim to a grant of land "four thousand acres more or less." This land lay on the north side of the Potomac River and "was bounded on the South and East," the patent of October 26, 1649, tells us, "with said river, on the west with a line drawn North west and by North from a well by Potomeck River called St. Raphaells well, until it fell into a branch of St. Raphaells Creek formerly called Nangeny Creek" and on the north "with said Creek and Branch."[7]

That the Catholic laity soon became interested in such schools is attested to by the fact that some forty-two legacies for school purposes were left between 1650 and 1685.[8] In one such legacy, the importance of Ralph Crouch's school was recognized. On April 4, 1653, Edward Cotten made his will, in which he appointed Thomas Matthews and Ralph Crouch as his executors "to have power to take and dispose of all my whole estate whatsoever in manner and form as followeth." Ninthly on his list of bequests, Edward Cotten wrote: "I doe give all my female cattle and their increase forever to be disposed of

[6] Wm. P. Treacy, "Some Early Catholic Grammar Schools," *United States Catholic Historical Magazine*, I, No. 1 (January, 1887), p. 71.

[7] *Maryland Land Records*, Hall of Records, Annapolis, Liber II, p. 537.

[8] Rev. J. A. Burns, C.S.C., *The Catholic School System in the United States* (New York: Benziger Bros., 1908), p. 94.

. . . unto charitable uses . . . the stocks to be preserved and the profits to be made use of to the use of a Schooll." And, "Twelfthly," he expressed his desire that "if they shall think convenient that the Schooll be kept at Newtowne."[9]

After Ralph Crouch returned to England, it would seem that the institution was closed but later reopened. Father Warner, later Jesuit provincial, speaks of a school in the Maryland mission in which "humane letters are taught with great fruit."[10] Just when the reopening took place is not certain. It would seem to have been about the year 1677, when Father Thomas Gavan arrived in Maryland.[11] In a letter of the English provincial in 1681 reference is made to a school opened four years earlier under the direction of two fathers. That the school was more than a "three R's" academy is indicated by the fact that its boys were deemed worthy of admittance into European colleges. Two, in fact, are mentioned as "second to few Europeans in talent and contended with the best of their class for the first place."[12] One of the teachers of this early school was Thomas Hothersall, a scholastic who used the alias Slater.[13] Mr. Hothersall had been trained at St. Omer's College, and entered the Society of Jesus on June 20, 1668. Although he studied theology, he was, for some reason not apparent, never ordained. He died in Maryland in the year 1698 at the age of fifty-six.[14]

The most important of the early schools was that of Bohemia Manor. About the year 1741 the growth of religious intolerance

---

[9] *Maryland Land Records*, Hall of Records, Annapolis, Liber I, pp. 46-48.

[10] Hughes, *op. cit.*, *Text*, Vol. 2, p. 136. He quotes from Cambridge, *Warner's Note Book*, giving the date of the letter as August 20, 1680. Treacy, *Old Catholic Maryland*, p. 71, gives the date of this letter which was to the Jesuit general as August 30, 1680.

[11] Hughes, *op. cit.*, *Text*, Vol. 2, p. 136.

[12] *Loc. cit.*

[13] Treacy, *Old Catholic Maryland*, p. 72. Treacy is here following the catalogues of the English Province, S.J.

[14] *Loc. cit.*

in the Maryland colony had induced the Jesuits to move the center of their activities to a remote location in the northeastern corner of Cecil County, not far from the Pennsylvania border. The question as to why the Jesuits chose such a wilderness for a school, is best answered by Father Thomas Hughes. His very reasonable estimate is that they feared another forced move, and sought this section which was closer to the friendlier and more tolerant neighbors in Pennsylvania.[15] Here a boarding school was opened at what was termed Bohemia Manor or the Bohemian Manor. Unfortunately, the absence of complete records concerning this institution leaves us in the dark even as to its opening date. Among the more likely dates are 1742 and 1745.[16] Father Thomas Poulton is mentioned as being at Bohemia in 1742, and it was under his direction that the school was opened.[17] Other indications make 1745 the more probable opening year of the school. "Jacky" Carroll, later Archbishop John Carroll, first bishop and archbishop of Baltimore and founder of Georgetown College, was one of the first pupils.[18] He is said to have been about eleven years old when he came there; this would be in 1745 or 1746.

It is hard to overestimate the importance of Bohemia Manor as an educational center. The number of youths from the colony who entered European colleges after their early training at the Manor school, testifies to the great role it played in the future of the Catholic Church in America. The Jesuit procurator in London, who was instrumental in placing many of these youths in European colleges, could hardly have realized the future

---

[15] Hughes, *op. cit.*, *Text*, Vol. 2, pp. 472-473.

[16] McCormick, *op. cit.*, p. 7, says that "it is probable that this school was in operation by 1742."; following Hughes, *op. cit.*, *Text*, Vol. 2, p. 123, p. 520.

[17] Poulton Hall at Georgetown University honors Father Thomas Poulton.

[18] Charles Carroll of Carrollton may also have been a pupil but conclusive evidence is wanting. See E. I. Devitt, S.J. "Bohemia," *Records of the American Catholic Historical Society*, XXIII, No. 2 (June, 1913), 105.

greatness to be attached to the names he scribbled in his register. Nor could the Jesuit who wrote such names as John Carroll and Leonard Neale in the day-book of Bohemia Manor, realize what careers were beginning on that day.[19] Among the first students with John Carroll was Robert Brent, of Aquia Creek, Stafford County, Virginia, whose ancestor had emigrated to Virginia in 1687 under the special protection of James II.

As the opening, so the closing of the school at Bohemia Manor is in doubt. The school was probably discontinued shortly after the death of Father Poulton in 1749.

Our records of the school at Bohemia Manor, as noted previously, are very meager. There exists but a sketchy outline of what constituted the course of study, the number of scholars, and so forth. Apparently there were two courses available: the classical course for which the tuition was forty pounds a year; and another English course, or perhaps a type of commercial course, the tuition for which was thirty pounds. Some have thought, rather, that there was a college preparatory course and an elementary course. The figures of forty and thirty pounds, respectively, are from the record of the schoolmaster, Mr. Wayt, and have been variously interpreted.[20] Considering the fact that the closing of Newtown had been brought about by an Act of the Maryland Assembly of 1704, it is not to be wondered at that the records are so scanty.[21] Secrecy and retirement from the public eye were at a premium. At one time there may have been twenty pupils, hardly a greater number.

What the exact nature of the college preparatory course was is hard to determine. One inquirer has conjectured that the New-

---

[19] *Day-Book of Bohemia Manor, 1745*, Woodstock College Archives (hereafter referred to as WCA), 174A.

[20] Hughes, *op. cit., Text*, Vol. 2, p. 520.

[21] Edward I. Devitt, S.J., "A Dark Chapter in the Catholic History of Maryland," *United States Catholic Historical Magazine*, I, No. 2 (April, 1887), 140.

town school offered a college preparatory course that was woven around, but not limited to, the "three R's." This surmise is based on the assumption that the two youths who were admitted to St. Omer's, had received their preparation at the earlier Jesuit school in Maryland.[22] That of Bohemia Manor would have been similar. It seems quite likely that the Jesuit teachers, trained to follow the traditions of their predecessors, and themselves products of that training, would have used some version of the *Ratio Studiorum,* or Jesuit Code of Liberal Education, and imitated the methods of the Jesuit masters in European schools. As we shall see, Carroll was quite anxious at the time of Georgetown's founding that the methods and courses of the English ex-Jesuit college of Stonyhurst be followed. Whatever the courses in detail offered there, Newtown school and Bohemia Manor school were of great importance in the early educational movements of Maryland. They were of significance to the future of the Church in America, for they were to prepare many students for entrance into European colleges, whence these young men were to return to be the leaders of the Church in Maryland and America.

But they were not Georgetown College in embryo. They have no genealogical link with the College on the hill overlooking the Potomac. Georgetown stands alone. It is a separate foundation. To say that it was but Newtown or Bohemia moved to a new location, is to stretch a point. But it was founded by a man who had attended the school at Bohemia Manor. That school had prepared him for entrance into college; and for that college training—as a mere youth—he had had to make an arduous journey across the sea, and be separated from his loved ones for many years. Is it fanciful to think that at least one of the motives that spurred John Carroll on to found his beloved "Academy,"

---

[22] Rev. James A. Burns, C.S.C., "Early Jesuit Schools in Maryland," *Catholic University Bulletin,* XIII (December, 1907), 388.

was the realization of what he had experienced in his struggle for a Catholic education? Another Bohemia Manor would be built, but it would also include its own St. Omer's. Nor can we overlook the fact that the men of 1789, though their beloved Society had been suppressed some sixteen years before, were still sons of St. Ignatius, imbued with the same tradition of the importance of education—a tradition which had formed so large a part of the thinking of the founders of Newtown and Bohemia Manor. We shall see that when opposition arose to the founding of Georgetown College, its supporters would appeal to the fact that education was dear to the heart of their holy founder, St. Ignatius, and they would argue that it would be to play false to their tradition not to further the plan for the establishment of the college. The minor premise of the argument might change, but the major was written large in the Jesuit tradition. It would be written large on the Georgetown seal: *Utraque Unum— Religio et Scientia.*

CHAPTER II

John Carroll
Returns to America

Seventeen seventy-four. The colonies were soon to disappear. In their place would rise states to be known as the United States, but much time would elapse before they could be called a nation. The materials for a nation were there, but the cohesive force was yet to be found. In 1774 the thirteen colonies had a total population of between two and a half and three million, with approximately equal distribution north and south of the Mason and Dixon line. Virginia still ranked first; with Massachusetts, Pennsylvania, North Carolina, and Maryland following. There were in round numbers half a million Negroes in the colonies in 1775, with but one in every seven above the Mason and Dixon line.[1]

The American of 1774, still stood on the edge of the vast forest of the interior, but he had begun to peer into it more intently. It was yet to be conquered. In 1800, more than two-thirds of the people would still be clinging to the seaboard within fifty miles of tidewater, and the center of population would be resting within eighteen miles of Baltimore, north and

---

[1] E. B. Greene, *The Revolutionary Generation, 1763-1790* (New York: The Macmillan Company, 1943), p. 67.

east of Washington.[2] By 1790, there would be only six cities
in the United States with a population of eight thousand or
over, and their combined numbers totaled but three percent of
the total number of persons in the nation. The American was
not, in general, conspicuously wealthy, but neither did he know
the poverty of many of his European contemporaries. He was
predominantly agricultural, but by 1775, there were more
forges and furnaces in the thirteen colonies than in England
and Wales. Little of the output was sent overseas. Of course,
too, by this time a goodly portion of the output of pig and bar
iron was being made into forms previously prohibited by
British law.

The great danger for the American was that he might
become provincial. Communication was difficult; the postal
system was but spotty, and roads were few and poor. As a
result, community of interests suffered. By 1773, it is true,
stages had begun to operate between Boston and Providence
and New York, and between New York and Philadelphia; but
the New York-Philadelphia round trip required five days, with
only a day at the journey's mid-point for the transaction of
business.[3] Travel by water was improving, but a sea voyage
from Boston to Charleston was still a hazardous and arduous
undertaking.[4] The colonies of 1774 were much farther from
each other, physically, than is the old from the new world
of today. To produce anything like the singleness of aim and
interest needed to keep the thirteen commonwealths together,
was to be a task calling for the highest statesmanship.

Pennsylvania, which with Maryland was to occupy most
of Carroll's interest in the early years of his return, would
soon replace Massachusetts as the second largest state. In 1790,

---

[2] Henry Adams, *The Formative Years*, condensed and edited by Herbert Agar
(Boston: Houghton Mifflin Co., 1947), Vol. 1, p. 3.

[3] Greene, *op. cit.*, p. 37.

[4] *Ibid.*, p. 36.

its population would be numbered at 435,000. Philadelphia, which almost became the first episcopal see in the United States, was in 1790 the first city in the United States for commerce, architecture, and culture. Until 1800 it would be the seat of the Federal Government. A few miles from Philadelphia were the most fertile lands of eighteenth-century America, a region that extended into Maryland and the Valley of Virginia. But twenty-five miles south of Philadelphia the Mason-Dixon line divided Pennsylvania from Delaware, and divided also the farming or commercial from the plantation states. Maryland in 1790 had a population of 320,000, one-third of them slaves, and it was the northernmost state where slavery was fixed in the economic system. Baltimore was growing fast in 1790, and rapidly approaching the population of Boston.

Immigration had been interrupted by the French and Indian War, but had begun again not only from England and Scotland, but also from Germany and Ireland. In a two-week period of January, 1744, two hundred and sixty-four persons sailed for Maryland, Pennsylvania, or the Carolinas, from London.[5] Most of these newcomers would, of course, be from England, but some were from Ireland or Scotland. During 1774-1775, more than a thousand persons departed from Scotland alone, for New York.[6] The high point of early Irish immigration seems to have been reached at this period. One estimate has it that forty thousand persons sailed from five northern ports in Ireland between 1769-1774.[7] In 1773 Daniel Carroll had settled some immigrants from Galway on his land and suggested to George Washington that he do the same.[8]

---

[5] M. L. Hansen, *The Atlantic Migration, 1607-1860*, ed. by A. M. Schlesinger (Cambridge: Harvard University Press, 1940), p. 52.

[6] *Loc. cit.*

[7] Greene, *op. cit.*, p. 70.

[8] Stanislaus M. Hamilton (ed.), *Letters to Washington* (New York: Houghton Mifflin Co., 1901), Daniel Carroll to Washington, September 1, 1773, Vol. 4, pp. 256-257.

The Catholics of Maryland were mostly of English and Irish origin; in Pennsylvania the Germans predominated, with a scattering of Irish, Scots, and French. In the other colonies there were but a few scattered Catholics, although the zealous missionary, Father Ferdinand Farmer, was laying the ground-work of congregations in New Jersey and New York.[9]

When Carroll reached America in 1774, a new era was being inaugurated in the history of America and in the history of religious liberty. The revolution in a few short years would remove the bonds under which his fellow priests had labored in the mission. No longer would they fear religious intoler-ance. The established Anglican Church would fall from its privileged, exclusive station in 1776 in Maryland and North Carolina, in Georgia in 1777, and in South Carolina in 1778. Virginia would hold out, but, through the efforts of Jefferson and Madison a Statute of Religious Freedom at last was passed in January, 1786, proclaiming that no man could be compelled to attend or support any church not of his own preference. Carroll was always proud of the free air of his native land, and in his letters to an old friend, Father Charles Plowden in England, often boasted of the religious freedom to be found in America.[10] Intolerance did not yield without a struggle but it did yield and the freedom to teach, to preach, and to admin-ister the sacraments was recognized. Anything less would be unworthy of America. As far as in him lay, Carroll would labor to preserve that freedom, and to preserve it as an Ameri-can freedom. Later years would need other Carrolls, but he

---

[9] John M. Daley, S.J., "Ferdinand Farmer, S.J.: 1720-1786," *Woodstock Letters*, LXXV, Nos. 2, 3, 4.

[10] E.g., "I believe that in my last letter I gave you a proof of the decay of religious prejudice here, by informing you that Mr. Thomas Sims Lee who embraced the Catholic faith about four years ago and is a zealous observer of its pre-cepts, is lately chosen Governor of this State." Carroll to Plowden, June 1, 1792, MS WCA, 202 B 43.

led the way. When Carroll returned to America in 1774, the difficulties facing the new states paralleled in many ways the difficulties confronting the Church in America. For both the future was promising, but a false step could prove fatal. Both were building for posterity, and every move became a precedent. It is apparent to any student of American history that the founding fathers of the new nation were acutely aware of the importance of their every action. They had an awareness, awesome at times, that they were forging the first links of a great tradition. John Carroll, courageous, wise, clear-thinking, prudent, a man of keen vision, was equally aware that every move he and his fellow priests made was to become part of the permanent record of the Catholic Church in America.

John Carroll was born at Upper Marlborough, Prince George's County, Maryland, on January 8, 1735, the son of Daniel Carroll and Eleanor Darnall. Whether he received his boyhood training from one of the private, itinerant school-masters then becoming common in the colonies, we cannot ascertain. It is more likely, as John Gilmary Shea believed, that his elementary education was obtained at home from his mother whose own school days had been spent in France. "It was this training," observes Shea, "that gave him the ease, dignity, and polish which marked him through life."[11] At the age of twelve, John, or as the now tattered page of the register styles him, "Jacky Carroll," was sent by his parents from Upper Marlborough to the recently opened Academy at Her-men's Manor of Bohemia, Cecil County, on the Eastern Shore of Maryland.[12] Here, the Jesuits had opened an academy under the title of Saint Francis Xavier, and within half a mile of the boundary line of the three counties on the Delaware, perhaps

---

[11] John Gilmary Shea, *Life and Times of the Most Rev. John Carroll* (New York: John G. Shea, 1888), p. 27.
[12] Devitt, "Bohemia," *op. cit.*

to facilitate removal in case of necessity beyond the jurisdiction of the Maryland officials.[13] Among other students at Bohemia were the Neales—Benedict, Edward, Charles, and Leonard—James Heath, and Robert Brent.[14] The classes taught at Bohemia were both elementary and preparatory, including in the latter Latin, algebra, and probably Greek. The board and tuition fees were forty pounds a year for preparatory and thirty pounds for elementary. No doubt John Carroll entered the preparatory school.

On July 8, 1748, Carroll left Bohemia to prepare for the voyage to St. Omer's in French Flanders. The courageous sacrifices undergone by the Catholic parents in the colonies to educate their children in surroundings that would not destroy their faith marks a glorious page in the history of American Catholicism.[15] It requires no flights of imagination to realize the sorrow that must have been in the heart of Elizabeth Darnall Carroll when she prepared young John for the trip across the Atlantic. It was not the sacrifice of a first day at school; it meant at least a sojourn of ten or fifteen years away from home. It meant the sacrifice of her beloved son in his early years. In Carroll's case, it was to be an absence of some twenty-six years. It is not to be wondered at that an unauthenticated tradition grew that upon Carroll's return to the colonies his mother did not recognize him. Bitter, too, to the parents, must have been the thought that even when the children did return as educated men and women, they were still, because of their faith, political outcasts. Charles Carroll and John were the

---

[13] Shea, *op. cit.*, p. 28. Penal laws forbidding such education were still in force if bigoted judges chose to interpret them strictly.

[14] Robert Brent in later life married the sister of John Carroll. As noted earlier, it seems doubtful that Charles Carroll (of Carrollton) attended Bohemia with his cousin. (Devitt, "Bohemia," *op. cit.*)

[15] See, e.g., Thomas Hughes, S.J., "Some Educational Convoys to Europe in the Olden Times," *The American Ecclesiastical Review*, XXIX (1903), 24-39.

victims of the bigotry of 1748, but both benefited by the training they received abroad, and would scarce forget on their
return what the lack of religious liberty had meant to them.

Charles was still to know the effects of religious prejudice
after his return. But a few years before the Revolution he
was prominent in a successful fight against Daniel Dulany over
an attempt to establish the fees of officers by proclamation
of the governor without the concurrence of—and in fact in
opposition to—one branch of the assembly. One of the newspapers tried to weaken the force of his arguments by injecting
the religious issue into the debate, describing Carroll as "this
patriotic nursling of St. Omer's . . . who doth not enjoy the
privilege of offering his puny vote at an election."[16]

Of the voyage across the Atlantic, and of the years at St.
Omer's, little has come down to us.[17] Charles, modestly omitting
reference to himself, gave a good report of his cousin. "I believe," he wrote to his father, "Cousin Jack Carroll will make
a good scholar as he is often first. Most of our Marylandians
do very well, and they are said to be as good as any, if not
the best boys in the house."[18] The college of St. Omer was
well known in the colonies and the assemblies of Virginia and
Maryland; both sent petitions at times to London, disclosing
the danger which St. Omer's represented to the Protestant
ascendancy.[19] Shea reflects that the results of the St. Omer

---

[16] *Green's Gazette,* March 25, 1773, cited from B. U. Campbell, "The Life and
Times of Archbishop Carroll," *The United States Catholic Magazine,* III
(1844), 99.

[17] John Carroll's letters from home would no doubt have given us his mother's
reflections on his musings as a student, but they were lost in the confiscation
of Bruges College in 1773. (Peter Guilday, *Life and Times of John Carroll,
Archbishop of Baltimore, 1735-1815* New York: Encyclopedia Press, 1922,
Vol. I, p. 19).

[18] Charles Carroll of Carrollton to his father (no date, c. 1749-1750), "Extracts
from the Carroll Papers," *The Maryland Historical Magazine,* X (1915), 144.

[19] Guilday, *op. cit.,* p. 21.

training were easily noticed. The continental education received by the young Catholic men and women was vastly superior to that received by their Protestant neighbors at home. The former were more conversant with languages, with literature, and with science, and had a far less insular store of ideas.[20] John Carroll had spent over five years at St. Omer's when he left to join the Society of Jesus at the novitiate at Watten, a small abbey town about six miles from the college. He entered the novitiate on the eve of Our Lady's Nativity, September 7, 1753. Having completed his noviceship on September 8, 1755, he was sent to Liége to begin the study of philosophy. In 1758 he returned to St. Omer's to teach the classics. He was still teaching when the suppression of the Society of Jesus was decreed by the Parlement of Paris and St. Omer's was confiscated and transferred to the English secular clergy.[21] On August 9, 1762, the college boys were assembled and told the news, and informed of the decision to move to Bruges. The students decided to follow their masters, and the journey began. Without baggage, and in parties as if on a walking tour, the fugitives continued on to the frontier, and arrived at Bruges on the eleventh.[22] John Carroll was but a scholastic of twenty-seven years of age at the time, and it must have recalled to him his own journey from his beloved home in Maryland. Bruges soon became St. Omer's in all but name.

It is probable that Carroll returned to Liége about the year 1763, or possibly 1765, to begin the study of theology. In normal circumstances it would have been easy for him to resume the life of study. The prospect of ordination would have made the months speed by. Each day, however, brought new anxiety. The enemies of the Society were busy. When he was

---

[20] Shea, *op. cit.*, p. 29.

[21] Guilday, *op. cit.*, p. 29.

[22] Edwin H. Burton, *Life and Times of Bishop Challoner* (London: Longmans, Green, and Co., 1909), Vol. 2, p. 39 ff.

ordained to the priesthood in 1769,[23] his joy was marred by the shadow of the suppression of his order. By that year, the Society of Jesus had already been at least partially suppressed in Portugal, France, French Louisiana, Spain, Naples, and Parma. By 1773, save for two countries, Prussia and Russia, which did not recognize and promulgate the brief of Clement XIV, the Society of Jesus had been deprived of its corporate existence throughout the Catholic world.

Sometime after February of 1771, when Father Carroll had pronounced his final vows in the Society of Jesus, Lord Stourton, an English Catholic nobleman, asked that the young American Jesuit be permitted to accompany his son on a year's tour of Europe. The permission was granted, and Carroll set out with his young charge through Alsace and Lorraine, across the Rhine and into the German Empire. He visited Heidelberg with its famous university, Cologne with its yet unfinished Cathedral, Augsburg and Munich, and at last the Tyrol, and continued on to Rome.[24] Carroll's stay in Rome is not recorded in the incomplete journal of the trip now extant. Shea adds:

> How under more favorable circumstances the Eternal City would have impressed the American priest cannot be known; but it chilled rather than inflamed his devotion. Rome . . . now looked with such disfavor on the Order to which he belonged that the American Jesuit was compelled to conceal his character;

---

[23] The chronology given follows that of Guilday, who in turn is following Daniel Brent, *Biographical Sketch of the Most Rev. John Carroll, First Archbishop of Baltimore, with Select Portions of His Writings,* ed. by John Carroll Brent. (Baltimore: John Murphy, 1843). Shea and B. U. Campbell omit the period of teaching, etc., since they follow the ordination date as 1759. Francis X. Reuss, *Biographical Cyclopedia of the Catholic Hierarchy of the United States, 1787-1898* (Milwaukee: M. H. Wiltzius, 1898), p. 20. says that Carroll was ordained in 1761. He claims as authority for the date the records at Liége. Guilday, however, in 1914 could find no such record *(loc. cit.)*

[24] D. Brent, *Biographical Sketch,* Appendix. The *Journal* as published by Brent, ends very abruptly with a few observations on Italy and the Italian Government.

he endeavored to see Fathers of his province who were personal
friends; but as they were out of Rome, he could hold no inter-
course with members of the Society. He saw sold in the streets
without restraint libels on the Jesuits in which the prayers of the
Mass were burlesqued, and treatises assailing the Devotion of the
Sacred Heart of Jesus. The overthrow of the Society of Jesus was
the common topic, and was expected when Spain declared her
will.[25]

Shea's source may have been the letters sent by Carroll to
Father Thomas Ellerker, one of the professors at Liége. These
communications, written from Rome during the period January
23, 1772, to June 23, 1773, are faithful reflections of the
thoughts of one Jesuit regarding the imminent suppression of
the order.[26] Occasionally, there escapes from the pages a note
of bitterness, but one could hardly expect a constant note of
serenity as Carroll watched the complaisance of some of the
authorities of the Church, while the Bourbons completed their
work of intrigue against the Society of Jesus. Against this background one sees more clearly Carroll's later insistence on the
independence of the American Church, never from the Holy
See, but from unfortunate interference by mistaken members
of the Roman congregations. Carroll must certainly later have
feared the rise of another Cardinal Marefoschi, Secretary of
the Congregation *de Propaganda Fide*, and an avowed enemy
of the Jesuits. In the last of the letters written from Loreto,
Carroll's grief is manifest at the approaching end of the Society.
The Spanish ambassador was rumored to be on his way to
Rome with the final demand. In actual fact, the brief of sup-

---

[25] Shea, *op. cit.*, pp. 36-37. There is a possibility that Shea may have seen a complete text of the journal. It would seem, however, that his source was the
Carroll-Ellerker letters.

[26] Guilday, *op. cit.*, p. 36, has published the letters entire. They, along with other
letters, were copied for him in the Stonyhurst Archives. The Stonyhurst
Transcripts are now in the Archives of the Catholic University of America.

pression, *Dominus ac Redemptor Noster*, was even then being prepared. It was signed on July 21, 1773, by Clement XIV, and was being promulgated at the time Carroll had settled down again at Bruges. It was made known to him there on September 5. In a letter to his brother Daniel, we are able to see the effect this dreadful news had on him. "I am not," he wrote, "and perhaps never shall be, recovered from the shock of this dreadful intelligence." His thoughts went out, too, to the fate of the congregations in Maryland, and those of the German fathers in Pennsylvania. Although he had been offered the vacant post of prefect of the Sodality of the Blessed Virgin Mary in Bruges, he felt that his usefulness in Europe was at an end, and he resolved to return to Maryland.[27] On the evening of October 14, 1773, the Austrian commissioners forced entrance into the college at Bruges, and arrested Fathers Angier, Charles Plowden, and Carroll.[28] At length they were released, and Carroll continued on to England, while Plowden went again to Liége, where the English ex-Jesuits were to set up a college. Finally, when nearly forty, Carroll set sail for Maryland in the late spring of 1774. He had left home at the age of thirteen; and one of his earliest biographers describes the young priest's feelings as he returned to his native land after an absence of over twenty-six years:

> A care-worn man of forty, destitute of fortune and disappointed in the hopes he had formed for the triumphs of religion, to be achieved by the Society to which he had pledged his faith forever. Its banner had been struck down, but the glorious motto, *Ad majorem Dei gloriam*, was inscribed upon his heart; and while

---

[27] John Carroll to Daniel Carroll, September 11, 1773, in D. Brent, *op. cit.*, pp. 25-27.

[28] Charles Plowden, S.J., "Account of the Destruction of the English Colleges at Bruges in 1773," in Henry Foley, S.J. (ed.), *Records of the English Province of the Society of Jesus* (London: Burns, Oates, 1883), Vol. 5, pp. 173-183.

he bowed in submission to the decree of Heaven, he sought to make himself useful as a priest in the station to which God had called him.[29]

Carroll had turned his back to Europe and the suppression of his beloved order, to return to a land noisy with rebellion. In the summer of 1774 he arrived at Richland, Virginia, the home of his brother-in-law, William Brent.[30] The year had seen Lord North's coercive policy, the Intolerable Acts, and, in September, the First Continental Congress at Philadelphia. The colonies which Carroll had known were gone. That he entered fully into the new movement, is well known. No reminder need be given of his sympathy with the Revolution, or of his appointment by the Continental Congress in 1776 as a member of the Commission to Canada, in company with Benjamin Franklin, Samuel Chase, and Charles Carroll of Carrollton. Most of John Carroll's life had been spent in Europe, but at the time when the Revolution broke out, he had remained an American.

After a short visit with his sister Ann, who had married Robert Brent, Carroll's old classmate at Bohemia Academy, and with his other sister Eleanor, who had married William Brent, Father Carroll proceeded to his mother's home at Rock Creek, Montgomery County, Maryland, now Forest Glen.[31]

What must have been the joy of that reunion can be inferred from the evidence of devotion to his mother that is found in line after line of his long correspondence with Father Plowden. Here for the next ten years he would remain, ministering to the Catholics in the neighborhood and on occasion in Virginia. The

---

[29] B. U. Campbell, "Memoirs of the Life and Times of the Most Rev. John Carroll," *United States Catholic Historical Magazine*, III (1844), 36.

[30] D. Brent, *op. cit.*, p. 35. Carroll's return is given the date of June 26 by Campbell, "Memoirs," p. 35. He gives no source for this information. Although his account leans heavily on Brent, *op. cit.*, the date of June 26 is not contained in the latter work.

[31] D. Brent, *op. cit.*, p. 37.

stations in Virginia had been attended for many years by his
brethren, but, with the lack of replacements from Europe, many
of these stations had of necessity been neglected. Writing in
1844, Bernard U. Campbell says of the chapel at Rock Creek,
then standing:

> At the distance of half a mile from his residence was the church
> in which he officiated on Sundays and holidays, an humble frame
> building of about thirty feet square, which still remains, though
> often patched and seldom painted, a frail and tottering memorial
> of its saintly pastor, and an evidence of the humble condition of
> Catholics sixty years ago.[32]

The suppression of the Society of Jesus, John Carroll, the
American Revolution, the Catholic Church in America—how
they would all be intertwined! The suppression had driven
Carroll from Europe, and the events of the American Revolution were to create circumstances that were to mean that upon
Carroll's judgment and courage would devolve the organizing
of "the distracted Church in the United States into a compact,
learned, and thoroughly patriotic body of clergy and laity."[33]

It would be a tremendous task. The Church in the United
States could scarcely ever be placed again in so perilous a
position as that which it faced at the time of the suppression
of the Jesuits in 1773.

From 1634 until 1756, it is unfortunately true that little,
if any, attention had been given to the Maryland Mission by
the Sacred Congregation *de Propaganda Fide*, or by the London
vicar-apostolic under whose care, presumably, the Maryland
mission had been placed. Bishop Challoner had frankly stated

---

[32] Campbell, *op. cit.*, III, 365.
[33] The Reverend Peter Guilday, "The Priesthood of Colonial Maryland," *The
Ecclesiastical Review*, January, 1934. Reprint, p. 17. See also, "Narrative of
the Establishment of the Catholic Religion in Maryland and Pennsylvania,"
The Woodstock Letters, IX (1880), 165. Carroll is credited with authorship
of this document.

that he was unwillingly saddled with the burden of the Catholics on the mainland and in the West Indies,[34] and he had tried often to rid himself of the responsibility. Actually, then, from 1634 to 1773 twenty-four superiors of the Society of Jesus, who were holding faculties of jurisdiction from the English provincial, directed the work in Maryland and in the surrounding colonies. Then, the death blow, the suppression of the Society of Jesus. When the Act of Submission sent to them by Bishop Challoner, October 6, 1773, was signed by Father John Lewis, the superior, and his twenty fellow Jesuits, the Church in the future United States was on the brink of disaster.[35] If Bishop Challoner contemplated any aid to the stricken mission in the shape of other missioners, or by another form of ecclesiastical jurisdiction, there is no evidence of it in any of his letters of the time.[36] With the rebellion of the colonies the split was made all but complete, and the vicar apostolic in London felt himself free of all responsibility for the Church in America.

After the suppression no appreciable change took place in the various congregations of the American Church. The priests of the Maryland-Pennsylvania mission continued to live under the leadership of Father Lewis until the year 1784, when John Carroll was appointed prefect-apostolic of the Church in the new nation. Fortunately for the Church, the twenty-one Jesuits who signed the Act of Submission were true missionaries. Cut off from the religious bonds of that Society by the Holy See

---

[34] *Loc. cit.*

[35] Hughes, *History of the Society of Jesus in North America, Documents*, Vol. 1, Part II, facing p. 607.

[36] Guilday, "Priesthood of Colonial Maryland," p. 19. Bishop Challoner died in 1781 and was succeeded by Bishop James Talbot who not only gave no aid, but actually refused faculties to two American priests—Fathers John Boone and Henry Pile— in 1783, declaring that he would exercise power no longer over the American church (Guilday, *Life and Times of John Carroll*, p. 164).

which their members had vowed to defend, they were broken in spirit. But they carried on in their mission stations, quietly, submissively, helplessly adrift, it is true, but waiting for the better day to come. A remarkable feature of their attitude was their constant trust and hope that some day their Society would be restored to serve the Church.

Such were the conditions facing John Carroll when he returned to his native America in 1774. Feeling free to decide his own course of action, he informed Father Lewis that he did not wish to be subject to removal from place to place now that he was no longer entitled to the merit of a vow of obedience, and that he chose to live with his mother, "for whose sake alone I sacrificed the very best place in England."[37] He exercised his ministry whenever occasion offered, in the Rock Creek district and surrounding territory.

Gifted with rare foresight, an abundant fund of common sense, and ever aware that situations are not met by ignoring them, he was not long to remain hidden in seclusion at Rock Creek. He recognized the need of some organization to preserve the landed property on which the missions depended for support, some ecclesiastical connection with Rome for jurisdiction and some method of obtaining worthy successors. He was more than aware that the Church must be ready to care for its members in the new America that was in formation.

As early as February 20, 1782, Carroll's keen appreciation of the problems facing the American church is evidenced in a letter to his life-long correspondent, Father Charles Plowden. The need, in his opinion, for clerical organization was paramount. Yet the clergy continued to live in the old form to which they were accustomed. As far as the present was concerned, the needs of each congregation were assured, but

---

[37] Carroll to Father Chas. Plowden, February 22, 1779. MS WCA, 202 B 1.

Carroll feared the future. He regretted that indolence had prevented the adoption of some form of administration which would not only secure to posterity a succession of Catholic clergymen, but also provide a comfortable subsistence for the latter. Jurisdiction, too, must be clearly established if any hope of permanency was to be looked for. Everything was still left in the hands of the ex-Jesuit superior, but he was free of those checks and balances that had been placed on him by the constitutions of his order. Fortunately, remarked Carroll, Father Lewis was a person free of selfishness and personal ambition. But it would not be Carroll writing had he not observed further that this offered no security for the future. The main drawback, he felt, was his brethren's empty hope of a quick reestablishment of the Society. This, plus the irresolution of Father Lewis, seemed destined to kill any hope of a move for clerical organization.[38]

At the time when this letter was written, Carroll held no official position, and was not even in regular communication with his brethren. Since his return he had, as we have seen, kept closely to Rock Creek, and he did not share the hope entertained by so many of his brethren that the Society would soon be restored. He had felt the blow of the suppression keenly, and throughout his life would be ever anxious for the vindication of the Society's name. But to him the suppression had been complete, and nothing would merit the name of restoration but a brief as complete as that of suppression had been. It is important to note this difference of view between Carroll and the other ex-Jesuits at this early date of 1782, for, once he has become bishop and archbishop, the difference will be a cause of separation and suspicion and disagreement—though not disunity—between himself and his brethren. Again and

---

[38] Carroll to Plowden, February 20, 1782, MS WCA, 202 B 3.

again the restoration of the Society, and the various rumors and hopes of the same, will cross the Georgetown story. Carroll's was ever the larger view. He loved the Society of Jesus as truly as any of his brethren, but he did not hesitate to blame the indolence of his fellow priests. He knew that the indolence was caused by the suppression of their beloved Society, but he knew, too, as few others seemed to know, that they were standing on the threshold of a great era. If American Catholicism was to have the proper start, it was a time for action, and not for licking the wounds of the past. He knew, also, that this organization must be stamped very clearly as being American. Independence had been won, and it would be asking too much of his fellow Americans to distinguish clearly in the height of victory between London and Rome. It had to be made very plain to all in the new republic that this new Catholic ecclesiastical organization meant no threat of foreign interference in American affairs.

The plan drawn up by Carroll in 1782[39] for the guidance of the clergy, dealt mainly with the problem of property and its secure management, but it shows clearly the grasp he had of the situation. Some organization, agreeable to all and hence workable, must be formed that the work of the mission might go on. Hughes has observed that a copy of the plan must have been presented or circulated among the clergy, since all the main points of the program were adopted in the formal meeting of 1783. The ex-Jesuits in Maryland held meetings at Whitemarsh, Prince George's County, on June 27 and November 6, 1783, and on October 11, 1784.[40] Although the call went out from Father John Lewis, it would certainly seem that John

---

[39] This is the date assigned to the plan by Hughes based on the information contained in certain Carroll letters such as that of September 26, 1783.

[40] Hughes, *History of the Society of Jesus in North America, Documents*, Vol. 1, Part II, p. 617.

Carroll was the active spirit behind these first moves to extri-
cate the clergy from the bonds of indolence. On September 26,
1783, he brought Father Plowden up to date, informing him
of the efforts of the ex-Jesuits to establish some regulations
which would lead to provision for a steady flow of reinforcements for the laborers on the mission, and which would tend
to preserve the morals of the clergy, prevent idleness, and
secure as well an equitable and yet effective administration
of the temporalities.

The move was imperative, for the young republic offered
a vast field for apostolic endeavor. The harvest was white. With
great numbers of Roman Catholics moving into the new regions
bordering on the Mississippi, and with the vast country blessed
with universal toleration, thousands would be impatiently clam-
oring for clergymen. In Carroll's mind the most important need
was that of a school. At present he could see no prospect of
success in this regard, but the object nearest his heart was,
he declared, "to establish a college on this continent for the
education of youth, which might at the same time be a seminary
for future clergymen."[41]

At the meeting of June 27, 1783, the clergy of Maryland
entered upon preliminary discussions and the mission was
divided into three districts—the Northern, Middle, and Southern—each of which was to meet and appoint two delegates to
a General Chapter. The final meeting of this first chapter was

---

[41] Carroll to Plowden, September 26, 1783, MS WCA, 202 B 5. Carroll had also
heard of the existence of the Society of Jesus in White Russia at this time. A
remnant still remained there since the Brief of Suppression had not been
promulgated. A brief comment in this same letter shows at once Carroll's
desire for the restoration of the Society but his fear of any questionable, half-
way measures. "God grant that the little beginning in White Russia may prove
a foundation for erecting the Society once again; but I cannot help wishing
that the protectress of it [Catherine of Russia] were a more respectable character than she has been represented."

held on October 11, 1784.[42] Two events of this assembly can not be passed by without mention. The first was the appointment of a committee of five at the meeting in November, 1783, to draw up a petition to the Holy See, asking that Father John Lewis be formally constituted the superior of the Church in America with episcopal privileges.[43] When the form of this request was objected to by some of the clergy, a second committee was appointed to draw up a second petition and have it submitted to the Holy Father through a friend of Carroll's in Rome. Along with this petition Carroll sent a clear exposition of the situation in the new republic, and a cogent explanation why "we think it not only adviseable in us but in a manner obligatory, to solicit the Holy See to place the episcopal powers, at least such as are most essential, in the hands of one amongst us, whose virtue, knowledge, and integrity of faith, shall be certified by ourselves."[44]

The second event that must be recorded as forming part of the background of Georgetown's origin was the presentation by Father Carroll at the last meeting of the chapter on October 11, 1784, of the letter from Rome announcing the appointment of himself as prefect-apostolic of the Church in America.[45] The appointment was totally unexpected by Carroll, but more disturbing was the additional news that as soon as the necessary information could be gathered, the Holy See would appoint him to the dignity of a bishop. The chapter quickly went on record

---

[42] Hughes, *History of the Society of Jesus in North America, Documents*, Vol. 1, Part II, p. 617, has a complete account of the proceedings of this meeting most important to the history of the Church in America.

[43] Shea, *op. cit.*, p. 208.

[44] Baltimore Cathedral Archives (afterward BCA), Special C A-4.

[45] The letter was from Father John Thorpe, Carroll's correspondent in Rome, who resided at the English College in Rome from 1756-1792 and acted on many occasions as Carroll's agent here (Campbell, *op. cit.*, pp. 376 *et seq.*). The letter dated June 9, 1784, arrived at Rock Creek on August 20, 1784 (Guilday, *Life and Times of John Carroll*, p. 173).

as opposed to the introduction of episcopal government into the United States at this time, and appointed a committee to prepare a memorial to the Holy Father expressing their views. Carroll did not aspire to episcopal office. None more than he realized the great responsibilities the office would entail. He was opposed to the memorial, however, and to its chief author, Father Bernard Diderick, whom he feared as "not sufficiently prudent, and conversant in the world or capable of conducting such a business with the circumspection necessary to be used by us toward our own Government and the Cong. of the Propaganda."[46]

It is of importance to note this opposition to the appointment of a bishop on the part of some of the clergy, because it forms part of the pre-history of Georgetown College. The establishment of a college and the appointment of a bishop were to be considered as of a single piece, and the opposition to each stemmed from the same source.

At least as early as the first meetings of the chapter at Whitemarsh, the Maryland and Pennsylvania clergy—the gentlemen of the Southern and Northern districts respectively— were in disagreement over the preservation or use of the landed property of the mission. The Southern group was definitely of the view that everything should be looked upon as still belonging to the Society of Jesus, and that it was the clergy's duty to preserve such property intact until the day of restoration.[47] The Northern group held, on the contrary, that the property should be handled with more freedom and utilized for the purposes of the Church just as would have been the case if the Society were still alive! The Middle district—at least in its representatives,

---

[46] Carroll to Father Thorpe, Feb. 17, 1785. Shea Transcripts, Georgetown University Archives (afterward GUA), 255.1. Carroll's copy of this letter is preserved in the Baltimore Cathedral Archives, 9A Fl.

[47] Hughes, *History of the Society of Jesus in North America, Documents,* Vol. 1, Part II, p. 625.

Diderick and Carroll—might be said to be divided.[48] As mentioned previously, Carroll could not abide any evasion of the
facts. He longed for the restoration of the Society, and
considered that its general restoration would exhibit "a won-
derful display of divine providence over the wily politicks
[sic] of wicked and oppressive tyranny of powerful men." It
must be, however, he believed, a restoration in the full sense
of the word, for, as he vehemently insisted to Plowden, "with
all my penetration I cannot discover the arguments made use
of by some to evince that it was never totally destroyed: and
I do not chuse [sic] to surrender the clearest principles of
reasoning for the sake of supporting the credit of some pious
prophecies or visions."[49]

During all the Whitemarsh proceedings it is evident that
the object nearest the heart of John Carroll remained the establishment of a school. As early as July 7, 1784, obviously in
answer to a letter of Carroll's, we have the views of Father
William Strickland, procurator of the English ex-Jesuits.[50] He
gave his complete approbation of the plan, but warned Carroll
not to expect too much in the beginning. His own experience
with Liége Academy was his authority for the warning. That
institution had suffered from a lack of planning. The one in
America, he was sure, would not labor under this defect, as was
obvious from Carroll's request for advice from England. Father
Strickland, in transmitting a plan for a school from Father
Barrow, warned that, however good the plan chosen might be,
care must be taken to adapt it to the instruments at hand.
Unfortunately, though he could supply a plan, he did not see
much prospect of success in the search for such a superintendent

---

[48] *Loc. cit.*, Hughes lists Bernard Diderick with Carroll as a liberal. Carroll would
not have considered Diderick as such if we are to judge from his correspondence.

[49] Carroll to Plowden, April 10, 1784, MS WCA, 202 B 6.

[50] Father William Strickland to Carroll, July 7, 1784, MS BCA, 8 A 1.

as Carroll had asked for—"a man of extensive learning, great abilities, prudence and knowledge of the world."[51] Such men, he observed, were not easily found. There were three in England, Fathers Kemper, Barrow, and Plowden, but they were too necessary there for their superiors to think of parting with them. Strickland did not believe that Carroll would need a superior man, but merely one who could carry out the details arranged by Carroll, who would retain the principal superintendence of the establishment.[52] There is evidence, too, that Carroll sought advice from other sources. Father Thomas Talbott wrote to him on September 21, 1784, again obviously in answer to a previous letter, "I see only two ways possible, either by setting up schools and forming a seminary of your own or depending on foreign assistance." The possibility that the academy at Liége under the direction of the English ex-Jesuits, would supply workers for the school in America, Carroll himself had seen as unlikely. "Liége," wrote Talbott, "will not be able to supply you with grown up and trained plants for the reason you allege: 'tis well if it can support long its own establishment."[53]

At home Carroll found an advocate in his friend, Father Robert Molyneux, to whom Carroll must have communicated some of his own enthusiasm for a school, and who fully agreed with the plan of organization for the proposed institution of learning. On December 7, 1784, Molyneux expressed the wish that Father Ashton might have success in the administration of the temporalities during the next term, so that the Body of the Clergy might then agree to have something of the revenue applied to the foundation of a college.[54] At about this time,

---

[51] *Ibid.* The plan, unfortunately, does not seem to have survived with the letter.
[52] *Ibid.*
[53] Father Thomas Talbott to Carroll, September 21, 1784. MS BCA, 8 F 3.
[54] Father Robert Molyneux to Carroll, December 7, 1784. MS BCA, 5 K 8.

however, Carroll, seeing little hope of success for his cherished venture, was preparing to settle for a second best.

There was a college already established in Pennsylvania, and proposals were being considered to establish two more in Maryland. In these schools Catholics could be admitted not only as pupils, but also as presidents and professors. Perhaps he could hope for some vocations to the ministry from among the graduates of these institutions, and hence the first task would be to supply a small seminary. Among others to whom Carroll spoke of this plan, was his friend and faithful correspondent, Father Plowden.[55] He admitted that there was danger in these mixed colleges, but perhaps the danger could be offset. And after all, as he had written earlier, "are we able to do anything better?"[56] In the seminary, the aspirants to the priesthood might be formed to the virtues of that state, and would receive a theological education. Such, Carroll declared, was the plan now in his mind. What a fortunate thing it would be if Plowden could supply him with some young men who would seek posts as professors in the colleges of Pennsylvania and Maryland! By the end of that same year, however, Carroll saw that the employment of the non-sectarian schools as sources of vocations to the ministry was not the answer to the problem. Earlier he had written that, although there was as yet no hope of success, the object nearest to his heart was the establishment of a school. His determination that he would succeed can be dated from the end of 1785. No longer do we read estimates of the possibilities of success or failure. He repeats the same phrase: "the object nearest to my heart"; but now he adds that

---

55 Carroll to Plowden, February 27, 1785. MS WCA, 202 B 8. On the same day he had written to Cardinal Antonelli, as he informed Plowden. This letter known as Carroll's *Relatio* under date of March 1, 1785, also includes this plan. Earlier he had written to Father Thorpe along the same line (February 17, 1785, MS [Carroll's Copy], BCA, 9A F1).

56 Carroll to *(N. N.)*?, December, 1784. Shea Transcripts, GUA, 255.5.

the establishment of a school and afterwards a seminary for young clergymen is "the only one that can give consistency to our religious views in this country."[57]

At the meetings at Whitemarsh of 1783-1784 there does not seem to have been any formal discussion of the opening of a school in the mission. As we have seen, however, Carroll had expressed the great need of a school to some of his fellow priests and the question had, at least privately, been discussed. The next meeting of the chapter was scheduled for November of 1787. It was decided to anticipate the meeting by a year. The pressing problems of incorporation, the nomination of a bishop, and the question of the school, called for immediate decisions. It is probable that the earlier meeting was occasioned by a dispatch from Cardinal Antonelli to Carroll at the end of March, 1786.[58] Previously the latter had represented to Rome that his powers were insufficient. In informing Carroll of an extension of his powers, Cardinal Antonelli added that the nomination of a bishop had been suspended until the Sacred Congregation should receive word from Carroll that the proper time had arrived. Further, wrote Antonelli, the appointment of the first American bishop would not be made by the Roman tribunal without reference to the American clergy; when the proper time came, the clergy might choose two of their own number, one of whom would be appointed bishop. This last concession doubtless helped to sway the opinions of those who had formerly been opposed to the appointment. But this could wait. The school could not.

Through the summer and early fall, the project of the school was discussed. In his report to Cardinal Antonelli of August 18, 1786, Carroll informed His Eminence that consideration was being given to the opening of a school and a

---

[57] Carroll to Plowden, December 15, 1785. MS WCA, 202 B 10.
[58] Carroll to Plowden, July 11, 1786. MS WCA, 202 B 11.

seminary, and he requested the Cardinal to furnish him with a *ratio studiorum* for the two establishments.[59]

As the date for the meeting of the chapter drew near, Carroll's determination to have the school project succeed grew ever greater. He had received a glowing report of the success of the academy at Liége from his friend, Charles Plowden, who had written apparently with a view to inducing the American clergy to send the young aspirants to Liége for their education. In his answer written on the day the chapter was to convene Carroll expressed his pleasure at learning this good report, but hastened to add that it would not prevent him from pursuing the great object of a school and seminary in America. The deputies from the three districts, he informed Plowden, were meeting that very day and "one great point of their deliberations" was to be that very matter. Carroll would be late, not being able to join the deliberations until a day or two later; but written between the lines of the answer to Plowden may be read quite clearly that he intended that the school would be indeed "one great point of their deliberations."[60]

An interlude of the preceding March may have contributed to his determination. At Mt. Grant's tavern in Baltimore on March 28, 1786, a meeting had been held at the instance of several of the leading citizens of Baltimore to consider the "propriety of founding an academy" in that city. "The Rev. Dr. Carroll," the press reported, "was nominated to the chair."[61] This school later was established, but did not prove

---

[59] Carroll to Cardinal Antonelli, August 18, 1786. GUA, Shea Transcripts, 255.1. In answer to Father Strickland's request that he dispose people to send their children to Liége Academy, Father Ashton wrote on September 13, 1786, that he would do so but that he did not promise much since "we are about to institute a school in this state" Hughes, *History of the Society of Jesus in North America, Documents*, Vol. 1, Part II, p. 658.

[60] Carroll to Plowden, November 13, 1786. MS WCA, 202 B 12.

[61] *The Maryland Journal and Baltimore Advertiser*, Vol. XIII, No. 26, Friday, March 31, 1786.

successful.[62] It is not unlikely that these proceedings further convinced Carroll that a school must be established by the Body of the Clergy for the proper formation of the Catholic youth of America.

The second chapter of the Clergy met from November 13-22, 1786, and in important decisions moved that measures be taken to form a corporation of the clergy, that a bishopric be advocated and "that a school be erected for the education of youth and the perpetuity of a body of clergy in this country.[63] Included with the resolve was a very general plan of the school and the terms of tuition, established at this date as "£10 currency per annum . . . to be paid quarterly and always in advance."[64] The first directors were also appointed by the delegates of the chapter. These directors were the Reverend Messrs. John Carroll, James Pellentz, Robert Molyneux, John Ashton, and Leonard Neale. Not long after the close of the chapter, this committee, the directors of the proposed school, circulated a prospectus which was at the same time an appeal for funds to aid in its construction. The chapter had voted £100 toward the building, but this would hardly be sufficient.[65]

The proposed plan of education, states the prospectus, "solicits and, it is not presumption to add, deserves public encouragement." The plan is briefly and succinctly stated thus:

> The object of the proposed Institution is to unite the means of communicating Science with an effectual Provision for guarding

---

[62] J. Thomas Scharf, *Chronicles of Baltimore* (Baltimore: Turnbull Brothers, 1874), p. 243.

[63] Hughes, *History of the Society of Jesus in North America, Documents,* Vol. 1, Part II, pp. 665-666.

[64] *Loc. cit.*

[65] *Loc. cit.* The £100 was to be realized by the sale of a piece of property. Hughes surmises that the land was that known as "Campbell's Chance" because its sale had been authorized in the meeting of October 11, 1784 (*Ibid.,* p. 631). Shea, *op. cit.,* p. 241, quotes from another resolve of the chapter which gives the value of £100 sterling as $444.

and preserving the Morals of Youth. With this View, the Seminary will be superintended by those who, having had Experience in similar Institutions, know that an undivided Attention may be given to the Cultivation of Virtue and literary Improvement, and that a System of Discipline may be introduced and preserved incompatible with Inattention in the Professor, or with incorrigible habits of Immorality in the Student. The benefit of this Establishment should be as general as the Attainment of its Object is desirable. It will therefore receive Pupils as soon as they have learned the first Elements of Letters, and will conduct them through the several Branches of Classical Learning to that Stage of Education from which they may proceed with Advantage to the Study of the higher Sciences in the University of this or those of the neighbor· ing States. Thus it will be calculated for every Class of Citizens; as Reading, Writing, Arithmetic, the easier Branches of the Mathematics, and the Grammar of our native Tongue, will be attended to no less than the learned Languages. Agreeably to the liberal Principle of our Constitution, the Seminary will be open to Students of every religious Profession. They, who, in this Respect, differ from the Superintendent of the Academy, will be at Liberty to frequent the places of Worship and Instruction appointed by their Parents; but with Respect to their moral Conduct, all must be subject to general and uniform Discipline.[66]

On January 12, 1787, Father Carroll informed Cardinal Antonelli of the project, and expressed his expectation of success if the Catholics of America and Europe responded to the appeal.[67]

---

[66] *Proposals to Establish an Academy at George Town, Patowmack River, Maryland.* One of the originals preserved in the Georgetown University Archives.

[67] Carroll to Cardinal Antonelli, January 12, 1787, in Guilday, *Life and Times of John Carroll*, p. 452, citing *Propaganda Archives, Scritture originali*, Vol. 876, No. 13, f. 120.

CHAPTER III

George Town,
Patowmack River, Maryland

Carroll was now pushing ahead fast. He realized fully that much must be done before his academy could be what he wished it to be, but the work was under way. He would send copies of the prospectus to England, but he would not suffer his friend Father Plowden to be limited to such meager details as that document afforded. On January 22, 1787, he began a very long letter in which he entered into particulars regarding the regime of the new academy. In the beginning boarders would not be received; they must provide themselves with lodgings in town. The conduct of the students, however, would be under the surveillance of the academy both in and out of school; for it was precisely in this attention to supervision that other American schools were deficient. The president, when he should be appointed, would live at the academy to exercise over it a general superintendence. There would be no dearth of good secular masters, for men of all professions and talents had arrived in the States from Europe, and many of these had already solicited appointments. Although in the beginning it would be necessary to use these secular teachers, this was not intended to be the regular system. It was hoped that many of the youths would feel called to the service of the Church, and, after finishing at the academy, would be sent on to the seminary which was also projected. After some years at the seminary they would return to the academy prior to receiving holy orders, and would teach there for a time. Typically, Carroll remarks, "the difficulties indeed perplex, but do not dishearten me."[1] The assistance of Plowden, he hoped, would be of great aid in lessening the difficulties. Although he realized that he could hardly obtain the services of his English friend as president, it would be a great blessing to the academy if Plowden might then obtain someone to take the post, who would be imbued with the same ideas.

Carroll could not stress too much the importance of a worthy president. He knew just what qualities were necessary for that post, particularly in America, but he had been unable to find anyone to match his standard. For the president must be "a man old enough to carry a considerable weight of authority and respect; experienced in the detail of government for such a place of education, and capable of embracing in his mind a general and indeed universal plan of studies, of which the academical institution is only a part."[2] It would be necessary that he have considerable knowledge of the world, as he would be required to converse with many different persons. Conscious ever of the *new* world, Carroll required that the president be a man "capable of abstracting his mind from the methods used in the colleges, where he has lived, so as to adopt only as much of them, as is suited to the circumstances of this country, and of substituting such others as are better adapted to the views and inclinations of those with whom he has to deal."[3] Carroll was well aware that his requirements were high, but as other institu-

---

[1] Carroll to Plowden, January 22, 1787. MS WCA, 202 B 13.
[2] *Ibid.* Here we have concrete evidence that the "Academy" was to develop into a school of higher studies.
[3] *Ibid.*

tions had secured educators of a very high quality from Europe, he must be content with none but the best if reputation and permanence were to mark his beloved school. As Fathers Kemper and Barrow[4] had been spoken of very highly, he would be pleased if one or both could come to the assistance of the new school. He could offer in the beginning but £60 a year, but hoped that later it might be "in our power to make the superintendent's situation exceedingly comfortable indeed."[5]

Although the prime requirement was the obtaining of an outstanding man for president, Carroll called upon his friend for other assistance as well. What kind of books would Plowden recommend for "teaching English, Latin, Greek, Geometry, and the first principles of Mathematics?" Besides the elementary books, Carroll desired to know what were the best books "for forming and improving the taste of students and enlarging their minds without endangering their moral principles."[6] Plowden must have felt that it would have been far less difficult for him if he had accepted Carroll's invitation to come to America. The enthusiasm of his American friend seemed boundless. "Above all," Carroll had written, "be not afraid of tiring me by descending into too great a detail: you may see by my inquiries, how much information I want, and particularly with respect to the minutes of the business. At the same time inform me where the elementary books, the Classics, Maps, Globes, etc. may be had on the most reasonable terms."[7] Finally, of course, he hoped that Plowden would do his utmost to induce some of the opulent Catholics in Great Britain to render financial assistance to the school. The great expense would be the salaries

---

[4] It will be recalled that it was the plan of Father Barrow which Father Strickland had sent on to Carroll in July of 1784. See *supra*, p. 29.

[5] *Ibid.*

[6] *Ibid.*

[7] *Ibid.*

of the masters. Salaries, notwithstanding the debt of an expensive war, were quite high. The ordinary grammar master in the colleges and academies received £150, £180, and even £200 a year.[8] Carroll could not hope to match these, but he would hardly evade the payment of at least £60 to £80 a year, which, in the beginning of the academy, would be a heavy burden to meet.

It has been noted that this letter was begun on January 22. It was not signed and sent until February 28, 1787. An important event had intervened to require all the attention of Carroll, and perhaps, too, he wished to acquaint Father Plowden with the latest episode in the school venture. The event in question was the opposition raised by "some of our good brethren"[9] against the establishment of the school.

In the chapter minutes of November 26, 1786, there is mention of the appointment of Father Molyneux to draw up a record of the proceedings to be sent out to the various districts. Some time between January 22 and February 7[10] Carroll learned that the report had met with opposition, particularly on the part of the members of the Southern district, but also from Father Diderick of Carroll's own district. This opposition, as Father Carroll fairly observed, was based on a very laudable motive. The Southern district priests and Father Diderick, desired, as we have seen, to restore intact to the Society of Jesus at its restoration the property it possessed at the time of the suppression, and considered themselves but stewards of another's goods. Any alienation of property to assist in the

---

[8] £150 was equivalent, at this time, to approximately $400. It is difficult to give an exact figure, as the value of the pound fluctuated from time to time and state to state.

[9] Carroll to Plowden, January 22-February 28, 1787. The section quoted is in the February 28 portion of the letter. MS WCA, 202 B 13.

[10] We are able thus to fix the time-span, since Carroll wrote on this date to a clergyman in Maryland telling him of the opposition.

foundation of the school[11] they considered to be an alienation of the rights of the Society.

How they could thus view the case Carroll could not see, for, as he estimated the situation, it was impossible for a right of property to exist in a non-existing body. The opponents, fortunately, were but few and he hoped that they would soon see that "a very uncertain prospect of the revival of the Society ought not to hinder so essential a service to Religion: that the Society was instituted to save souls and that souls were not made subservient to the temporal benefits of the Society."[12] Furthermore, although it was true that at the time of the establishment of a form of government for temporal concerns the clergy promised to each other that, if it pleased God to restore the Society in this country, they would surrender back into her hands the former property, yet at the same time a power was expressly reserved to alienate for the common good or for pious uses any part of the property. It was this power, argued Carroll, that would justify the transfer of some of the proceeds of the Society's lands to Georgetown College. In Carroll's view "the Gentlemen who have objected have considered the promise of re-delivery to the Society; but have not attended to the power expressly granted to the Chapter."[13]

Carroll had no doubt that when the matter was sufficiently explained to the "Gentlemen," agreement would be reached. He did not hope for complete harmony, however, for he was sure that "Mr. Diderick" would never agree. Carroll recalled that Plowden himself had listed Diderick among those "whom . . . Mr. Howard's undistinguishing charity admitted into our

---

[11] The same arguments were used against a provision from the estates for the bishop's support. As the founding of the school is our main interest, it has been thought better to omit the arguments against the salary for the bishop.

[12] Carroll to Plowden, January 22-February 28, 1787. MS WCA, 202 B 13.

[13] *Ibid.*

province, and sent hither."[14] The founder of Georgetown was
sure that Diderick had spearheaded the opposition and for a
personal motive: "The secret cause, though perhaps unknown
to himself, is that your [Plowden's] school fellow Ashton is
very strenuous for the measures adopted, as indeed are
Molyneux, Matthews, Pellentz, Digges, Mosely, Sewall, Boarman, Lewis and your humble servt." Diderick, Carroll
observed, had made it a point to oppose anything that Ashton
was for, and Carroll did not believe that he himself came in
"for a great share of his good will." He felt that Diderick
would prove an obstacle to all progress, and he would not be
sorry were Diderick to return to Europe. "For," Carroll wrote,
"I fear he will do mischief sooner or later," Confidently, and
we may add determinedly, the founder warned Plowden not to
let this adverse news slacken his efforts to accomplish the
various missions asked of him in the earlier part of the letter,
for he could be assured "that the Gentlemen will soon withdraw
their objections."[15]

On February 7, 1787, Carroll wrote to one of the members
of the Southern district regarding the opposition, and repeated
some of the views which, as he noted, he had expressed in his
letter to Father Leonard Neale. He was surprised to learn that
one of the points of objection referred to the extensiveness of
the plan for the college. Unfortunately, the needs of the Church
in America would not permit it to be otherwise. "Perhaps," he
admits, "my hopes are too . . . sanguine, but God is my witness

---

[14] *Ibid.* "Mr. Howard" was the Rev. John Holme (alias Howard) rector of the
House of Studies at Liége 1768-1773. At the time of the suppression he
was also viceprovincial. When in 1773 the college became known as "the
Academy" he continued as president.

[15] *Ibid.* Carroll's hopes and determination for the academy may be read in every
line of his correspondence of this period. In this same letter, referring
obviously to an earlier one of Plowden's he says: "With Mrs. Fitzherbert I
had myself the honor of some acquaintance. Is it impossible to obtain from
her a donation toward our academy?"

that in recommending a school at first, and in still persisting in that recommendation, I think that I am rendering to religion the greatest service that will ever be in my power."[16] It was a matter, too, of great surprise to him to find opposition coming from men so devoted to the Spiritual Exercises of Loyola and who had preserved such an attachment to the Institute of St. Ignatius: "For, amongst all the means prescribed by him for the salvation of souls, every one who considers the past services of the Jesuits, or the present decay or religion in Europe . . . the great scarcity of pastors and Priests . . . must acknowledge that the Society rendered no service more extensively useful than that of the education of youth."[17] Georgetown College would be continuing that tradition. The members of the opposition must recognize their great opportunity.

A more detailed and official reply to the objections was prepared and sent to the "Reverend Gentlemen of the Southern District" under the signatures of: "T. Digges, J. Ashton, C. Sewall, Sylv. Boarman, and J. Carroll." A comparison of Carroll's letter of February 7 and this reply would seem to indicate that he was author of the latter as well. The document answers completely all the objections regarding alienation of property formerly belonging to the Society, but our interest is mainly focused on the arguments it contained regarding the school. The colleges of the Society in Europe, the reply points out, were not calculated merely to supply the order with members or the Church with ministers, but to diffuse knowledge, promote virtue, and serve religion. "This," urged Carroll, "is just the end we propose by our School, and though no members should take to the Church, we conceive this end alone well worth our most earnest concurrence, since it is the object

---

[16] Carroll to "a priest in Southern Maryland," February 7, 1787. Shea Transcripts, GUA, 398.1.
[17] *Ibid.*

of our daily labours and the establishment of this mission."[18]
This was offered in rebuttal to the objection that the plan was
"too extensive" in scope. In Europe the Jesuits did not have to
begin with the teaching of the first elements, but in America
they would have to start at the beginning and prepare to carry
the plan through to higher studies. The reply closes with the
statement that in the view of the signers, the plan proposed "for
the glory of God and edification of our neighbor" is "such as
St. Ignatius would glory in coming from his most zealous
children, whose spirit we wish may subsist amongst our successors to the end of time in spite of every opposition which may
be made to so laudable an undertaking."[19].

Happily, the reply was successful. By March 29 Carroll
was able to write that not only the school project, but the
application to Rome for a diocesan status was now seen as
reasonable by the Southern district.[20] As he had expected, however, "The Rev. Mr. Diderick" must be excepted from the
number who agreed. Carroll was certain that nothing would
bring him around. "I have my doubts," he wrote "whether
anything would remove his opposition but an assurance that the
whole government of the Academy should reside in him, and
that he should be the first Bishop of the American Church."
Without so much as a backward glance, Carroll then quaintly
concluded, "therefore a perfect unanimity prevails amongst us
. . . I recommend again and again to your consideration the
points of my former letter."[21] There had been a slight interlude,
and now the work must go on. On the following day Carroll

---

[18] Answer to the Reverend Gentlemen of the Southern District, February 1787.
   Shea Transcript, GUA, 398.1. The main portions of the letter less some of the
   sections quoted above, may be found in Hughes, *History of the Society of
   Jesus in North America, Documents*, Vol. 1, Part II, pp. 676-679.
[19] *Ibid.*
[20] Carroll to Plowden, March 29, 1787. MS WCA, 202 B 14.
[21] *Ibid.*

sent out the proposals of the academy to his friends in England authorizing and urging them to solicit and receive donations for the school.[22]

In the meantime the founder had been seeking the approbation of the Holy See for the project. Father Thorpe, from Rome, urged Father Neale to have the petition presented to the Holy Father through Cardinal Borromeo, as in this way the Cardinal also would become interested, and would aid with a generous contribution.[23] Officially under date of August 8 of the same year Cardinal Antonelli informed Carroll that the "design of establishing a school for the instruction of youth in piety and learning and a seminary for the training of clergymen, is warmly commended."[24] The Sacred Congregation, in answer to Carroll's previous request for a *ratio studiorum*, declared that it would offer none but would leave it to Father Carroll to devise one suited to America and then submit it to the consideration and approbation of the Holy See.

Another indication of the determination of Georgetown's founder should be noted. During all the period of the Southern district's opposition he never slowed his pace. He was busily engaged in trying to attract an outstanding man to come to America to assume the post of president of the new academy. One such was Father William Aston of Liége who wrote to Carroll in high approval of the plan of establishing the school, but who begged to be relieved of consideration for the presidency. "For the treasures of Peru," he wrote, "I would not undertake the management or direction of a College. I am intimately persuaded that such an employ is of all others the

---

[22] Authorization Notice, GUA, 398.1. "Edw. Weld, Esq. and Lady" were in charge of the collections and empowered "to appoint any other person or persons to execute the same liberal office." *Ibid.*

[23] Father John Thorpe to Father Francis Neale [then at Liége], July 25, 1787. MS WCA, 202 F 1.

[24] Cardinal Antonelli to Carroll, August 8, 1787. Shea Transcripts, GUA, 30.6.

Old South

most disagreeable when not relieved by the advantages which accompanied our former state."[25]

In the meantime, too, the site of the new academy had been obtained at "George Town on the Patowmack" from Colonel Deakins and John Threlkeld. The negotiations were not completed, but the site had been obtained, and building could begin whenever the necessary capital should become available.[26] The year 1787 had been in truth the year of decision. Georgetown College was not to provide a story of uninterrupted progress. There were to be many dark days ahead for Georgetown and for Carroll, but the determination which Carroll had displayed in the preliminaries to its founding was to continue in its organization, in its development, and, when necessary, in its restoration. Succeeding years were to bring new interests and new problems but it is not an exaggeration to insist that the college was ever an object close to his heart.

From the beginning of 1788 onward, Carroll's one aim was to see the building erected. With a view to easing his financial difficulties, and in order to convince his brethren that they would not shoulder the burden alone, he sent a request to Rome for financial help for the new academy.[27] In January Cardinal Antonelli promised to lay the appeal before the Sacred Congregation.[28] Father John Ashton, meanwhile, had been appointed to superintend the building, and by March there was every hope that construction would get under way early in the summer. The plans were drawn for a modest beginning, but with an eye to the future. Carroll was jubilant in his announcement to Plowden:

---

[25]Father Wm. Aston to Carroll, Liége, August 13, 1787. MS BCA, 1 B 12.

[26] Carroll to ——, January 25, 1787. *American Catholic Historical Researches*, X, 40.

[27] Carroll to Father John Thorpe, January 16, 1788. White Transcripts, GUA, 55, p. 252.

[28] Cardinal Antonelli to Carroll, January 19, 1788. Propaganda Transcripts, GUA, 30.6.

We shall begin the building of our Academy this summer. In the beginning we shall confine our plan to a house of 63 or 64 ft. by 50, on one of the most lovely situations that imagination can frame. It will be three stories high, exclusive of the offices under the whole. Do not forget to give and procure assistance. On this Academy is built all my hope of permanency and success to our H. Religion in the United States.[29]

This last sentiment was not written merely to afford quotable material for future historians of Carroll and Georgetown. The importance of the academy was becoming clearer the more one considered the state of religion in the United States. The academy must not fail. The results would be disastrous. The spirit of the Jesuit missionaries had accomplished great things for the cause of religion, but that spirit was not being caught by those whom Carroll so aptly termed "missionary adventurers." These clergymen, generally malcontents or failures in European posts, were to be a heavy cross for the Church in America and for its prefect-apostolic and future bishop. Already Carroll had had occasion to fear some of their bad effects on the American congregations.[30] The spirit of the great pioneers, he was afraid, would die out once those who had been trained in its discipline would be gone. The academy was the one hope. Here might be found a seed-ground of vocations to supply the future American seminary with students and the Church in America with zealous, devoted, and apostolic American priests. A Liége education for young ecclesiastics would be of great advantage, but "even that without the restoration of the Society is liable to degeneracy." It was a haunting thought that in the event of the school failing, "our houses and foundations will probably fall into the hands of

---

[29] Carroll to Plowden, March 1, 1788. MS WCA, 202 B 17. (See "Earliest Ministrations of the Society in Baltimore," *Woodstock Letters*, III (1874), 57).
[30] For Carroll's difficulties with these unfortunate priests, see, e.g., Guilday, *Life and Times of John Carroll*, chap. xxxv et passim.

such missionary adventurers as we have lately seen."[31] That
the academy was the hope for any permanent success of religion
in the United States, was a long and very thoughtfully considered conclusion.

Great, then, must have been the joy in Carroll's heart when
the college building was begun in mid-April of 1788.[32] Father
Ashton had obtained as "Commissioners to superintend the
building" Bernard O'Neale, William Deakins, junior, Notley
Young, and Charles Beatty, senior. These gentlemen entered
into a contract with one Henry Carlile, who agreed along with
his partner John McHenry, "according to the best of his art and
skill well and substantially [to] erect, build and set up one
House or College in Georgetown . . . sixty-three by fifty feet
from out to out." An interesting feature of the building trade
of 1788 is revealed in the stipulation that "the said Henry
Carlile [is] not to be obliged to be at the charge of glazing nor
of doing anything on the inside of the said house except the
laying of the joysts [sic]. The said Henry Carlile having agreed
and hereby stipulated only for the erecting the Hull or Carcase
of the said House."[33]

---

[31] Carroll to Father Francis Beeston, March 22, 1788. White Transcripts, GUA, 255.4.

[32] Carroll to Cardinal Antonelli, April 19, 1788, Shea Transcripts, GUA, 30.6. While
in this letter and in another of May 26 to Father Plowden Carroll speaks of
the building as "just been commenced," he was probably referring to the
preparation of the site. The contract of June 4 speaks of "the materials to be
brought to the site."

[33] Contract between Henry Carlile and Bernard O'Neale, Wm. Deakins, Jr., Notley
Young, and Charles Beatty, Sr. MS WCA, 56 P 3. For this work Henry Carlile
and John McHenry were paid (or credited, as it seems they were indebted to
the commissioners for one thousand pounds) four hundred and fifty pounds,
Maryland currency. It was strictly a pay-as-you-go transaction. £100 were to
be paid after "the first floor of joysts [sic] were laid, £100 after the second,
£100 after the last, £100 after the raising of the roof and £50 when all the
rest is finished." *Ibid.*

The interior of the "Hull or Carcase" seems to have been completed by
William Eaton. His estimate for the work was found with Henry Carlile's
contract and estimate.

While Carroll was happy to see the work under way, and had hopes of "seeing the building covered in this year [of 1788]," such progress served only to heighten the need for an outstanding man to head the new institution. The founder had hoped that the English ex-Jesuits would have come to his assistance, but the success of Liége Academy was absorbing all the available men abroad. Carroll would be able to obtain masters in the United States and it was hoped that, once the academy was under way, it would supply in turn its own masters from the graduates; but the burning need was for a "general Director or President." "Do look out," wrote Carroll, "for some Gentleman of abilities and judgment and inspire into him a desire[34] of rendering this eminent service."[35]

At the same meeting at Whitemarsh, at which the plan for the school had been approved, it will be recalled that a second proposal had been joined to it and also approved. This was the momentous motion to request the Holy See to appoint a bishop for America.[36] Although he had thrown himself wholeheartedly into the first project—that of the school—Carroll had delayed on the subject of the request for a bishop. He had been busily engaged on the selection of the site for the school, the choice of a president and the raising of funds. Further, it would be highly desirable to prepare the ground slowly and carefully so that episcopal jurisdiction would be received favorably in

---

34 He had at first written "love" and then crossed it out and wrote "desire."

35 Carroll to Plowden, May 26, 1788. MS WCA, 202 B 18.

36 A committee had been appointed to draw up the memorial and petition. The members chosen were Father Carroll, Father John Ashton, and Father Robert Molyneux. Father Ashton was engaged as temporal agent of the clergy, and as general supervisor of the building of Georgetown College. Father Robert Molyneux, as we shall see, could hardly be called a man of quick and resolute action. The result, in Carroll's words, was that "they, as it happens to easy people like myself, devolved the whole trouble of framing memorials, petitions, etc. on me" Carroll to Rev. Wm. O'Brien, O.P., May 10, 1788, White Transcripts, GUA, 255.1.

the new States. Lastly, and by no means the least important reason for delay, Carroll knew that the dignity and responsibility of first American bishop might well be placed upon his own shoulders. At length, however, the difficulties encountered in the Nugent schism in New York convinced him that it was no longer safe to put off the petition.

Father Andrew Nugent was an Irish Capuchin who had come to New York, presumably to assist Father Charles Whelan, a priest of the same order and a fellow-countryman who was then ministering to the Catholics of New York City.[37] His congregation became, in 1786, the first congregation of Old St. Peter's Church. It was not long before there was dissension between the two priests, arising, it would seem, from Nugent's ability as a preacher, a quality which had gained him the support of the predominantly Irish congregation, and filled him with stubborn pride. Soon the congregation was split into two camps.

On December 18, 1785, two of the Nugent faction, with Nugent's knowledge, seized the collection taken up at Mass. The first schism in the American Church was the result. Boldly and openly, the rebels meant to force the prefect-apostolic and the pastor to submit to their choice by refusing any support to Father Whelan. The schism was to drag on for over three years. Father Whelan later withdrew from the city, and Father Nugent was left apparently the victor. Being refused faculties and eventually suspended by Father Carroll, he continued to rule from his stronghold. In 1788, when Carroll appointed Father William O'Brien as pastor of the St. Peter's congrega-

---

[37] Father Whelan had arrived in New York in October 1784. He had first served as a chaplain in Count De Grasse's fleet and had either decided to remain here to aid the Catholics of New York or had returned to Ireland after the war and then made a second journey to America. Carroll had had his difficulties with Father Whelan as well. "It was a sign of coming difficulties," says Shea, "that Father Whelan officiated without waiting for faculties." Shea, *op. cit.*, p. 265.

tion, open rebellion took place. As Father Carroll was about to say Mass on Sunday morning, Nugent began a tirade against him to the people. Carroll announced to the people that Nugent was suspended, and then left to celebrate Mass in the home of the Spanish ambassador. Father Nugent said Mass in St. Peter's in order to show his defiance of Carroll's suspension. Eventually, after other shocking and disturbing scenes, the Nugent faction, which had almost split earlier over the question of the pastor's salary, was forced to yield after the decision of the court was against them. Father O'Brien assumed charge of the parish; and the first schism, the result of lay intrusion into the sanctuary—"a fatal dagger into the vitals of true religion,"[38] as Carroll termed it—was at an end.[39]

Carroll was more convinced than ever by this series of events, that he could not trust the future of the Church in America to volunteer clergymen immigrants to America. The Georgetown academy must be a success in order to supply a future seminary with candidates for priesthood. American Catholics could not be left to the mercy of priests who had left Europe under a cloud, nor could the Church in this country depend on European bishops who would rid themselves of troublesome clergymen by urging them on to America.[40] Again the academy and the appointment of a bishop are seen to be intertwined. The academy was to supply vocations, the bishop would supply jurisdiction. When it was seen that it would be possible to have an American appointed bishop[41] after having been elected by the Body of the Clergy, the memorial and petition was sent to Rome. Carroll described the occasion thus:

---

[38] Carroll's Address to the Catholics of New York, cited by Guilday, *Life and Times of John Carroll*, p. 279.

[39] *Ibid.*, pp. 262-281.

[40] Carroll to Father Thorpe, November 7, 1787. MS BCA, 9 M6.

[41] See *supra*, p. 32.

Being very unwilling to engage in this last affair [the episcopacy],
I delayed it till Nugent's misconduct convinced me it was not longer
safe to do so: and a prospect having opened itself of procuring a
Bishop eligible by the officiating clergymen in America instead
of being appointed by a foreign tribunal (which would shock the
political prejudices of this country) the Memorial for that purpose
is now gone to his Holiness.[42]

During the summer while Carroll was anxiously awaiting
the completion of the building of the academy, a joint letter
was sent to him from the clergy of the Southern district asking
his views on the state of the Society of Jesus, now that the
news had come that the Society still existed in Russia. Carroll's
reply must be noted at this early date. He had given long
thought to the question, and had formed his conclusions. As he
had himself stated earlier in a letter to Plowden, he could not
let his heart rule his head. It was with genuine grief that he
reached the conclusion that "the Clementine Brief has had its
full operation here. We stand in the same situation in that
respect as our brethren at Liége, in Poland and everywhere else
but in Russia."[43]

The question of the state of the Society, its possible restoration, and the manner of procedure in requesting that restoration,
were to remain divisive points between Carroll and his brethren
down to the final restoration of the Society of Jesus throughout
the world in 1814. The Clementine, or "Ganganellian" brief,
as he occasionally would term it, had, to his mind, been a
complete and official document. The restoration of the Society,
in his opinion, would never be complete and secure until an
equally all-inclusive brief had been issued. Many of the ex-
Jesuits disagreed with both of these opinions. The controversy

---

[42] Carroll to Rev. Wm. O'Brien, O.P., May 10, 1788. Shea Transcripts, GUA, 255.1.
[43] Carroll to the Rev. Gentlemen of the Southern District, July 15, 1788. [Carroll's copy.] MS BCA, 9A G1.

would become increasingly sharp as the years went on, and would at many points cross the early history of Georgetown. The vision of Father Carroll, and his constant awareness of being engaged in a great pioneering work, is thus evident early in his reply to his fellow-priests of the Southern district. He gives some of the reasons which guided him to his conclusion:

> In forming this opinion I have endeavored to make the general interest of Religion my first concern and the restoration of the Society my next. The last, if really effected, would be of great advantage to the first but if it be attempted unsuccessfully, especially by any application to Rome, I fear the attempt would be harmful not only to the cause of the Society, but even of Religion.[44]

The work on the building did not progress as rapidly as Georgetown's founder had hoped, but the disappointment only slightly dampened his enthusiasm. In a note of thanks to his friend, Father Plowden, for a sizable contribution to the academy, he added that he had not yet lost hope of having the building under cover before the year was out. The contractor for the bricks had depended on two kilns of 60,000 each, and when the first lot had been refused by the superintendents of the building, the work had suffered a long stoppage. Carroll was anxious to have the building erected, not only so that he might get his academy under way, but also that he might be able to report some tangible results to his benefactors in England from whom he hoped for further support for the early years of the academy. "I hope," he wrote to Plowden, "you will not be disappointed this fall, for you own sake, as well as the academy's."[45]

Written at about this time, it would seem, is a document still extant. It has no date, nor was it addressed to anyone. It would

---

[44] *Ibid.*
[45] Carroll to Plowden, November 12, 1788. MS WCA, 202 B 19.

seem that it was drafted to be read to or circulated among the clergy. It gives in complete detail Father Carroll's plan for the general government of the new academy.[46] The document begins:

> It is proper before the academy is opened to determine on its general government. 2o the particular branches to be taught and the duties of the professors. 3o the duties and discipline to be observed by all scholars. 4o the public exercises to be required and rewards to be conferred on them. 5o the special duties to be performed by, and the attention to be bestowed on the religious instruction of R. Cath. students.[47]

The general government of the academy was to be in the hands of the president, subject to the control and supervision of the Board of Visitors to be chosen from among the members of the Body of the Clergy. Among other of his duties the president was to be present at all public exercises, and himself take part in the examination of the students. He should visit the classes frequently, and should recommend often to the professors "to excite their respective scholars to study and a desire of improvement by means of persuasion and motives which are fitted to act on their understanding and affections rather than excite their fears." The rod, however, was not to be banished completely from Carroll's plan: "As there are always some ungovernable by generous motives, the president shall make general regulations concerning the degrees of punishment to be inflicted in this academy."[48] It was not the office of the president to establish policy; that was to be the function of the supervisors. The president was to be the executor of the plan of studies and discipline established by them. Besides promoting literary

---

[46] BCA, MS 9A N3.

[47] *Ibid.*

[48] Father Carroll here inserted a question for future consideration: "Shall this be left to the presidt. or regulated by the Visitors?" *Ibid.*

improvement he was, however, to watch over the morals of both teachers and scholars, and he must dismiss any "whose habits of immorality shall be found incorrigible and of a tendency dangerous to the virtues of others."[49] Carroll's final provision for the president should be seen in its entirety. It is a witness to the wisdom of the founder of Georgetown:

> The President must incessantly bend his attention to the points here mentioned; but though his attention should be unremitted and minute, yet it is advisable for him not to interfere personally, unless circumstances render it absolutely necessary. His authority will be so much the greater as it is seldomer exerted. Whenever business can be done by the professors themselves, let it be left to them. The President and the academy will find great advantage in this; and in general his government will be made easier for him by his testifying a confidence in, and where it may be done, consulting concerning all business relative to the conduct of education, with the head professors who will be flattered by such attention.[50]

One feature of Carroll's plan, which he outlined in the draft and later noted as "suspended for the present", was to be realized later. "The students of the academy," he directs, "are to be distinguished by some peculiar badge in their dress, without which they are never to appear in publick [sic], and if they neglect wearing it, they shall be liable to punishment."[51] During the presidency of Father William DuBourg this "peculiar badge" was to become an eye-arresting uniform of blue coat, blue pants, and red waistcoat with large yellow buttons, dazzling enough on one occasion, when he was visiting the town, to fascinate even George Washington.[52]

The last general item covered in the draft of Carroll's

---

[49] *Loc. cit.*
[50] *Ibid.*
[51] *Ibid.*
[52] Christian Hines, *Early Recollections of Washington City* (Washington, D.C.; Chronicle Book and Job Print, 1866), p. 15.

plan was the uncomfortable one of finances. The salaries of the professors would have to depend on the funds of the academy. As these funds, for the first years at least, would inevitably be very scanty, it would be necessary to prefer as professors, if they were equally capable, those who might solicit admission to the clerical state. English teachers, it must be reported, did not possess a very high academic standing. "But as it cannot be expected that the meer [sic] English teacher will be a candidate for H. Orders, it is proposed to give him £80 per annum."[53] The other professors, if candidates for holy orders, were to be engaged for the same sum. Perhaps later expenses might be lowered by boarding these professors who would be candidates for holy orders, with the president, and allowing them £30 per year for incidental expenses. The professors who would already be ordained clergymen would live with the president, and be allowed "a yearly allowance for cloathing [sic] etc." The tuition for the school, Father Carroll thought, should be £5 a year in the English school, and £8 for the other scholars payable half-yearly in advance. Realistically, the provision was made that "if any scholar die or be removed before the expiration of the half year, a proportionate part of payment advanced will be refunded, *if demanded.*"[54]

January, 1789. Throughout the colonies the successful candidates in the recent elections were making plans to travel to New York to take office on March 4 under the new Constitution of the United States. The future Federal District of Columbia would not be fixed by that Congress until the following year, and Washington was not yet even the cleared space and scattered buildings it was to remain from 1790 until 1800.

---

[53] *Ibid.* The "meer [sic] English teacher" suffered a cut in salary before ever being engaged. Father Carroll first had written £100 and then corrected it to £80.
[54] *Ibid.* Italics mine.

But to the northwest, in the busy town of George Town, John Carroll was living one of the proudest days of his life. On January 23, 1789, "for and in consideration of the sum of seventy-five pounds current money" which had been "in hand paid", John Carroll, Robert Molyneux and John Ashton received from Colonel William Deakins, Jr. and John Threlkeld the deed to the first plot of ground to bear the name George-town College.[55]

With the deed in hand and the building rapidly nearing completion, the old burning question of the director or president must have an answer. Financially the picture had grown brighter. In a meeting of the General Chapter of the clergy held at the White Marsh in May, it was resolved that a sub-scription be proposed to the general officers and members of the clergy to relieve the "'public exigencies to which it is likely the General Fund will not be adequate." The procurator was directed to apply all sums arising from the subscription "to the finishing of the Academy at Georgetown." He was further authorized to apply to the same purpose, all the savings of his office until the next meeting of the chapter.[56] Just two months later Cardinal Antonelli informed Father Carroll that the Sacred Congregation had subscribed one hundred crowns a year for three years to aid in the establishment of the academy.[57] But 1789 still brought no president. Again and again note has been taken of the fact that the two projects—the bishop for America and the establishment of the academy—are intertwined in the origins of Georgetown. The knot became tighter when word was received from Rome approving the choice by the American clergy of John Carroll as the first bishop of

[55] Deed to Parcel #1 [original]. GUA, 1.1.

[56] Proceedings of the General Chapter at the White Marsh, May 11, 1789. MS WCA, 2 N 9. The business of the academy was discussed on May 15.

[57] Cardinal Antonelli to Father Carroll, July 11, 1789. Propaganda Transcripts, GUA, 30.6.

the American Church. At the moment, one can well wonder of which project Carroll was thinking.

In anticipation of the event, his friend Thomas Weld had invited Carroll, should the choice fall upon the latter, to be consecrated in his chapel of Lulworth Castle.[58] In a letter to Plowden telling of his great appreciation of the invitation, and after expressing his hope that Divine Providence would still provide a worthier subject to be its instrument in founding the Church in America, the bishop-elect launched into an account of the new academy. A fitting president must be found:

> I am greatly obliged to you for your anxiety respecting our proposed academy as well as your generous intentions respecting it. I think we shall get enough of it compleated [sic] this summer to make a beginning of teaching; but our great difficulty will be to get a proper President or Superintendent. The fate of the school will depend much on the first impression made upon the public and a President of known abilities and reputation would contribute greatly to render that impression a very favourable one. Many seminaries of education have been raised in the United States within these few years but in general they are exceedingly defective in discipline.[59]

Father John Carroll's consecration as Bishop of Baltimore took place in the chapel of Lulworth Castle on August 15, 1790. The consecrating prelate was Bishop Charles Walmesley, O.S.B., assisted by Fathers James Porter and Charles Plowden. In his sermon, Carroll's life-long friend, Father Plowden referred to him as "the first Father and Bishop of the new

---

[58] Thomas Weld to Bishop Charles Walmesley, June 28, 1790. Printed from the archives of the Bishop of Clifton, *Catholic Historical Review*, I, 249-250. "Dr. Carroll's own thoughts 'would naturally have turned,' he writes to Archbishop Troy (July 23, 1790), 'to Ireland or Canada' had he not already promised 'unwarily' to be consecrated in Mr. Weld's chapel." (C. M. Antony, "Lulworth Castle: Its History and Memories," *The Catholic Historical Review*, I (April, 1915-January, 1916), 250.

[59] Carroll to Plowden, February 24, 1790. MS WCA, 202 B 26.

church.["60] The Welds urged him to remain for a long stay, but he was anxious to return to America.[61] After a brief visit, he went to London to prepare for his trip to America. Just two weeks after his consecration, he was busy again on academy business. He had received an invitation from Mr. Talbot to come to Bury to receive a donation for the academy and the gift would not be bestowed on any other condition. Bishop Carroll paid the visit. In relating this event to Father Plowden, his thoughts again go to the academy and the desperate need for a president. "Our Academy," he wrote, "from its situation will be conspicuous. The great object is to procure for it an eminent president and good instructors."

Carroll had received news from America that the Congress had decided that the future Capital of the United States and permanent residence of the Congress would be fixed on the Potomac River. The particular spot had not been chosen, but it would be in a district of about fifty miles on that river. He was confident from his knowledge of the locality, that it would be placed "either at George Town or what would answer better for our school, within four miles of it."[62] His confidence was not misplaced. On his return from the trip to Bury, he was in better spirits than when he had started out, for the journey had been a profitable one for his beloved academy. "Mr. Gage, £25, Messrs. Thomson, Lane and Beeston ten guineas each," he noted; "twenty guineas more from a person who will be incog-

---

[60] *A Short Account of the Establishment of the New See of Baltimore in Maryland and of the Consecration of the Rt. Reverend John Carroll First Bishop Thereof on the Feast of the Assumption, 1790* (London: John Coghlan, 1790). On the title page of this is a reproduction of the coat of arms of Bishop Carroll. The figure of the Blessed Virgin Mary is surrounded by thirteen stars. The usual representation in Christian art, based on *The Book of the Apocalypse*, 12/1, contains twelve stars. Did Carroll have the thirteen states in mind?

[61] Carroll to Plowden, September 2, 1790. Stonyhurst Transcripts, Archives of the Catholic University of America (afterward CUA).

[62] *Ibid.*

nita and other benefactions to the amount of £85."[63] He had
learned that the Reverend Joseph Pierre Picot de Cloriviere
had applied to go to America. Perhaps de Cloriviere might be
able to secure a president for the new academy to come along
with him. There had been a possibility of securing Pere le Grou,
whose "superior talents and learning adapt him" for the post
of president, but unfortunately he did not know English, and
the handicap would be too much to overcome.[64]

Back in America, Carroll found the college almost completed, but he still was at a loss for a president.[65] In September
of 1791, he was able to report that the academy would be
opened to students in the following month, but as yet he could
find no one to head the institution. This, in masterly understate-
ment, he termed a "terrible inconvenience."[66] Nothing daunted,
a notice was inserted in the press announcing the opening of the
new academy:

> The academy lately erected at Georgetown Potomac will be open
> before the end of this month and admit scholars provided they have
> received some instruction in reading and writing, from which stage
> of education they will be conducted through the several branches of
> useful and classical learning till they be fitted to proceed with
> advantage to the higher sciences of this or of those of the neigh-
> boring states.[67]

On October 12, 1791, Carroll wrote to Father Plowden to
announce the impending opening of the school. Had he the man

---

[63] Carroll to Plowden, September 7, 1790. MS WCA, 202 B 28.
[64] *Ibid.* In this same letter Carroll thanked Plowden for sending on to him a letter
from Father Chas. Sewall. Among other news the letter had reported the
arrival of Father Robert Plunkett. Father Plunkett was to become eventually
Georgetown's first president but, as is evident, Carroll had not yet decided
upon him, nor brought him to America for that purpose. "Pere le Grou" was
the famous ascetical writer Jean Nicolas Grou (1731-1803).
[65] Carroll to Plowden, March 21, 1791. MS WCA, 202 B 35.
[66] Carroll to Plowden, September 3, 1791. MS WCA, 202 B 37.
[67] *The Maryland Journal and Baltimore Advertiser*, October 4, 1791.

in the president's chair that he had hoped for, the letter would have rung with joy and enthusiasm. As it was, it betrayed disappointment, but manifested likewise determination and confidence. "The academy will be opened in a few days," he wrote, "but not so advantageously as I hoped. No president *pro dignitate loci.* I can hardly forgive my friends at Liége. Here was an opportunity for infinite services to the cause of God and his Church."[68] He had tried to persuade Father Robert Molyneux to accept the post, at least for a while. Molyneux refused the office, but Bishop Carroll was not very much disappointed, for he felt that his good friend had not "the activity of body nor the *vivida vis animi* for such an employment." Carroll had then offered the post to Father Plunkett but had not yet received the latter's answer. In this last letter to Plowden, before the opening of the academy, the founder exhorted him to "pray for the success of this establishment after having concurred in it by your benevolence."[69] As noted earlier, Carroll would have been more than happy had Father Plowden been able to extend this "benevolence" to assuming the presidency of Georgetown or at least of supplying someone of equal stature. This was not to be and so anxious to proceed to the opening, Carroll had called upon Father Robert Plunkett.

Father Plunkett accepted the post, but it would seem that he did so unwillingly. Although he did not possess all the qualities listed in Carroll's prescription (as Father Strickland had remarked earlier, "such are hard come by"), he was a man of learning and ability. But he had not come to America to engage in educational activity. Apparently after volunteering his services, he had been commissioned by Cardinal Antonelli for missionary work in the United States in 1789, although his arrival was delayed until late in 1790 while Carroll was

---

[68] Carroll to Plowden, October 12, 1791. MS WCA, 202 B 39.
[69] *Ibid.*

still in England.[70] He would relinquish the post of president in 1793 to devote himself entirely to pastoral work on the missions in Maryland.

While the first president was preparing to change his residence from the White Marsh to the new academy, in Philadelphia, William Gaston, who was to be the first student, and apparently a match for the founder in determination, was preparing to set out for the second time for Georgetown. His widowed mother, learning that a Catholic college was about to be opened in Maryland at George Town, had decided to enroll young William. The lad had set out from his home in New Bern, North Carolina, in the Spring of 1791 in the care of John Devereux, an old friend of the family. Finding that the college was not yet ready to accept students, John Devereux took his young charge to Philadelphia and placed him in the care of the Dominican, Father Francis Fleming, until the college should be prepared to receive him. William was not allowed to remain idle. While he waited for the opening of Georgetown, Father Fleming prepared him for the classes ahead. The boy's day began with Mass at six o'clock. After breakfast, the schedule called for French exercises until eight o'clock, then English class until noon. Latin and Greek exercises were not neglected, and a further English class until five in the afternoon finished the day. This preparatory schedule was topped off with three hours of French conversation class each week at one of the schools in town. Perhaps William, even though quite the scholar, was glad to set out for Georgetown on November 2,

---

[70] Father Plunkett had sailed for America in the same ship with the four American ladies who had become Carmelite nuns in Belgium and who were to found the first Carmelite convent in America. Father Charles Neale, who was to be their chaplain and later superior of the Jesuits in America, accompanied them. See Mother Ann Louisa Hill to Revd. Mr. Carroll, August 8, 1790. *Records of the American Catholic Historical Society*, XX (September, 1909, 252 n.); and Carroll to Plowden, September 7, 1790, *supra*, p. 60.

1791, by which time it was thought that the school would certainly be ready to receive students.[71]

After three days' journey from Philadelphia, Father Fleming and William Gaston arrived at Georgetown, only to find that the academy was still not ready. To the great dismay of Father Plunkett, who had not known of his coming, young William had to be put up at the tavern of Joseph Semmes "at the sign of the Green Tree in the main street of the town"[72] for almost three weeks.[73] The welcome delay gave young William an opportunity to walk about the town. Once school began, there would not be many such excursions. He had gone up to the hilltop to inspect the new academy just three days after his arrival, and in words very reminiscent of Carroll's own description, gave the following account to his mother:

> A more beautiful situation than this in which the College is, could not be imagined; on a high hill with a view on one side of the river, on the other of the town, quite surrounded with trees, and everything that could make it either beautiful or useful, it stands as if it were made on purpose for the erecting of some such building.[74]

Finally on November 22, 1791, Georgetown's first student entered.[75] Carroll's hope was seeing fulfillment.

---

71 J. Herman Schauinger, *William Gaston, Carolinian* (Milwaukee: Bruce, 1949), p. 9. Father Fleming wrote to Mrs. Gaston, November 7, 1791, that the college would have been opened sooner but that an accident had delayed the completion (*ibid.*).

72 Advertisement in *Georgetown Weekly Ledger*, May 14, 1791.

73 Father R. Plunkett to Mrs. Gaston, June 23, 1792. Gaston MS quoted by Schauinger, *op. cit.*, p. 11. See *Treasurer's Ledger, A-1, 1789-1793*, GUA, p. 105.

74 Gaston to his mother, November 5, 1791. Gaston MS quoted by Schauinger, *op. cit.*, p. 10.

75 College students old and young who have crossed pens with college treasurers will be able to reconcile a difficulty here. Gaston's account for board and lodging dates from November 21 in the treasurer's accounts while his bill for Semmes' Tavern carried to November 22! *Treasurer's Ledger, A-1, 1789-1793*, GUA, pp. 2 and 105.

CHAPTER IV

The School
Bell Rings

As William Gaston climbed the hill to the new academy on November 22, 1791, his thoughts must have strayed far from school books, for George Town in 1791 was an exciting, bustling little town ranked as the greatest tobacco market in the state of Maryland, and perhaps in the Union. There was much to interest the young lad from North Carolina.

On May 15, 1751, the legislature of the state of Maryland had given a favorable reply to the petitioners who desired to lay out and erect a town "on the Potowmack river" above the mouth of Rock Creek. From the start, the town progressed and soon grew to be one of the important sea ports of the colony. It enjoyed a large foreign trade, and its wharves and warehouses were packed high with cases and bales. Thomas Corcoran, one of the pioneer merchants of George Town, counted ten squared-rigged vessels in the harbor on one day in 1788.[1] George Town, too, was blessed in remaining far from

---

[1] Hugh T. Taggart, *Old Georgetown* (reprinted from the *Records of the Columbia Historical Society*, XI (1908), 75). See also Henry Ridgely Evans, *Old Georgetown on the Potomac* (Washington, D.C.: 1933); Richard P. Jackson, *The Chronicles of Georgetown, D.C., from 1751 to 1878* (Washington, D.C.: Polkinhorn, 1878) for the general Georgetown scene.

the scene of the war, and had emerged physically unscathed
from the Revolution. But George Town's citizens knew the war.
Recruiters were active in the town, and military supplies had
been collected in large quantities. A large number of men from
its sixty families[2] had gained distinction in the famed Maryland Line, and later returned to George Town to resume their
civilian life. William Deakins, Jr., who attained the rank of
colonel, sold, along with John Threlkeld, the plot of ground
to Fathers Carroll, Ashton, and Molyneux, which was the first
land of Georgetown College. General Uriah Forrest, originally
from St. Mary's County, Maryland, lost a leg at Germantown.[3]
After the war he went to London to begin his business career;
but he returned to George Town, and the sign over his office
might have caught the eye of young Gaston as he made his way
to school for the first time. Colonel Charles Beatty was another
who entered into business in the town; there was also Benjamin
Stoddert, later first Secretary of the Navy, who was now con-
templating sending his boy to the new academy.

On December 25, 1789, the village had been incorporated
with Robert Peter, its first merchant, as its first mayor. This
fact was to be of small importance in the light of even more
notable developments for the town. In 1789 the leaders of the
nation were seeking a permanent home for the new government,
and various localities were considered. On Tuesday, September
8, 1789, a group from George Town presented its offer to the
House of Representatives, and on the following June 28 a presentation was made to the Senate in behalf of Robert Peter and
the other inhabitants of George Town. On July 16, 1790,
the act was passed for the establishment of the permanent seat

[2] Evarts B. Greene and Virginia D. Harrington, *American Population before the Federal Census of 1790* (New York: Columbia University Press, 1932), p. 133, n. h. quoting *Towns in Maryland* in "An Estimate of Produce" in Chalmers Coll. Md. II, NYPL.
[3] Taggart, *op. cit.*, p. 73.

of the government of the United States at some place on the Potomac between the mouth of the eastern branch of that river and the Conogocheague. The act further authorized the surveying and defining of the ten-mile district. As a part of Montgomery County, Georgetown was included in this ten-mile square. The arrival of President George Washington at Georgetown in late October of 1790 caused the odds to run high in favor of Georgetown's being chosen for the site of the national capital.[4] There is no need to carry the story through the details of the formation of the District and the determination of the eventual site of the capital, but it was at all events but natural that when the government was moved from Philadelphia, Georgetown became not only a business, but a social center as well. For, in those days, Georgetown with its fine mansions but poor and narrow streets, was termed by a French lady visitor, a city of houses without streets, while Washington was described as a city of streets without houses.[5] In 1790, Georgetown was made a port of entry, and a collector of customs was appointed. It could boast as well that it was one of the seventy-five post offices in the United States.[6]

The fine homes of later day Georgetown were not all in evidence as yet when William Gaston arrived, nor did he know any of the residents. A house soon to be built, however, was to become very familiar to him and its later occupants were to be very well known. In 1798, what is now known as the Worthington House was built at the northeast corner of the present Prospect Avenue and Thirty-fifth Street, by John Thompson Mason. The house was sold to John Teackle in 1807. On October 17, 1810, Teackle sold the mansion to Dr. Charles

---

[4] *Ibid.*, p. 91f. "George Town will hereafter be given its modern spelling "Georgetown."

[5] D. B. Warden, Account of the *United States of North America* (Edinburgh: Archibald Constable and Co., 1819), Vol 3, p. 214.

[6] Jackson, *op. cit.*, p. 100.

Worthington, who had first come to Georgetown in 1783, was elected one of the early mayors of the city, and became the first college physician of Georgetown College in 1791.[7] The records and diaries of the college show that William Gaston was at least an occasional visitor at the college in later years.[8] Perhaps he would have returned more often, but he must have found it difficult to get above Prospect Avenue and Thirty-fifth Street on his visits to the town, for Dr. Worthington's daughter, Eliza, became his wife on September 3, 1816.[9] The wedding took place in the parlor of the Worthington home, with Father John Grassi, S.J., then president of Georgetown, officiating.[10]

Naturally, William Gaston did not begin a full academic schedule, constituting as he did a class of one. Father Plunkett, it may well be imagined, did not permit the young lad to

---

[7] Evans, *op. cit.*, p. 55. "Dr. Charles Worthington was a gentleman of most distinguished presence. Dressed in old style, hair en queue, knee breeches, long stockings, shoe buckles, and driving a coach-and-four, he was able to carry with dignity the honor of being the first president of the Medical Society of the District of Columbia" (Charles Moore, *Washington, Past and Present*, New York: Appleton-Century, 1929, Vol. 2, p. 647). *The Treasurer's Ledger of Georgetown College, A-1, 1789-1793* reveals that on November 17 and 23, 1791, Dr. Worthington treated "Will: Gaston" and gave him "sundry medicines," p. 40, GUA.

[8] Father John McElroy, S.J., notes in his diary that Gaston dined with the Community at the college on June 6, 1813, and again on February 26, 1814. McElroy Diaries, GUA 256.

[9] *National Intelligencer*, September 5, 1816. Eliza Worthington was the third wife of William Gaston. To Gaston's great sorrow, he was early to lose Eliza. She died January 19, 1819. Gaston at the age of 41 became a widower for the third time. Schauinger, *op. cit.*, p. 91.

[10] In his note of appreciation to Father Grassi, Gaston showed a rare touch of neatness and delicacy. "I had flattered myself with the hope of seeing you personally before my departure for Carolina; but I have been forced to deny myself that gratification by the long continued bad weather which has confined me closely to the house. Suffer me to present to you the grateful acknowledgements of Mrs. Gaston and myself for the happiness we experience in an union formed under your holy ministry. Suffer me further in our joint names to request that you will be our agent in properly disposing of the little sum which is enclosed herein." William Gaston to Father J. Grassi, September 16, 1816. MS WCA, 205 W 10.

remain idle, but continued the preparatory work begun by Father Fleming. He saw in Gaston a youth with a very promising future. Later he was to write to the boy's mother that "Billy" was the best scholar and most exemplary youth at Georgetown, although "'perhaps he is deficient in paying that attention to outward gracefulness which is held in too high estimation abroad." In a later letter Father Plunkett praised him also for good management with money, and for his engaging manners and eminent merits.[11]

Meanwhile, the first faculty was being formed. Before Gaston arrived, Mr. John de Mondésir[12] had been engaged, and Father Francis Neale and Mr. Samuel Brown would be added to the staff in a few months. It was December 20, however, before Gaston was to have a classmate. Philemon Charles Wederstrandt, later to have a brilliant career in the United States Navy, entered on that date.[13] The routine of the college day was much like that followed in most colleges of the time. It would seem logical that Carroll's plan, which we have seen in its general aspects, was also followed in the minutiae of the school's discipline. What indications we have all point to Carroll's plan being accepted in substance. Carroll did not give

---

[11] Robert Plunkett to Mrs. Gaston, June 23, 1792; September 19, 1792, in Schauinger, *op. cit.*, p. 11.

[12] John de Mondésir had come to America with Father Nagot in 1791 as one of the first seminarians of the projected seminary of St. Mary's. Bishop Carroll asked that he be sent to Georgetown to teach. He taught there until July 30, 1796, when he returned to the seminary. He was ordained to the priesthood on September 30, 1798. He returned to France in 1801. *The Entrance List St. Mary's Seminary*, in Joseph William Ruane, *The Beginnings of the Society of St. Sulpice in the United States* (1791-1829). (Washington, D.C.: The Catholic University of America, 1935), p. 40.

[13] At the age of 18 Philemon Wederstrandt received his warrant as a midshipman, U.S.N., and was assigned to the *Constellation*. In 1808 he received the command of the *Argus*. He has served in the Tripolitan wars and assisted, too, in the apprehension of Aaron Burr. *Notes for a Life of P. C. Wederstrandt* by his daughter Mrs. Isaac Edward Morse. MS GUA, 311.5.

a complete order of time, and one may well wonder whether he could have foreseen the difficulty implied in Father Plunkett's letter to Mrs. Gaston when the president of the college informed the good lady that he did not permit the boy to rise until six.[14]

Although, as we have seen, it had been decided earlier that the school would have to provide elementary education as well as advanced, it was a stipulation of Bishop Carroll's plan that only those who had learned to read and were at least eight years of age would be admitted.[15] These were to be perfected in their reading, writing, English grammar, arithmetic, geography, and, if required, were to receive the first elements of French. A teacher of "the elements and useful branches of mathematics" would be provided. There was to be a teacher for each class of Latin and Greek, particularly if the number of scholars was large. Care should be taken, however, that besides the daily exercises to be performed in Latin and Greek, there should be exercises in English. Besides the explanation of the Latin and Greek authors in each class, particular English authors were to be read publicly. In the manner of the *Ratio Studiorum* there was to be a "prelection" or explanation of the lessons for the following day. The masters of the respective classes, if clergymen, would advance with their scholars until the commencement of poetry year. It will be recalled that in the beginning, at least, the boys were to lodge at homes in the town rather than at the college. The corridor prefect of today was, in Carroll's plan, a roving prefect. The professors were to visit the pupils at their lodgings, and give them some employment out of school hours "to prevent idleness and dissipation, as much as possible."[16]

That the task of the professor in his watch over his scholars

---

[14] Rev. Robert Plunkett to Mrs. Gaston, January 21, 1793, in Schauinger, *op. cit.*, p. 12.
[15] Carroll's Plan for the government of the Academy. MS BCA, 9A N3.
[16] Carroll's Plan for the Academy, MS BCA, 9A N3.

might be facilitated, obedience to the masters was enjoined under penalty of punishment and, for "incorrigible" offenders, expulsion from the academy. This obedience was due "not only in but outside the schools." The scholars were obliged "to keep themselves cleanly and decently clothed and never come otherwise to school" Notorious quarrel-makers, fighters, and bullies were warned to expect severe punishment. Students were enjoined to "shew [sic] extraordinary respect for the President and Professors, wherever they meet them, saluting them with great submission, and uncovering their heads, whenever they go into their presence, or to speak to them."[17] Even granting to the youth of 1789 a certain measure of precociousness, the next regulation must have looked to their future years in college when they had advanced far beyond the entrance age of eight. "They must," it reads, "avoid carefully all immodest conversation; the frequenting of disorderly company or houses; going to publick [sic] houses or gaming tables; they must never go beyond the limits assigned them, play at games of hazard or drink intemperately. These vices will be punished with the most exemplary severity."[18] The proximity of the inviting but dangerous waters of the Potomac urged the regulation that no student of the academy was allowed to swim except at stated times and places. Another task for the already burdened roving prefect is included in the last of the disciplinary regulations:

> Students not boarding in the academy, must be and continue all night at their lodgings, by six o'clock from Nov. 1 till March 1st; from March 1st till May 15 by half past seven; from May 15 till August 31 at the half past eight and from Sept. 1 till Nov. 1 at the half past seven. They who board at the academy must conform to the hours which will be determined.[19]

---

[17] *Ibid.*
[18] *Ibid.*
[19] *Ibid.*

The procedures for the classes were as equally detailed. Repetitions of the class matter were a strong feature of Carroll's plan of studies. On each Saturday there were to be exercises reviewing all the matter covered in each class that week. An interesting exercise was prescribed for the last hour or half-hour of school on each Saturday: "All the Masters and Scholars shall assemble in each school alternately, excepting the English school and the two lowest classes of Grammar, and hear the repetition of the class where they are assembled."[20] The monthly exercises were much more elaborate. On a specified day each month the president, professors, and scholars were to meet in "the great hall of the Academy."[21] Here some of each class would be called upon to demonstrate the progress they had made "by explaining their authors, by reciting by heart, by reading or delivering their own compositions; by answering historical or geographical questions, shewing [sic] their writing, arithmetic, resolving problems, etc."[22] It was to be the duty of the president on such occasions to confer marks of commendation and rewards, or to "testify his disapprobation of idle youths: who had neglected their studies."

The president, as is evident, had more than his share of presiding during the semesters, but his hours in the chair reached their high point at the end of the year. The yearly exercises consisted of a general examination of each student by the professors in the presence of the president! It was determined that the students' progress was to be noted, and those who proved deficient were subject to three sentences. They should be "remanded for further examination; publicly censured, or if necessary, shall be sentenced to remain longer in the same class while their fellow students proceed to a

---

20 *Ibid.*
21 *Ibid.*
22 *Ibid.*

higher."[23] The progress of the student was not determined by the examination alone. At about the same time when the examinations were being held, exercises for composition were to be given in each class to be performed in a limited time and for three days successively. The student's grade for the year was estimated "by the compound excellence of composition and . . performance in [the] examination."[24] Finally, regulations were offered for what was to become a regular feature for many years at Georgetown, the public reading of marks. This, as we shall see, in later years, assumed more and more the character of an academic day of judgment. The exercises were introduced with an address by the president and concluded with another by one of the professors. The best scholars of each class recited some of their best performances. "After which," Father Carroll proposes, "the names of the students of each class shall be called over, who have signalized themselves by their merit and proficiency with some commendation, and if possible, some reward. If any have deserved by uncommon negligence or irregular conduct to be publicly stigmatised, it must be done on this occasion."[25]

To a regime at least closely approximating this detailed plan of Bishop Carroll's, were the first young scholars introduced. Through 1791 and early 1792, Gaston and Wederstrandt were joined by more and more classmates, and the program of studies could settle down to routine procedures. George and David Peter, sons of Georgetown's first mayor, entered the college on April 16, 1792, and they were joined by Benjamin Stoddert, Jr.,[26] son of the first Secretary of the Navy of the United States. John Peter joined his brothers George and David

---

[23] *Ibid.*

[24] *Ibid.*

[25] *Ibid.*

[26] *Georgetown College Journal,* VIII (1880), 25; *Treasurer's Ledger A-1, 1789-1793,* p. 37.

on December 3, 1792.[27] At the close of 1792, there were sixty-
six boys in the college.[28] Carroll could well say on April 30,
1792, that the "Academy at Georgetown . . . is on foot, and
acquires reputation." He looked to it to be of "great service
hereafter if well conducted", and it was his hope as well that it
might prove to be a nursery for the "seminary of St. Sulpice
established here under my own inspection [and] which
flourishes with all that spirit of piety and regularity which was
observable in our own noviceships."[29]

It will be recalled that as early as 1785, the object nearest
Carroll's heart was the establishment of a school, and afterwards of "a seminary for young clergymen."[30] The opening for
that seminary in the designs of divine providence was to come
from the distressed state of the Church in persecuted France
following upon the French Revolution. When Father John
Carroll arrived in England for his consecration in the summer
of 1790, the Superior General of the Society of St. Sulpice,
James Andrew Emery, had already decided that the impending
persecution of the Church in France made it mandatory that he
establish a house of his Society abroad as a place of refuge.[31]
The Papal Nuncio at Paris, Archbishop Dugnani, to whom he
disclosed his plan, suggested to Emery the possibility of the
establishment being made in the new See of Baltimore, whose
bishop was at that very time in England for his consecration.
The archbishop would approve of the foundation of a seminary
at Baltimore for the good of the whole United States, if Bishop
Carroll were in agreement. Father Emery gladly consented to

[27] *Georgetown College Journal*, VII (1789), 43; VIII, 25; *Treasurer's Ledger A-1*,
  1789-1793, p. 55.
[28] John Gilmary Shea, *History of Georgetown University* (Washington, D.C. Collier,
  1891). p. 18.
[29] Carroll to Plowden, April 30, 1792. MS WCA, 202 B 42.
[30] Carroll to Plowden, December 15, 1785. MS WCA, 202 B 10. See *supra*, p. 32.
[31] Ruane, *op. cit.*, p. 20.

further the project. After he had secured the consent of the
Sulpician Assembly, both he and Archbishop Dugnani wrote
to Bishop Carroll at London. Although the proposal definitely
fitted hand in glove with Bishop Carroll's plans, he hesitated
to accept the offer. The time was not ripe now. As he wrote to
Father Plowden:

> . . . I have a letter from the Nuncio at Paris and another from
> M. Emery, Superior Genl. of the Seminary of St. Sulpice. They
> both solicit my passage to Paris to confer with some gentlemen of
> the Seminary, who wish to employ in the rearing of young clergy-
> men in America that experience, which is made useless by the
> revolution in their own country. They offer to bestow their services
> gratis. We certainly are not ripe for a seminary; it will take some
> years before we shall have scholars advanced to profit by this
> generous offer. I shall decline therefore going to Paris till I hear
> from them in answer to the letter I shall send tomorrow.[32]

In the letter to Father Emery referred to, Carroll proposed
to the Superior General an alternate plan. Would the Sulpician
fathers, while awaiting the formation of the seminary, be willing to start a mission among the congregations along with the
banks of the Wabash?

> Up to the present we have no seminary there. I have worked for
> three or four years to form an establishment for the education of
> Catholic youth in *belles lettres* and the principles of religion. This
> literary establishment is on the point of opening for the reception
> of youth. When I conceived the idea their instruction was not my
> principal object. I proposed to form there students for an ecclesi-
> astical seminary which will be prepared while the youths are
> making their first studies. Now it is in this seminary that the
> experience and the zeal of the Gentlemen of St. Sulpice would be
> useful above all. . . . Here perhaps is an object which would interest
> them while awaiting the formation of the seminary. Before the
> breaking up of the Diocese of Quebec there were flourishing con-
> gregations on the banks of the Ouabache (Wabash) which flows

---

[32] Carroll to Plowden, September 2, 1790. Stonyhurst Transcripts, Archives of CUA.

into the Mississippi. . . . Would the gentlemen, of whose desires you have informed me, be willing to engage themselves in those missions?[33]

It would be years before Georgetown would be in a position to offer students for the seminary. Carroll, man of vision that he was, could see that the unfortunate happenings in France were offering to him a golden opportunity. And yet, was Providence trying him? It would be imprudent to attempt a second foundation while the first was still being laid. To his great joy, the full plan of divine providence was revealed. The arrangement was made that two or three Sulpician fathers chosen by Father Emery, would come to America. They would bring with them the nucleus of a seminary, three or four seminarians who either were English or knew the English language. With these the seminary would begin, awaiting the day when Georgetown would be able to supply further candidates for the priesthood. Carroll was delighted at the prospect, for it fulfilled the "object nearest his heart." "Thus," he wrote to Lord Arundell, "we shall be provided with a house fit for the reception and further improvement in the higher sciences of the young men whom God may call to the ecclesiastical state after their classical education in our Georgetown academy.[34] After three months of voyage, the party of four priests and five seminarians arrived in Baltimore on July 10, 1791.[35] Among the seminarians was John de Mondésir who became a member of the first faculty of Georgetown at the request of Bishop Carroll.

---

[33] Ruane, *op. cit.*, p. 25, citing Faillon, "Histoire du Séminaire de Saint Sulpice de Baltimore, 1861"; manuscript in St. Mary's Seminary Archives. Ruane notes further that the original draft is also in the St. Mary's Seminary Archives.

[34] Carroll to Lord Arundell of Wardour, October 4, 1790. Stonyhurst Transcripts, Archives of CUA. Lord Arundell was a contributor to Carroll's subscription for Georgetown Academy.

[35] Ruane, *op. cit.*, p. 34.

Having put "on foot" these two projects which he considered most necessary for the future of the Church in America, it is not surprising to find them occupying an important section in the first pastoral letter of Bishop Carroll. This document is the first of its nature in the history of the Church in the United States. The dates of its composition and publication explain most fully why the academy and the seminary should be so thoroughly considered. Guilday states that the letter was composed shortly after the close of the first National Synod at Baltimore, November 7-10, 1791, and was published on May 28, 1792. As a summary of the origins of Georgetown, it is of no small importance. After treating of the advantages of religious education, Bishop Carroll wrote:

> These being the advantages of a religious education, I was solicitous for the attainment of a blessing so desirable to that precious portion of my flock, the growing generation. A school has been instituted at George-Town, which will continue to be under the superintendence of some of my reverend brethren, that is, men devoted by principle and profession to instruct all who resort to them, in useful learn-ing, and those of our religion, in its principles and duties. I earnestly wish, dear brethren, that as many of you, as are able would send your sons to this school of letters and virtue. I know and lament, that the expenses will be too great for many families, and their children will be deprived of the immediate benefit of this institution; but indirectly, they will receive it; at least, it may be reasonably expected, that some, after being educated at George-Town and having returned to their own neigh-borhood, will become in their turn, the instructors of the youths who cannot be sent from home, and by pursuing the same system of uniting much attention to religion with a solicitude for other improvements, the general result will be a great increase of piety, the necessary consequences of a careful instruction in the principles of faith, and Christian morality. The school, dear brethren, if aided by your benevolence, and favoured with your confidence, will be the foundation of an additional advantage to true religion in this our country. Many amongst you have experienced inconveni-ence and disadvantage from the want of spiritual assistance in your

greatest necessities, in sickness, in troubles of conscience, and counsels and offices of the ministers of religion. It is notorious to you all, that the present clergymen are insufficient for the exigencies of the faithful; and they will be more and more so, as the population of our country increases so rapidly; unless, by the providence of our good and merciful God, a constant supply of zealous and able pastors can be formed amongst yourselves; that is, of men accustomed to our climate, and acquainted with the tempers, manners and government of the people, to whom they are to dispense the ministry of salvation. Now, may we not reasonably hope, that one of the effects of a virtuous course of education will be the preparing of the minds of some whom Providence may select, to receive and cherish a call from God to an ecclesiastical state.[36]

It will be recalled that the original plan for the academy stipulated that in the beginning the college would not receive boarders, but that they were to lodge in the town nearby. The steady increase, especially of those from distant parts of the country, necessitated a change in the plan, and boarders soon became quite numerous. As early as September of 1792, it was necessary to reserve pews for them in the "Catholic chapel in G. Town" which had been erected a few years before.[37] In November of the same year the chapter of the clergy met at the White Marsh, and after considering the election of directors of the college, its visitors and their duties, voted to "approve an addition to be made to the College of George Town and empowers the directors to undertake and

---

[36] Rev. Peter K. Guilday, *The National Pastorals of the American Hierarchy 1792-1919* (Washington, D.C.: N.C.W.C. privately printed, 1923), pp. 4-5. Guilday notes that copies of this pastoral letter are scarce. He reprinted it from the *Catholic Miscellany* IX (1829), 297-299.

[37] Carroll's note regarding an agreement with Alexander Doyle of Georgetown whereby there was "sold and relinquished to Alex. Doyle of Geo. T. his first choice of one pew in the Cath. chapel in G. Town other than the pews reserved for the boarders at the academy, for the sd. Alex. Doyle, his heirs, etc. forever; he and they continuing Catholics." BCA, 9A 12.

execute the same to the best of their skill so as to make it convenient for the purpose of schools,[38] study-place, hall and dormitories."[39]

Before the approved addition could be erected, Bishop Carroll was face to face again with an old problem, and one which would frequently recur: the need of a president for the college. Father Plunkett, while never losing interest in the college and while continuing to further it with his counsel, and on one occasion at least, with financial aid,[40] did not desire to retain the presidency once the college was under way. Carroll continued to beseech aid from his learned friends at Liége, and meanwhile persuaded his good friend Father Robert Molyneux to assume the post.[41] On June 14, 1793, Father Molyneux became the second president of Georgetown College.

Robert Molyneux was born in Lancashire, England, July 24, 1738, of an old Catholic family. He entered the Society of Jesus September 7, 1757, and, following the normal course of the English Jesuit of those days, went for his studies to St. Omers, Bruges, and Liége. He came to America in 1771, and was soon afterward stationed in Philadelphia. In 1788, he was placed in charge of the congregation at Bohemia, Cecil County, Maryland, and then later at Newtown, from which post he came to Georgetown.[42] Carroll considered him his "oldest friend" after his "relation and companion to St. Omer in childhood,

---

[38] The term "schools" was used for "classes" or "classrooms."

[39] Minutes of the Meeting of the Clergy at the White Marsh, November 7, 1792. MS WCA, 2 N 9.

[40] The minutes of the Corporation of the Roman Catholic Clergymen for the meeting of February 25, 1794, disclose that "the contract made by the Rev. J. Ashton with the Rev. Mr. Robert Plunkett for an annuity of 9% on $2000 for which the estate of the White Marsh becomes accountable is hereby ratified." The money was applied to the new building "of the College of George Town." Transcripts of the Minutes, GUA, 398.1.

[41] Carroll wrote to Plowden on February 24, 1793, " . . . you will not be unmindful of our deplorable want of a president for Georgetown."

[42] Shea, *Life and Times of the Most Rev. John Carroll*, p. 524.

Mr. Charles Carroll of Carrollton."[43] Father Molyneux was also a close friend of Father Charles Plowden, and from the Carroll-Plowden correspondence we are enabled to piece together a very heart-warming human picture of the character of their mutual friend. Father Molyneux was a large, jovial, good-natured man. Carroll once described him as "fat *comme un cochon*. He laughs as much as ever, and when he does so, he opens his mouth so wide as to put me in mind of Gresset's description of one of his Jesuit Superiors, *'rit a la toise'*."[44] He had his touch of half-humorous vanity. He was very proud that his funeral sermon on the venerable Father Farmer had been printed "in all the newspapers of Pennsylvania and translated even into German," and good naturedly defied Plowden to produce anything so honorable.[45] It was he who, upon hearing of a proposed visit of Carroll to Philadelphia in 1784, had written a very persuasive invitation. ". . . but if you chuse [sic] to take up yr. lodgings with me, I have a cask planted at yr. bedside of what is said to be excellent."[46]

On another occasion, describing a visit made to him by the good father, Carroll informed Plowden that Father Molyneux had left that afternoon after staying exactly one week longer than he proposed. Apparently with great humor, Carroll added that if a "Gentleman who was to travel the same road had not dragged him away, he would still be here." In a more serious vein, he judges that Molyneux was the same now as he was when Plowden knew him at Bruges, "fond of beginning mischief but sure of being worsted; never calculating today for tomorrow; more absent if possible than ever; but of sound judgment in things where he is not to be an actor; but of the greatest timidity

---

[43] Carroll to Plowden, February 21, 1809, in Foley, *Records of the English Province*, Vol. 7, p. 514.
[44] Carroll to Plowden, January 22, 1787. Shea Transcripts, GUA, 255, p. 39.
[45] *Ibid.*
[46] Molyneux to Carroll, December 7, 1784. MS BCA, 5 K 8.

and irresolution where he is—in other respects a most valuable man."[47] Father Thomas Hughes and Monsignor Guilday, in associating Father Molyneux merely with "good-natured indolence" and "easy-going inoffensiveness", are harsh in their judgment.[48] Seen against the light of Carroll's dynamic activity, the accomplishments and worth of Molyneux do not gleam brightly. His counsel and good judgment were, however, as Carroll justly perceived, a great support to the founder. His "good-natured and torpid disposition"[49] did not fit him for bustling executive posts, but he was a man capable of rendering great aid to more active men. That Carroll sought his counsel, esteemed it, and requested him twice to preside over his college speaks high praise for Robert Molyneux.

Soon after Molyneux became president, preparations were made for the erection of an additional structure to meet the needs of the expanding student body. Although the project had been approved in November of 1792, it was not to be until November of 1795 that Carroll could inform his friend Plowden that the building was nearing completion, and that it was a noble edifice presenting a front of 154 feet, and an elevation of three stories on one side and four on the other. Plowden would be, noted Carroll, extremely fortunate to have such a building at Stonyhurst.[50] The delay in the building was due to a perennial difficulty—lack of funds.

Whatever initial objections had been raised by some of its members against the establishment of the college, the faith and support of the chapter of the clergy in the building of the new addition merit high praise. We have seen that an annuity was settled on Father Plunkett in return for the two thousand

---

[47] Carroll to Plowden, May 8, 1789. MS WCA, 202 B 21.
[48] Philip S. Hurley, S.J., "Father Robert Molyneux, 1738-1808," *Woodstock Letters*, LXVII (1938), 291.
[49] Carroll to Plowden, September 24, 1796. Shea Transcripts, GUA, 255.
[50] *Ibid.* Carroll to Plowden, November 13, 1795.

dollars given by him to the Corporation of the Roman Catholic Clergymen.[51] This sum was allotted to the completion of the new building. At the next meeting at St. Thomas Manor, July 2, 1796, it was further resolved that "whereas a very considerable sum of money has already been spent on the building of the college and more is necessary to complete the work the Board of Trustees now met agree that the Rt. Rev. John Carroll, Rev. Messrs. Robert Molyneux and John Ashton or either of them be authorized to make up the necessary sum on interest to be paid out of the moneys yet due from the sale of the Pipe-Creek lands."[52] A limit was imposed of four thousand dollars and this sum was to be used to discharge the debts of the college. That Father Molyneux's financial worries were not limited to the larger scale ones relating to the new buildings, is evidenced by his following interesting note to Ignatius Fenwick:

> Being out of meat and finding none in our Great City, if it be convenient to you to kill a Calf, College will take what you can spare and with Cr [credit] for the same.[53]

At length the new building was opened. Standing directly north of the first building of Georgetown, it came in later years to be known as Old North. Its counterpart—Old South Building —was razed in 1904 to make way for the present Ryan Building. Not long after the construction of the new building, it was found that it was in need of strengthening, and thus the two octagon towers were added. That they supplied the needed support to Old North, has been evident to generations of Georgetown men to the present day. The upper story of the building supplied needed dormitory space for the increasing number of boarders. The second floor was devoted to class rooms, the chapel, and—at least in later years—the president's

---

[51] See above p. 78, note[40].
[52] Transcripts of Corporation Meetings, 1794-1798, GUA, 398.1.
[53] Robert Molyneux to Ignatius Fenwick, July 6, 1793. MS WCA, 56 V O.

room. In the basement were the wash-rooms and play room.
This last was opened only in rainy weather. Whether the
custom arose at once at the opening of the building, has not been
established, but at least as early as the 1820's, the first corridor
of Old North was the scene of ceremony at meal times. Before
dinner the entire college would gather here to be arranged in
line according to size, single file along the walls. At a given
signal, silence reigned. A second signal started the silent
procession across the yard to the student dining-room in the
Old South Building.[54]

In Georgetown's early years personnel changes were frequent. Considering the shortage of priests and of educated
Catholic laymen, it was not to be wondered at that teachers
were not easy to obtain and, when obtained, were not easy to
retain. Priests would be needed for work in the parishes, and
the school would have to yield. Among others who joined the
faculty during the presidency of Father Molyneux, were
William Matthews, a future pastor of St. Patrick's Church in
Washington and future administrator of the diocese of Philadelphia, and the Reverend Benedict J. Flaget, better known to
Catholic history now as the Bishop of Louisville and Bardstown,
but who, upon hearing of his appointment, desired ardently to
be freed of that honor and allowed to continue as a teacher
in the college.[55]

At a somewhat later date, Carroll could not help but be
heartened and a smile must have crossed his face at two
applications he received for posts in his diocese. The first came
from Herman de Monti of Augusta, Georgia, who offered
himself for a teaching post in the college for Latin, Greek, or
music. When questioned if he knew any mathematics, the appli-
cant had to decline, but expatiated again on his ability in Latin,

[54] Description of Old North by Father F. Barnum, S.J., GUA 444.3.
[55] Flaget to Carroll, October 26, 1808, Shea Transcripts. GUA, 30.8.

Greek, and particularly in "good Church music," which he lamented was a neglected field. He was willing to come on trial, being "thirty-six years of age and sound of mind and body."[56] The second speaks for itself. The writer was the Reverend Michael McCormick, an Irish Franciscan who wrote from Naples:

> The purport of my troubling your Lordship was, and is no other than that, as being informed there is a scarcity of horses in your new found world, to cultivate the vineyard of the Lord, should your Lordship be under the deplorable necessity of supplying the defect of applying even asses, I should most humbly offer myself for one, tho' I can boast of nothing to recommend me for so sublime a function.[57]

The year 1793 had brought forty-seven new students and necessitated the enlarging of the teaching staff. Three new teachers were added.[58] A sampling of the statements of Matthew Carey, bookseller, in account with Father Robert Molyneux, reveals that among others, the students wrestled with such printed companions as Young's *Dictionary of English,* Fenelon's *Telemaque,* editions of Sallust, Caesar and Xenophon, Webster's *Spelling Book,* Perrin's *Grammar,* Gouth's *Arithmetic,* Simpson's *Euclid,* Moore's *Navigation* and Gibson's *Surveying.*[59] The tuition at this period had been set at £10 per year, to be paid half-yearly in advance. Board on the same terms was to be £30 per year. Each boarder was to come pro-

---

[56] Herman de Monti to Bishop Carroll, September 20, 1796, and November 12, 1796. MS BCA, 5 M 6. De Monti obtained a post. On July 5, 1801, Carroll wrote to L. Neale, "I now send a packet from De Monti containing the music for your conclusion of the scholastic year. . . . " MS WCA, 203 Z 6.

[57] Reverend Michael McCormick to Bishop Carroll, February 19, 1797. Shea Transcripts, GUA, 255.5.

[58] *Treasurer's Ledger, A-1, 1789-1793.* GUA Cabinet 3. The new teachers were Felix Kirk, Peter McDonald and Peter Barre.

[59] *Ibid.* and "Matthew Carey in account with Father Robert Molyneux." MS GUA, 1.4.

vided with a definite list of articles. A note in the last page of the first ledger reads:

N.B. The following articles to be found by the parents at entrance or will be furnished by the College at the rates subjoined. —viz.—

2 blankets £1. 10
1 Rug £1. 15
1 Matrass [sic] £2. 10
1 Silver spoon £1. 5
1 knife and fork £0. 1.6
1 Glass tumbler £0. 1.0
2 pair sheets £2. 15
Doctor's charges per annum: 10/   £0. 10
Mending charges per annum: 15/   £0. 15

Books, paper, quills at the expense of the Parents. Item cloathing [sic] at the same.[60]

To this list in a short time we may note that a few other "extras" were added. Such items as "candles furnished for studies use," and "six months fire wood for schools and recreation" created problems for parents like Ignatius Fenwick.[61]

As was not wholly unexpected, once the new building was under way, Father Molyneux begged to be relieved as president of the college. He had found it "impossible to bear the burden any longer as he found it daily increasing with increasing infirmity."[62] He had made many entreaties to be released and Bishop Carroll finally judged that "the employment of president [was] too bustling and requiring too much energy for his good

---

[60] This would seem to have been a first draft of a possible prospectus. Some markings on the page indicate that the doctor's charges and mending charges were to be deleted. Perhaps this was at the urging of the doctor, hardly flattered to be considered as valued at five shillings per year less than the mender. The proportion did find its way into the 1798 prospectus where the doctor's fee was three dollars per year while the mender received four. *Treasurer's Ledger, A-1, 1789-1793,* Georgetown University, GUA, Cabinet #3.

[61] Messrs. Enoch, Benedict, F. Fenwick in a/c with GeoTown College. MS WCA, 56 P. 2.

[62] Molyneux to Carroll, October 16, 1796. MS BCA, 5 L 3.

Old North

natured and somewhat torpid disposition."[63] He was replaced
by the Rev. William DuBourg, a native of Cape Francois, in
the island of San Domingo, and a member of the congregation
of Saint Sulpice. Carroll described this priest as "a French
clergyman of abilities and pleasing character."[64]

In view of the fact that Father DuBourg was to resign due
to difficulties with the trustees, and since, as Carroll was to
judge later, it was difficult to discover just where the fault lay,
it is important to note that there were some hints of opposition
to DuBourg from the beginning of his term. Apparently in
answer to a letter of inquiry, Father Molyneux informed
Carroll that upon receipt of the latter's letter intimating or
offering the appointment of Father DuBourg, he had shown
it to Father Leonard Neale. Neale replied that it was well—
"An answer," notes Molyneux, that Neale generally gave when
speaking "as an [oracle]."[65] Father Neale further had travelled
to Port Tobacco, Charles County, Maryland, with Father
DuBourg, and had made no objection to the appointment during
all that journey. Father Sewall and Father Charles Neale, likewise, had expressed no objection, although they had offered
some suggestions regarding the government of the college. As
far as Father John Ashton was concerned, he had been very
civil to Father DuBourg, and had expressed but a desire that
Father Molyneux remain with the new president for a short
time to settle the affairs of the building. Molyneux's own
opinion was that the trustees had "not a person among them
so fit for the place of president as the present one."[66] The cloud
over Father DuBourg's appointment was very disappointing to
Bishop Carroll.

---

[63] Carroll to Plowden, September 24, 1796. Shea Transcripts, GUA, 255.1.
[64] *Ibid.*
[65] Molyneux to Carroll, October 16, 1796. MS BCA, 5 L 3. "Oracle" was the best
    reading the writer could make of the document.
[66] *Ibid.*

Father DuBourg was not to be spared the financial harassments that fell to the lot of all Georgetown's presidents at this period. He, too, was to be handicapped by the lack of ready money.[67] A little over a month after he took office, he found it necessary to apply to a Baltimore leather firm for shoe leather on the deferred payment plan. "Wanting," he wrote, "for the college of GeorgeTown to the administration of which I have been lately called, a quantity of good soale [sic] and upper leather I am confident I cannot place our custom in better hands than yours." He felt obliged to add that he could not offer ready money but that a "credit of four or five months is made necessary by the present circumstances of the house."[68]

At a meeting of the clergy at St. Thomas Manor on September 1, 1797, it was resolved that there should be a board of directors for Georgetown College consisting of five members elected every three years from amongst the "Select Body of the Clergy."[69] It was further decided that a president and vice president be appointed by, and removable at the pleasure of, the directors. The directors also were to determine the respective duties of the president and vice president, would fix their salaries and those of the prefects and professors, and in general, would superintend the government and economy of the college.[70] At the next meeting of the directors, resolutions were passed continuing Father DuBourg as president and appointing Father Francis Neale as vice president. The president was commissioned to rent a house in the town for non-Catholics who might

---

[67] The debts of the college in the begining of October, 1797, amounted to £1,329 6s. 2d. Note in GUA, 1.4.

[68] Father Wm. DuBourg to John Hillen, November 16, 1796. MS GUA, 1.4. This letter was found behind some wainscoting nearly a hundred years later when repairs were being made on the Hillen building. *The College Journal*, XIV (1886), 104.

[69] The first directors were "the Rev. Messrs. Francis Neale, Robt. Plunkett, John Ashton, Charles Sewall and Francis Beeston."

[70] *Minutes of the Directors, 1797-1815*, GUA, 398,

wish to board, and was further "to establish a uniform of dress decent and suitable for all students of the said college and compel compliance."[71] This instruction regarding the house for non-Catholics may explain why Father DuBourg has sometimes been credited with being the first to open the academy to non-Catholics.[72] This, if we recall Bishop Carroll's pastoral letter, was not the case. That letter had said that "the reverend brethren were ready and able to instruct all who resort to them in useful learning and those of our religion in its principles and duties."[73] But it was Father DuBourg who wisely advertised the fact that the college was open to non-Catholics.[74]

In fulfillment of the resolutions of the directors, the first prospectus[75] of the college issued on January 1, 1798, announced that a house had been provided for boarders "professing other tenets" than the Catholic religion.[76] In this house, which was under the inspection of the president and a supervisor appointed by him, the students were subjected to the same rules, religion excepted, as were the boarders in the college. "A widow lady," the local press account adds, "of most respectable character . . . will take care of the household, and

---

[71] Meeting of the Directors of Georgetown College, October 3, 1797. *Minutes of the Directors, Georgetown College 1797-1815.* GUA, 398. An item of the uniform is indicated in the bill of D. Williamson to Rev. Wm. DuBourg for "40 Dble gro: gilt buttons with the inscription around the border Geo:Town College." MS GUA, 1.4.

[72] Shea, *History of Georgetown University*, p. 23.

[73] Bishop Carroll's Pastoral of 1792. See *supra*, p. 76.

[74] *The American Gazeteer* of Zedekiah Morse (Boston, 1798) noted that "The Roman Catholics have established a college here [Georgetown] for the promotion of general literature which is at present in a very flourishing state."

[75] The president had been directed to publish immediately a prospectus of the college in the English, French, and Spanish languages. Meeting of the Directors, December 20, 1797. *Minutes of the Directors, Georgetown College, 1797-1815.* GUA, 398.

[76] Prospectus of the "College of George-Town (Potomack) in the State of Maryland, United States of America — January 1, 1798," Regulation IX, GUA, 62.11. The board was one hundred and thirty-two dollars a year.

bestow a particular attention upon the health and cleanliness of the young boarders."[77] The second commission, also, Father DuBourg duly carried out. The tenth provision of the prospectus declares:

> To check the natural propensity of youths to extravagance, and stop at once just complaints of some parents on this subject, all boarders shall wear an uniform dress, to be furnished them by the College on the cheapest terms, unless their parents should chuse [sic] to take the trouble themselves, in which case they must scrupulously conform to the due quality, colour and form.[78]

The word "colour" in this regulation was not to be taken lightly. As mentioned earlier, Christian Hines recalled that on the occasion of a visit of George Washington to his nephew Thomas Peter, college boys were all formed in a line on the north side of the street and nearly opposite where he stood. "They were dressed in uniforms consisting in part of blue coats, red waistcoats, and presented a very fine appearance. They seemed to attract the attention of the general very much."[79]

The presidency of Father DuBourg saw many features of the college administration clarified, and patterns were formed which were retained for many years. Up to 1798 the title of the property had remained in the names of the temporary trustees —Bishop Carroll, Father Molyneux, and Father Ashton. Since, however, there had been created by an act of the Maryland Legislature in 1793 a legal entity called the Corporation of Roman Catholic Clergymen, empowered to receive any of the

---

[77] *Centinel of Liberty and Georgetown Advertiser*, November 21, 1797. Transcript. GUA, 62.11.
[78] Prospectus of the "College of George-Town (Potomack) . . . . January 1, 1798," Regulation X. GUA, 62.11.
[79] Hines, *Early Recollections*, p. 15. This was the Sunday uniform. Although the 1798 prospectus does not enter into all the sartorial details, it does mention the uniform for the season. From later editions of the prospectus we learn that the weekday uniform consisted of a black frock coat or jacket and white pants and vest (in summer), and blue or grey pants and black vest (in winter).

Jesuit estates in trust, the trustees in virtue of an act of the legislature at its November session, 1797, transferred the Georgetown property to this body.[80] The corporation was further authorized to receive donations in behalf of Georgetown College sufficient for the maintenance and education of thirty scholars, provided that the sum in any one year did not exceed four thousand dollars.[81] The college prospectus,[82] while admitting that the sphere of education was for a time unavoidably contracted, declared that gradual expansion had now brought the institution to a point where it was able to boast of "the promising prospect of being a complete nursery of learning equal to those in the United States whose institution was earlier, and which have taught this to emulate the same."[83] At this time the curriculum included "the study of the dead languages, English, French . . . writing, arithmetic in all its branches, mathematics, geography, the use of the globes, and the art of an elegant elocution." Plans had been made by 1798 for the introduction "of the study of the higher sciences, as history, moral and natural philosophy," when the students had advanced in their scholastic career. Spanish was being added, for it was, next to English and French, "considered as the most valuable in a country, naturally connected by the double tie of neighborhood and trade with the Spanish territories."[84]

The formation of the board of directors, and regular meetings of that board, resulted in a greater uniformity of college direction. The salaries of the professors were fixed at

---

[80] Parcels #1 and #2. *Property File.* GUA. The actual date of transfer was December 4, 1798.

[81] *Shea, History of Georgetown University,* p. 24.

[82] In this prospectus it is interesting to note that the fees are listed in dollars and cents instead of the English system of pounds, shillings, and pence formerly used.

[83] Prospectus of 1798. GUA, 62.11.

[84] *Ibid.*

two hundred dollars a year. The schedule of vacations was drawn up, and included vacations from Christmas Eve to New Year's Day inclusively, the Saturday preceding Shrovetide to Shrove Tuesday, from the Wednesday in Holy Week to the Wednesday in Easter week, and the Saturday before Whitsunday to the Tuesday following and from July 31 to September 1. The students were not allowed to go home during any of the short vacations, and the president was directed by the directors to discourage all absences from the college at undue times, and absolutely to forbid absences at night. The "long vacation" of 1798 was to be the last "during which it will be permitted to the students who are boarders . . . to be absent therefrom."[85] The prospectus explains this last measure:

> No student shall be allowed . . . to go abroad during the vacations: the many inconveniences attending that indulgence having induced the directors, after mature consideration, finally to adopt this measure, which, although it may affect the feelings of some fond parents, cannot fail of meeting with the applause of every one who will reflect on its happy tendence, and of proving unequivocally the disinterestedness of the administration of the College, when it is considered that it puts itself thereby to a considerable addition of expence [sic] and trouble, merely for the sake of the greater improvement of its pupils.[86]

In order that there be no overlapping of authority the duties of the president and vice-president were defined. The president

---

[85] Meeting of the directors, Georgetown College, at St. Thomas Manor, November 28, 1797. *Minutes of the Directors, 1797-1815*, GUA, 398. The professors and masters "were permitted to see their friends during the course of the long vacation, but so that not more than one half of them be absent at the same time at the direction of the President." *Ibid.*

[86] Prospectus of 1798. GUA, 62.11. Private study was encouraged on days of vacation and "students were allowed free access to the study place for that purpose: but notwithstanding that all be obliged to walk out once a month at the discretion of the president or of any other person by him appointed." Minutes of the November 28, 1797, meeting of the directors, *Minutes of the Directors, 1797-1815*, GUA, 398.

was to carry into effect the resolves of the directors, execute the plan of studies, maintain discipline, admit and discharge students, correspond with parents and guardians, and supervise the professors and prefects.[87] The vice president was to look after the temporal affairs of the college, the keeping of the accounts, and was to make sure that "a due and suitable diet be daily provided."[88] He was charged finally with seeing "that the wardrobe of the students be under good and careful keeping and that the cleanliness of their persons be strictly attended to."[89] Prefects and professors were to be discharged only upon the joint concurrence of president and vice president.

Mention has been made earlier that Father DuBourg did much to advertise the school, and the name of Georgetown College came into current use during his administration. He received, also, however, some publicity that he would have willingly foregone. On Saturday, November 15, 1797, about noon, the citizens of Georgetown came to know the college at first hand. They very kindly came to the aid of the school authorities in extinguishing a fire that had broken out in the second floor of Old South. "The Gentlemen of the College" acknowledged gratefully in the press their debt to the "inhabitants of Georgetown for the kind and active assistance they received from them in the tremendous disaster which (on the 15th instant) threatened their house with total destruction."[90]

---

[87] Meeting of the Directors, Georgetown College, held at the college, December 20, 1797. *Minutes of the Directors, 1797-1815.* GUA, 398.

[88] *Ibid.*

[89] *Ibid.*

[90] *Centinel of Liberty,* November 21, 1797. GUA, 302.3. The account further stated that the "Gentlemen of the College think it their duty to justify the workmen who had put up the fireplace, in which the conflagration originated, from the rash imputations started against them. Their work, being examined, has been found unexceptionable; and it has been proved to a demonstration that a log rolling down from the hearth was the only cause of the havock [sic]." *Ibid.* The damages of the fire amounted to £21.5.0. *Account Book of the Agent of the Corporation,* MS WCA, 190 A.1, p. 5.

Shortly before "the catastrophe" the directors had found it necessary to meet in order to clarify one previous resolution and retract another. The salary of two hundred dollars per year for each professor and prefect was not to apply to such professors as were in holy orders. The uniform yearly salary of the clerics was fixed at forty pounds Maryland currency "without distinction of persons or employment."[91] To the delight of the students, the directors retracted their decision that the boys must remain at the college during the long vacation, and referred the matter to further consideration.[92]

A more serious difficulty than the fire soon occupied the thoughts of Father DuBourg. Just as the school was beginning to fall into a smooth running routine he lost two of his teachers. Mr. John de Mondésir,[93] who had been one of the original faculty, and Mr. St. Tour left in the middle of the school year of 1797.[94] The burden of their classes and prefecting henceforth fell on the shoulders of the president. The cloud, however, had its silver lining. In order to meet the difficulty, Father DuBourg entrusted the young beginners to Enoch Fenwick, "the best scholar in the college who is in every respect perfectly qualified to teach a higher school, and whom the most uniform and exceptionable behaviour entitles to my entire confidence." Father DuBourg added that the votes of the masters, scholars, and parents were unanimous in favor of the appointment.[95]

---

[91] Meeting of the Directors, Georgetown College, September 25-26, 1798. *Minutes of the Directors, 1797-1815.* GUA 398.

[92] *Ibid.* Later the ruling was made that "such of the students who have merited censure for their misconduct and negligence during the course of the year shall not be permitted to absent themselves from the college during the long vacation." Meeting of December 18, 1798, at the White Marsh. *Ibid.*

[93] Mr. de Mondésir left to resume his studies for the priesthood at St. Mary's Seminary, Baltimore. He was ordained on September 30, 1798. In September, 1801, he returned to France. Ruane, *The Beginnings of the Society of St. Sulpice in the United States*, p. 40.

[94] DuBourg to Carroll, May 22, 1797. MS BCA, 8A H5.

[95] *Ibid.*

Enoch Fenwick was thus early introduced to the administrative details of Georgetown College. He would become its eleventh president in 1820.

In March of 1797 a man who but a few days before had compared himself to "the wearied traveller who seeks a resting place, and is bending his body to lean thereon,"[96] stopped at the village of Georgetown. General George Washington was on his way to a well-earned rest at Mount Vernon. He had received the compliments of the citizens of Washington and the good citizens of Georgetown were not to be outdone. They, too, on March 15, assembled to pay their tribute. Among the addresses delivered that day was one in the name of the president and professors of Georgetown College.[97] The "partiality to seminaries of learning" exhibited in the general's recent speech to the people of America had encouraged the faculty to extend an invitation to the general to visit the college. In the academic and rhetorical style of 1797 they declared:

> . . . your late address to the people of America which has earned to you the additional praise of being friendly to the Muses, and the Patron of those who introduce others to their acquaintance emboldens us now to invite you to an asylum we have prepared for them, not doubting that your presence will be a signal for them to take their flight to our Hill, and consecrate it as they did of old, those of Thessaly and Greece.[98]

The address further affirmed in much more glowing words than these, that upon that hill religion and sound policy presided "along with the nine Sisters." It was the hope of the president

---

[96] George Washington to Henry Knox, March 2, 1797. *The Writings of George Washington*, ed. by John C. Fitzpatrick (Washington: U.S. Government Printing Office, 1940), XXXV (March 30, 1796-July 31, 1797), 408.

[97] John C. Fitzpatrick (ed.) *The Diaries of George Washington* (Boston: Houghton, Mifflin Company, 1925), Vol. 4, (1789-1799), p. 255 and n.1.

[98] The president and professors of Georgetown College to George Washington. Received March 15, 1797. MS Division, Library of Congress.

and professors that that union of the muses, religion and sound policy, already begun, would continue successfully, for, if General Washington would visit them upon the hill, all could claim with equal emulation to be under his auspices, since "they will be at a loss to discern to which of them he has done more honor."[99] In a very gracious reply of gratitude to his fellow citizens, Washington expressed his "sincere thanks" and reciprocated "most cordially all the good wishes . . . to me and my family for our temporal and eternal happiness."[100]

Later that same year, probably on August 7, occurred the visit of the general to the Georgetown campus.[101] Mr. William Matthews, who was later pastor of St. Patrick's in Washington and practically pastor of Washington city, seems to have been the first to greet the distinguished visitor on this occasion.[102] Robert Walsh, later a journalist, brilliant editor, and—on the testimony of Edgar Allan Poe—one of the finest writers in America, was chosen to give the speech of welcome on behalf of the boys. Walsh, one of Georgetown's most eminent sons, retained almost sixty-two years later a very vivid recollection of the event in "the old edifice."[103] His speech, in verse, unfortunately has not been preserved.

---

[99] *Ibid.* Augustine and Bushrod Washington, grandnephews of Gen. Washington, had entered Georgetown on April 8, 1793.

[100] Washington's reply to the Citizens of Georgetown, MS Division, Library of Congress. See Fitzpatrick, *Diaries of Washington, Loc. cit.*

[101] The date affords some difficulty. Washington's diary records that he was in Georgetown on May 18 and August 7. Robert Walsh who gave the speech of welcome did not enter the college until June 21, 1797, and so the probability of the August 7 date. Perhaps the students were held over from July 31, normal close of the year, for the visit. The decision referred to earlier to keep the boys at school during the long vacation which was later retracted, was not to go into effect until 1799.

[102] Rev. Chas. H. Stonestreet, S.J., "Georgetown College," The *Philadelphia Catholic Instructor*, February, 1854. Father Stonestreet had heard the story of the visit from Father Matthews.

[103] Robert Walsh to Edward Everett, November 12, 1858, *Massachusetts Historical Society Proceedings, 1858-1860* (Boston, 1860), p. 232.

It has not been possible to ascertain whether Bishop Carroll
was also at the college on the day of Washington's visit. It can
be said, however, that if at all possible he would have been on
hand when America's first citizen visited the academy. We
know that Carroll held Washington in high esteem and enjoyed
more than a passing acquaintance with him.[104] George Washington Parke Custis, adopted son of Washington, declared that
"he [Carroll] stood very high in the esteem and affections of
the *Pater Patriae* from his exalted worth as a minister of God,
his stainless character as a man and above all his distinguished
services as a patriot of the Revolution."[105] Custis is the
authority, too, for the fact that Carroll often met the general.
He tells us that in the time of Washington's first term as president, it was the custom of a group of revolutionary stalwarts to
assemble at Grant's Fountain Inn in Baltimore to receive
Washington on his journeys to and from Philadelphia. This
chosen group generally consisted of Colonel Howard, General
Smith, Colonel Rogers, Colonel McHenry, General Otho Williams, Bishop Carroll, and others. "As if by common consent,"
notes Custis, Bishop Carroll was in the center of the group as it
was ranged before the steps of the inn, and "received the first
grasp of the president's hand." Generally, inside the Inn
distinguished foreign visitors would be waiting. Bishop Carroll,
having known these people during his residence in Europe,
would present them to the president.[106] Carroll was most cer-

---

[104] On June 11, 1799, Bishop Carroll, Dr. Digges, and his sister Carroll dined with
Washington at Mount Vernon. Fitzpatrick, *Diaries of Washington*, Vol. 4,
p. 306. See also Benson J. Lossing, *Recollections and Private Memoirs of
Washington by His Adopted Son, George Washington Parke Custis* (New
York: Derby and Jackson, 1860), p. 173, where Custis numbers among the
bosom friends of Washington "the late excellent prelate and ardent friend of
American liberty, Doctor Carroll, Archbishop of Baltimore."

[105] Robert Walsh to Edward Everett, November 12, 1858, *Massachusetts Historical
Society Proceedings, 1858-1860* (Boston, 1860), p. 232.

[106] *Ibid.*

tainly disappointed if he was not present on the day of Washington's visit to Georgetown College.

Father DuBourg was to have the pleasure of returning Washington's visit. On July 10, 1798, in company with one of the professors and two of the students, "a son of Mr. Law's and a nephew of Barry's" and some other guests, he accepted the gracious invitation of Washington to dine at Mount Vernon.[107]

107 Fitzpatrick, *Diaries of George Washington, 1748-1799*, Vol. 4, p. 280.

CHAPTER V

Stress
and Strain

Father DuBourg was not to complete the year of 1798 as president of Georgetown College. The opposition, felt but unexpressed, though referred to in Father Molyneux's letter to Bishop Carroll as the beginning of Father DuBourg's term, gradually grew until the matter had to be resolved. Bishop Carroll was at a loss to explain the situation. Father DuBourg was a man of great merit and amiable accomplishments. He had been a very able president under very trying circumstances, financial and otherwise.[1] And yet, "somehow or other," he was unable to get along with, or receive the approbation of, the directors of the college. He was irked often by their regulations, and, after repeated difficulties, had resolved that there was but one solution. He offered his resignation to take effect at Christmas, 1798. Bishop Carroll doubtless made a fair estimate of the situation when he declared that the fault probably lay on both sides. The root difficulty as he saw it was national attachment. On his side, Father DuBourg was fond of introducing into

---

[1] The debt of the "old College" rose to £2741 7s, that of "new College" to £332 6s 5d by April 24, 1799. Meeting of Directors, April 24, 1799. *Minutes of the Directors, Georgetown College, 1797-1815.* GUA, 398. There were some who too easily placed the entire responsibility for the debt on Father DuBourg.

any vacant post his own countrymen. The directors, on the other hand, had extreme prejudices "against everything which was derived in any shape from France."[2] The international scene repeatedly cast its shadow over the relationship between the English and French clergy. Even Father Plowden, Carroll's good correspondent, was not free of an anti-French bias. In 1810 on the occasion of Father Grassi's departure for America, Plowden expressed the wish that the archbishop would find him "a station untainted by Frenchmen."[3] The feeling among many was much the same in 1798. The natural result was that every move of DuBourg's was viewed from this point of prejudice. Carroll expressed his confidence that in the providence of God all would turn out for the best, but feared that the college would suffer in public opinion.[4]

In this same letter Bishop Carroll returned to a topic that was causing him no little concern for the success of his twofold plan. Few young men had entered the seminary recently established at Baltimore, and very few of these had come from Georgetown College. It had been Carroll's hope that from such a source of supply would come not only pastors for the congregations, but also a succession of capable teachers for the college. But until the day when the school would be "blessed with masters acting with one spirit"[5], little could be expected. "Hired professors," however devoted and diligent, could not supply the need.[6] It was a vicious circle. Clerical teachers, animated with a single spirit, were needed if vocations were to be expected, and vocations must increase in the infant American church if priests were to be spared to enter the classroom. The directors of the college, in an attempt to resolve the dilemma,

---

[2] Carroll to Plowden, December 11, 1798. MS WCA, 202 B 52.
[3] Plowden to Grassi, December 26, 1810. MS WCA, 203 M 10.
[4] Carroll to Plowden, December 11, 1798. MS loc. cit.
[5] Carroll to Plowden, September 24, 1796. Shea Transcripts. GUA, 255.
[6] Carroll to Plowden, December 11, 1798. MS loc. cit.

requested the bishop to "spare such persons of the clergy from the diocese as they may jointly approve of for that end until such time as others . . . can be formed."[7] The dilemma was to receive no permanent solution until the restoration of the Society of Jesus in the United States, for then there would be a steady flow of professors. The prospects of that happy event, however, were not bright.

Christmas of 1798, if we can believe the testaments left to us, was a sorrowful one at Georgetown. On the evening of December 18 at the close of grace after supper, the students and professors expressed their sorrow at Father DuBourg's departure. By a happy inspiration, one of the students assumed the role of amateur reporter and procured copies of the addresses for the local newspaper.[8] The address of the students, which was not expected by the president, was delivered by James Bankhead of Virginia. It was spoken, the student reporter tells us, "amidst the sobs and emanations of the heart so sincerely expressed by the amiable and juvenile audience." The young spokesman stressed the fact that Father DuBourg had been truly a "father" to the boys. He declared that "no loss whatever can be compared to that which we now sustain, and we dare to venture to assert that our grief is proportionate to our misfortune."[9] The professors, through their spokesmen, apologized for having been anticipated by the students in expressions of devotion to their departing president. They gloried "to have been preceded, as they can but be the indications of that warmth of heart, that generosity of sentiment, which in youth must be the sure forerunner, the pledge of the most pleasing prospects

---

[7] Meeting of the Directors at Georgetown, April 24, 1799. *Minutes of the Directors, Georgetown College, 1797-1815.* GUA, 398.

[8] William Williams to Messrs. Green and English, December 20, 1798. Shea Transcripts, GUA, 15.3.

[9] The students of Georgetown College to Father Wm. DuBourg, December 18, 1798. Shea Transcripts, GUA, 15.3.

of manhood."[10] Father DuBourg gave an extemporary speech of thanks for the touching expressions of esteem, but unfortunately our reporter was unable to make a draft of his remarks. He tells us, however, "it drew tears from every eye."[11]

Before leaving his post, Father DuBourg gave to the press the notice of his resignation and call to a new appointment. He very graciously returned "his heartfelt acknowledgement" to the directors, professors, pupils, inhabitants of Georgetown, and other friends throughout the Union. Letters concerning collegiate matters he requested to be directed henceforth "to the Reverend Mr. Leonard Neale."[12]

The latter gentleman had, just a week previously, been chosen by the directors to head the college, and his appointment had been sent to Bishop Carroll for approval.[13] At the same time, the post of vice president, suspended for a time, was resumed and given to Father Francis Neale, brother of the president. A new office was voted, that of prefect of morals, and the president and vice president were to determine upon the duties of this functionary.

Father Leonard Neale at the time of his appointment to the presidency of Georgetown was coadjutor bishop-elect. The bulls for his consecration had been issued at Rome in 1795, but had not yet been received in America.[14]

---

[10] The professors of Georgetown College to Father Wm. DuBourg, December 18, 1798. Shea Transcripts, GUA, 15.3.

[11] William Williams to Messrs. Green and English, December 20, 1798. Shea Transcripts, GUA, 15.5.

[12] *Centinel of Liberty and Georgetown and Washington Advertiser*, Tuesday, January 8, 1799. DuBourg's notice had been written on December 24, 1798.

[13] Meeting of Directors, Georgetown College, at the White Marsh, December 18, 1798. *Minutes of the Directors, Georgetown College, 1797-1815*, GUA, 398.

[14] "These Bulls were expedited through the 'Congregation de Propaganda Fide,' and forwarded by some devious route, the French Revolution making it impossible to transmit them through the Nuncio at Paris, as on the former occasion." Shea, *Life and Times of Archbishop Carroll*, p. 414. The necessary documents eventually arrived in 1800.

Father Neale was born on October 15, 1746, near Port Tobacco in Charles County, Maryland. In many respects his long and brilliant career parallels that of Bishop Carroll's. At the age of twelve he was sent to St. Omer's by his widowed mother, who continued the tradition of the long line of heroic Catholic mothers of Maryland who made the great sacrifice, so that their sons or daughters would be assured of a Catholic education. After St. Omer's he continued his studies at Bruges and Liége, and entered the Society of Jesus at Ghent on September 7, 1767. He had been ordained, but was still in his theology course when the Society was suppressed in 1773. He accepted a post in England for a short time, but not long afterwards volunteered to serve in the mission colony of Demerara in British Guiana.[15] Here he labored for ten years, and did not return to his native Maryland until 1783. His first post in America was the very congenial one of attending the congregation in the neighborhood of his home at Port Tobacco. Father Neale had attended the White Marsh meeting of 1786 which had resolved to establish the academy, and had been appointed one of the first directors. Later, however, he joined the members of the Southern district in their opposition to the venture. His opposition stemmed from his firm belief in the eventual re-establishment of the Society of Jesus. He seems, remarkably, never to have doubted it. For this reason, he felt strongly that the properties of the Society should be kept intact, awaiting the day of the "inevitable" restoration. After Father Carroll had convinced him of the necessity of the school for the future of the Church in America, Neale became, instead of an opponent, an ardent advocate of the college at Georgetown. When called to the presidency of the institution, he was laboring in Philadelphia which was still suffering from the ravages

---

[15] By a happy coincidence, the county seat of Demerara was Georgetown, founded in 1781.

of the yellow fever plague which had first visited the city in 1793.[16]

"Undazzled by the honor awaiting him," as one writer phrased it, Bishop-elect Neale "left the active exercise of the ministry to guide the rising college."[17] Brother Mobberly, S.J., has left in his diary an estimate of the new president. "He was," says Brother Mobberly, a "sincere friend and an upright man." He may have been abrupt, continues this frank critic, for he was "too candid to be agreeable in his transactions with the foolish world." He neither courted the good opinion or applause of men, nor held in esteem those who did so. Plain, simple, never elegant, he was polite but without ceremony. Sincerity was his characteristic, and he had very little patience with fraud. He was slow to make a decision, but once he had made that decision he did not change it. He was tenacious of his opinion once formed, and "He always supported his authority with vigor and enforced regularity of life in very strong terms."[18] Even after his consecration Bishop Neale continued as president of the college, and resided there in the same simple manner he had always known. His room was in the Old South building of the college opposite the community chapel and next to the ascetory, or study room, of the students. There John McElroy, then a young man residing in Georgetown, and destined to have later a long and fruitful career as a Jesuit, used

---

[16] Altogether, from 1793-1800, eight priests died of the fever. Among those who died in Philadelphia was the Rev. Lawrence Graessel, coadjutor-elect. Upon Graessel's death, Father Neale had been chosen coadjutor. See "The Most Reverend Leonard Neale," *The United States Catholic Magazine and Monthly Review*, ed. Charles I. White, III (1844) 505-512; Sister M. Bernetta Brislen, "The Episcopacy of Leonard Neale," *Historical Records and Studies*, XXXIV (1945), New York: The United States Catholic Historical Society, 20 ff.; John Gilmary Shea, *History of the Catholic Church in the United States* (New York: John G. Shea, 1890), Vol. 2, *passim*.

[17] Shea, *History of Georgetown University*, p. 26.

[18] Diary of Bro. Joseph Mobberly, S.J. MS V, 35, GUA, 4.5. Printed in *Woodstock Letters*, XXXII (1903), 18-19.

to visit the bishop for spiritual direction. He tells us that Bishop Neale's room was at the same time the library of the college. His bed was folded up in the form of a cupboard during the day, and each evening was spread out by the colored man who attended the refectory. Father McElroy recalled that even in old age and feeble health Bishop Neale retained the same regularity that had always marked his life. He invariably rose at four o'clock, made a visit to the Blessed Sacrament, and returned to his room for his hour of meditation before celebrating Mass.[19]

Toward the close of Bishop Neale's first year as president, Georgetown College joined with the rest of America in mourning the death of George Washington. As on the occasion of Washington's visit to the college, Robert Walsh was again chosen to express the sentiments of the student body.[20] The exercises were held in Trinity Church, Georgetown. The press account stated that "Master Robert Walsh . . . a young gentlemen of the college, draped in badges of mourning, made his appearance on a stage[21] covered with black and delivered, with propriety and spirit, an ingenious and eloquent academical eulogium.[22] Unfortunately, this address has been lost. The

---

[19] Father John McElroy to the Editor (?) of *Woodstock Letters*. A Conversation. *Woodstock Letters*, III (1875), 90.

[20] Robert Walsh, although he did not complete his studies at Georgetown, is considered among Georgetown's most brilliant sons. He never enjoyed good health and his parents, residents of Baltimore, transferred him to St. Mary's College, lately opened in that city by Father DuBourg. Here, apparently, they considered they could keep more careful watch over him. There is some reason to believe, too, that he was dissatisfied under Bishop Neale after the departure of the genial, kindly Father DuBourg. See Sr. M. Frederick Lochemes, *Robert Walsh: His Story* (New York: American Irish Historical Society, 1941). Four generations of the Walsh family were to be represented on the student rolls of Georgetown.

[21] Walsh said that the address was delivered "from the pulpit." Robert Walsh to Edward Everett, November 12, 1858, *loc. cit.*

[22] *The Centinel of Liberty and Georgetown Advertiser*, February 25, 1800.

"eulogium," however, would tell us little of Walsh's ingenuity and eloquence, for he has recorded for us the fact that it was written by his professor of rhetoric.[23]

In July of 1800, presumably at the urging of Bishop Neale, the directors decided to inaugurate the course of philosophy which had been promised in the prospectus of 1798.[24] The proposal was far from being greeted with universal acclaim. Bishop Carroll believed that the move, good in itself, was ill-timed and that it was motivated not a little by prejudice on the part of the directors of the college against the Sulpicians and the seminary at Baltimore. This feeling against the Sulpicians was to him "very ill-founded." The opposition he looked upon as "violent and . . . unexpected," and he considered that the sudden resolution to open a course of philosophy in the college was calculated to counteract the seminary. Notwithstanding these reasons, he would still give his approval, but only after he had been assured of the fulfillment of two conditions:

> . . . if there were amongst us a man fit to undertake a course of philosophy, without disgracing himself and the College; and unless this appeared to be evidently an attempt to wrest from the Bishop the government and superintendence over the studies and education of his clergy which the canons and decrees of the Church confer on him.[25]

Bishop Neale was not opposed to the seminary, but he was very desirous of completing the curriculum at Georgetown by the introduction of the course in philosophy. He was, as were his fellow directors, opposed to the school opened by Father

---

[23] Walsh to Everett, November 12, 1858, *loc. cit.*
[24] Meeting of Directors of Georgetown College, July 1 and 2, 1800, at the White Marsh. *Minutes of the Directors, Georgetown College, 1797-1815.* GUA, 126.6.
[25] Carroll to Plowden, September 3, 1800. Stonyhurst Transcripts, Archives of the Catholic University of America. See also Carroll to M. Nagot, August, 1800 (undated on transcript). Shea Transcripts, GUA, 255.1.

DuBourg in Baltimore upon the latter's return from Havana.[26]
He considered that institution as constituting a very definite
threat to the success of Georgetown. Bishop Carroll had not
favored the establishment of the Baltimore school, but had been
forced to a compromise on the issue when Father Emery
threatened to recall the Sulpicians to France. Carroll needed the
Sulpician Fathers for the seminary and, as he had hopes that
they would soon have enough students to devote themselves to
their proper field, the training of ecclesiastics, he permitted
them to continue their academy for two or three years. He
further stipulated that no American students should be admitted. At the same time, the number of students was limited
to twelve, although Carroll later extended his approval to
twenty-four students.[27]

Bishop Neale was very anxious that Bishop Carroll should
understand the considerations that had persuaded the directors
to make the addition of the philosophy course to the curriculum
at Georgetown. The breach between Carroll and some of the
clergy had reached alarming proportions. Carroll had observed
to Plowden that the want of a sufficient number of men was not
the only cause for the little advantage that had accrued to
the diocese from the college. Errors committed at the beginning,
and national prejudices above all, were responsible. He
regretted bitterly that:

> . . . amongst our few remaining brethren here to whom is com-
> mitted the administration of the temporalities, there are some whose
> violence will listen to no lessons of moderation; and others whose

---

[26] Father Peter Babade conceived the idea of establishing an ecclesiastical college
in Havana and had interested Father Benedict Flaget and Father DuBourg
in the enterprise. His accounts may have contributed to DuBourg's decision
to leave Georgetown. The Spanish government forbade the proposed establishment and DuBourg returned to Baltimore, bringing with him three Cuban
boys who had been desirous of entering the new school. These formed the
nucleus of the college at Baltimore. Ruane, *op cit.*, pp. 100-104.

[27] *Ibid.*, pp. 104-108.

knowledge and observations are too confined to comprehend that anything can be learned beyond what they know; or that any change of circumstances should suggest improvements suitable to times and situations, and cause the slightest deviation from the track in which they once walked themselves.[28]

Doubtless it was such a feeling that prompted Carroll to believe that the decision of the directors in the matter of the philosophy course was part of an attempt to "wrest from the bishop the government and superintendence over the studies and education of his clergy."[29]

It was this "misunderstanding" between Carroll and the directors which gave "serious concern" to Bishop Neale.[30] He consulted with two of the directors, Father Plunkett and his brother Father Francis Neale, and they assured him that "such a thought never entered their minds and that they were fully convinced that none of the directors entertained such an idea." They had considered the new college at Baltimore with "its new and strangely enforced plan of a course of humanities introduced into the house destined for the Episcopal seminary" as being directly aimed at outstripping Georgetown. If they were to send on to Baltimore the students of the college who were then destined to begin their philosophical studies, they would be falling in with the "calculated plan above mentioned." St. Mary's College in Baltimore would accordingly add to its course of humanities a course of philosophy. This could have but one result. Georgetown would steadily decline and the

---

[28] Carroll to Plowden, September 3, 1800. Stonyhurst Transcripts. Archives of the Catholic University of America.

[29] *Ibid.* "Six or seven young men who intend to embrace an ecclesiastical state, were to have entered into the seminary and commence their philosophy this month."

[30] Bishop Carroll spoke of it as a "jarring" between himself and "some of our good brethren." It would be his "endeavor," however, "and hope to compose these differences." Carroll to Plowden, December 15, 1800. Stonyhurst Transcripts, CUA.

"sanguine expectations formed by the Clergy of Maryland in regard of the College . . . providing a sufficient supply of able *operarii* in the vineyard of the Lord" would be frustrated. As directors of Georgetown, they were charged with the support of the dignity of the college, and felt themselves obligated to take all measures necessary. Obviously, the introduction of the course of philosophy was such a measure. Such alone, they insisted, were their motives, and "they never conceived their conduct in that regard as in the smallest degree derogatory to that sincere respect which was due" to Bishop Carroll.[31] It is a tribute to the genius, prudence, balance, and good common sense of Bishop Carroll that he was able not only to recognize the ability, integrity, and zeal of the bodies of clergy in his diocese, but was adept also at mitigating the frictions that arose. He pointed beyond personalities to the cause common to the parties, and induced them to realize their full potential for the Church in America. This was evident in the case of the introduction of philosophy into the Georgetown curriculum. Although he was opposed to the measure, he was willing, in the interests of harmony and good order, to drop his opposition provided a fit professor could be obtained. Equally clear and impressive was the devotion of the clergy. Differences might arise, suspicions, jealousies, prejudices all so human, might develop between individuals or communities; but we would be hard put to it to show that in such cases the motive actuating the parties was one of personal gain. Each would hold to his opinion only because he felt that it was the best for the common cause. If it was seen that the cause which they all equally espoused might suffer, opinions were quickly yielded.

In the fall of 1801, the philosophy course was begun with Father Maréchal, a Sulpician, giving lectures in metaphysics,

---

[31] Leonard Neale to Carroll, July 21, 1800. MS BCA, 5 Q 1.

ethics and logic.[32] The fathers of St. Sulpice had accepted the opportunity, suggested by Bishop Carroll, in the hope of removing the friction engendered with the gentlemen of the clergy.[33]

At the close of the school year of 1802, however, Bishop Neale learned that Father Maréchal would not return for the next year, and at that date the president had little expectation of filling the post. It was at about this time, too, that Father Emery, despairing of any success for the seminary, was threatening to recall the fathers of St. Sulpice to France. If this threat were fulfilled, Neale remarked, "we shall be left perfectly bare."[34] He poured out his troubles to Father Stone in the hope that the recital would stir the latter to lend help speedily.[35] Neale was disappointed. Nor did the decision on the part of Father Maréchal (or his superiors) not to return to Georgetown

---

[32] Bishop Neale had been in correspondence with Father Marmaduke Stone, president of Stonyhurst College in England, in an endeavor to secure one or two ex-Jesuits but he was unsuccessful. For a while it seemed that some of the Paccanarists (termed by Hughes a "pseudo-Society of Jesus") might come to America but this did not materialize. Hughes, *History of the Society of Jesus, Documents*, Vol. 1, Part II, p. 813. See also enclosure in Strickland to Carroll, July 20, 1800. MS BCA, 8 D 2.

[33] *Régistre des Assemblées, St. Mary's Seminary* records: "We spoke in the assembly today of the proposition which the bishop made to Father Maréchal: that he go to teach philosophy at Georgetown College. We thought that this could become a means of reconciliation with the Gentlemen of the Clergy whom our Academy has so greatly offended. It is from this point of view and with this intention that Father Maréchal consents to accept the proposition." Cited from Ruane, *op. cit.*, p. 87.

[34] Neale to Father Marmaduke Stone, June 30, 1802. MS WCA, 4 S 1 (12).

[35] It was about this time that reports were beginning to reach America in greater volume of a *viva voce* reestablishment of the Society of Jesus. Neale persistently begged Father Stone for more news of this exciting report and for assistance from Stonyhurst for his depleted faculty. When the negotiations were being carried on with the Paccanarists, Neale cautioned that while Carroll had said he would receive them with open arms, he would do so only if he could not obtain some of the ex-Jesuits. See Neale's postscript to Carroll to Strickland, October 27, 1800. Brochure of transcripts of Carroll's Letters, GUA, 252.2, pp. 11 and 12. Some of the more important Neale-Stone correspondence has been printed in *Woodstock Letters*, XII, 81 ff.

fail to affect deeply the president. He was deeply troubled, for he saw that the vocations of some of the young clerics would certainly be endangered as a result. In his disturbed state of mind, doubts and suspicions were easily fostered, and Neale looked upon Maréchal's departure as "proceeding from some private policy or intrigue." He had frequently assured Father Maréchal that the young clerics would be sent to the seminary immediately after the conclusion of their philosophical course, and he had made the same very clear to the "Gentlemen of the seminary." It was impossible to give written assurance of this fact in the name of the board of trustees and directors due to the present angry state of "Mr. A—— whom no one wished to meet."[36] Neale deeply regretted that his reflections on the departure of Father Maréchal had caused Bishop Carroll to believe that the Sulpicians were held in little regard at Georgetown. On the contrary, averred Neale, they were held in high esteem there. He had blamed their conduct in opening a school to perform the same function as that given to Georgetown College, but other than that he had never passed any adverse judgment on the fathers of St. Sulpice. "I hope," he asserted, "that the Almighty will never suffer me either to depreciate or undervalue their merit which I have always been fully sensible of."[37]

In a move to establish harmony with "the gentlemen of the clergy," the Corporation of Roman Catholic Clergymen, "the gentlemen of the seminary," the Sulpitians, offered "to suppress immediately their academy at Baltimore; to transfer their students to the college; and to furnish it with a certain number of

---

[36] Father Ashton had become violently angry over injustices, real or fanciful, done to him. He later resigned from the Board of Directors and the Corporation of the Clergy. Carroll to Bishop Neale, Fathers Molyneux, Walton, and Sewall, September 1, 1801. MS BCA, 9 P 1. See, also, Carroll to L. Neale, July 5, 1801, MS WCA, 203 Z 6.

[37] Bishop Neale to Carroll, December 13, 1802. MS BCA, 5 Q 3.

subjects for teaching and other purposes."[38] This proposal was given serious consideration and varying degrees of approval in the form of preliminary conferences held by the representatives of the different districts of the Select Body of the Roman Catholic Clergy.[39] Unfortunately, the possibility of the union of the two communities was never to be actualized. In 1803 the Spanish government sent a corvette to convey the Spanish students back to Havana.[40] In order that their foundation might be sustained, the Sulpicians then decided with the consent of Bishop Carroll[41] to open the doors of St. Mary's College to "all applicants regardless of nationality or creed."[42] This move was necessary, they felt, until a sufficient number of applicants for the seminary should make it possible for them to return, exclusively, to the direction of the seminary. The enrollment expanded quickly and by 1806 there were one hundred and six students. Father DuBourg's move to expand St. Mary's was to have far-reaching consequences. Carroll was to be considered more and more by his ex-brethren as looking on them with disfavor, and even as desiring to replace them with the Sulpicians. Father DuBourg's own superior never approved of the expansion of St. Mary's College, nor would he adopt it as a work of St. Sulpice. Even the remarkable prosperity which the college began to enjoy, did not move him. His only conclusion

---

[38] Letter addressed to the members of the Select Body of the R. C. Clergy, residing in the different Districts, by the trustees of the said Clergy, October 15, 1802. Hughes, *History of the Society of Jesus, Documents*, Vol 1, Part II, pp. 793-794. The proposal had much to recommend it. It would have been a potent force for reconciliation of differences, would have restored Georgetown, which was diminishing in numbers, and from this increase would have come vocations to enable the seminary of the fathers of St. Sulpice to flourish.

[39] Hughes, *History of the Society of Jesus, Documents*, Vol. 1, Part II, pp. 794-795.

[40] Of a total of fifty-three students, twenty-three returned to Havana on the Spanish corvette. Ruane, *op. cit.*, p. 120.

[41] The consent of Bishop Carroll was obtained by Father DuBourg post factum. *Loc. cit.*

[42] *Ibid.*, p. 121.

was that Father DuBourg was "never meant to be a Sulpitian or to be confined within the limits of Sulpitian work."[43]

In the meantime, Georgetown was steadily declining in numbers and some very justly feared that it must soon close its doors. Bishop Neale attributed the smallness of numbers to two causes: the first was "the inability of some and the unwillingness of other Catholic parents to furnish the necessary expense for the education of their children." He was certain that if the college could offer free education, there would be no worry about numbers.[44] The second reason was, he felt, the "exclusion of foreigners which the college suffers in consequence of the erection of a rival within the nature [sic] verge of her influence." While giving this estimate, Neale was conscious of the fact that "Gentlemen of a censorious nature may wish to place it [the blame] elsewhere."[45] He was correct in his judgment.

Allowing for all the difficult circumstances under which he guided the college, the plain truth is that in the judgment of at least some of his fellow priests, and particularly of Bishop Carroll, Bishop Neale was not the man for the presidency of the school. Father Charles Sewall lamented to his brother Father Nicholas Sewall in England that the college had declined to such

---

[43] *Ibid.* Father Emery did not order the college to be closed. Although it continued until 1852, frequent were the representations against it as a work foreign to the Society of St. Sulpice. At the order of Rev. Father de Courson, the college was closed after negotiations had been entered into with the Jesuits to take over the education of the college men. Loyola College, Baltimore, thus came into existence.

[44] The financial history of the college offers some argument for Bishop Neale's case. The directors had found it necessary to place a limit of three months' grace on outstanding accounts and to discharge any student whose bill remained unpaid after that time. Meeting of the Directors, Georgetown, September 25-26, 1798; *Minutes of the Directors, Georgetown College, 1797-1815.* GUA, 126.6. A further measure found necessary was the "extra" charge to day scholars of £50 per year for the "fire wood and candles." Meeting of March 13, 1800. *Ibid.*

[45] L. Neale to Carroll, March 22, 1802. MS BCA, 5 A 2.

a point that by 1803 there were but twenty students. The cause of this, as he saw it, lay in "bad regulations" which displeased the parents and caused them to remove their boys from the college.[46] Bishop Carroll agreed with Father Sewall's judgment. Bishop Leonard Neale, the president, and Father Francis Neale, the vice president, were in his estimation "as worthy men as live," but as the principal administrators of the college they had deterred parents from sending their sons to Georgetown by "some regulations not calculated for the meridian of America."[47] A glance at a few of the regulations of 1829, which were considered very mild in comparison with those of Neale's time, will illustrate this point:

> 13. No one will ever be permitted to dine out of the college except with his parents, and that not oftener than once a month, and a note must be previously sent by the parent requesting this permission. Before he (student) can get his clothes,[48] he must ask a note of the prefect to whom he must on his return (which must always be before 5 o'clock) report himself.
>
> *   *   *
>
> 18. It is rigorously prohibited to any student to have money in his possession.
>
> *   *   *
>
> 22. At the end of school each student must salute the professor with a polite bow and silently depart.[49]

Carroll praised the motives of the brothers Neale, but their principles were, he thought, "too monastic"; and, "with a laudable view of excluding immorality" they had denied "that liberty which all here lay claim to."[50]

---

[46] Father Charles Sewall to Father Nicholas Sewall, November 21, 1803. MS WCA, 4 W 2. See also *Woodstock Letters*, XII, 83.

[47] Carroll to Plowden, March 12, 1802. Stonyhurst Transcripts. CUA. Unfortunately, we do not have any specific regulations of Neale's regime.

[48] This was the Sunday uniform.

[49] *Regulations for the Students*, 1829. GUA, 1.3

[50] Carroll to Plowden, March 12, 1802. Stonyhurst Transcripts, CUA.

At this point in his recital Carroll allowed himself the privilege of digression on the general topic of discipline. His idea would seem to be timeless in its value:

> Indeed it is difficult problem to solve, what degree of it [liberty] should be allowed in literary establishments, and never have I been able to satisfy my own mind on this subject, though it has been much employed in thinking of it. Theory and experience are constantly at variance in this case; for though the principles of religion and morality command, or seem to command, the instructors of youth to restrain their pupils from almost every communication with the men and things of the world, yet that very restraint operates against the effects intended by it, and it is too often found that on being delivered from it, young men, as when the pin that confines a spring is loosened, burst out of confinement into licentiousness, and give way to errors and vices, which with more acquaintance with the manners and language of the world, they would have avoided. . . .[51]

More than six years later Bishop Carroll had not changed his view of Bishop Neale as president of Georgetown. He deemed that the appointment had been a mistake. Father Francis Neale he considered to be "virtue and piety itself," and Leonard to have "equal perhaps superior virtue and equal constancy in pursuing what he deems to be right," but they were "too illiterate to have any share in the direction of a litterary [sic] institution." Bishop Neale had never made the study of "what is called polite litterature" [sic] the special object of his application, and it was precisely that kind of literature which must mark a college such as Georgetown. In America a college was judged by the talents of its president. Besides learning he must possess "affability, address and other human qualities," for which neither of the brothers was ever conspicuous.[52] The college had been founded for the education

---

[51] *Ibid.*
[52] Carroll to Plowden, April 2, 1808. Stonyhurst Transcripts, CUA.

of youth generally, and must not be "governed on the principles and in the system of a convent."[53] It was true that there was every hope and expectation that from the graduates would come candidates for the priesthood, but Carroll's pastoral of 1792 is ample evidence that that was not to be the exclusive function of the college. Unfortunately, Bishop Neale had chosen to manage the school as if it were a seminary. In 1803, he was not over concerned at the small numbers for "there was a respectable number of postulants for the clerical state." In 1808, two years after the first novitiate of the Society of Jesus had been established, he considered himself vindicated. There were eleven novices in the first course of the novitiate and seven in the second. "Thus the college of Georgetown," said Neale, complacently, "though short in point of numbers of scholars has not been unfertile in genuine productions." There could be but one conclusion: "The proof drawn from stubborn facts must be an ample support of the discipline and principles adopted in that college during my presidency."[54] He felt justified when he heard that many young men "were desirous of attending a course of natural philosophy in George Town College on account of its famed regularity."[55] Not long before this he had received an application from some young men from William and Mary College, Virginia. It appeared, judged Neale, that "They were totally disgusted at the irregularity and want of discipline observed in all their places of education."[56]

---

[53] *Ibid.* As we have seen often, Carroll stressed the American character of the enterprise. It could not follow European models. In this same letter he remarks that Father Kohlmann would be of great benefit when he had become more "informed of the customs of this country and understands that a college, founded like that of Georgetown for the education of youth generally must not be governed on the principles and in the system of a convent."

[54] Bishop Neale to Father Marmaduke Stone, February 16, 1808. Stonyhurst Transcripts, CUA.

[55] Neale to Carroll, November 5, 1804. MS BCA, 5 R 2.

[56] *Ibid.*

Jaspar Lynch apparently was not sufficiently appreciative of the "famed regularity" of the Neale disciplinary system. He merits our attention, for there must have been few culprits in academic history who occasioned correspondence between two bishops over their disciplinary problems. On October 17, 1805, Bishop Carroll received the indictment of Jaspar who had "eloped"[57] October 16, 1805, because he was reprimanded for his untoward conduct and "gross disobedience to several of his superiors for a considerable time." He was characterized as "disobedient," "discontented," and "a violent tempered boy." It was a pity, too, that his temper was so impetuous and unruly for he had "powerful abilities" and was an excellent scholar. Unfortunately, Carroll's answer has not come to light. Anyone familiar with Carroll would agree that he must have smiled benignly at Neale's excitement.[58]

Although, as we have seen, the student enrollment dropped considerably during the presidency of Bishop Neale, a student of those days recalled in later life that at the time of his entrance into the college there had been a "good number of scholars."[59] They were principally from the District of Columbia, but New York, Philadelphia, Baltimore, Virginia, and Maryland were well represented. Applications for admission, moreover, were occasionally being received from students in the more distant states of the Union. William Gaston, Georgetown's first student, had sent from North Carolina a very gifted and talented youth, Stephen Perry. Among the students from

---

[57] "Eloped" must be read as of the nineteenth century. It meant simply that the boy removed himself without leave from the care of the college.

[58] Father Charles Plowden, like Carroll, was an admirer of the virtue and piety of the Neales but he was inclined to believe that the spirit of inflexibility belonged "in some degree to the family." Plowden to Carroll, January 26, 1801. MS BCA, 6 Q 2; L. Neale to Carroll, October 17, 1805, MS BCA, 5 Q 5.

[59] The student was Joseph H. Clarke, who entered Georgetown about 1804. A teacher in later life, he had as one of his pupils Edgar Allan Poe. *Georgetown College Journal*, VIII, No. 3 (January, 1880), 26.

Washington city were Brents and Carrolls and Boarmans,[60] and from Maryland were members of the families of the Fenwicks, Digges, Bowlings, Sewalls, Brookes, Lancasters, Mudds, Neales, Youngs, and other well known names. James Ord, the reputed son by lawful marriage of George IV, King of England and Mrs. Fitzherbert, had entered in 1800. William and Richard Seton, sons of Mrs. Elizabeth Bayley Seton, foundress of the Sisters of Charity in the United States, entered in 1806 through the kindness of Bishop Carroll who had provided means for their education.[61]

These were indeed days of crisis for Georgetown. Never in good financial condition, the college knew even harder times in the later years of Neale's presidency.[62] "As far as I can recollect," wrote Father McElroy concerning this period, "there was for a long time but one vestment of *all colors* in the college, and this was old and worn. On Sunday morning this vestment was taken to Trinity Church with the missal, cruets, etc., for the celebration of Mass, and then brought back to the College."[63] In March of 1805, Neale, referring to a draft for two hundred and ten dollars which Carroll had undertaken to forward to him, asked that it be sent as soon as possible, "as it is much

---

[60] Charles Boarman, Jr., was a student at the college, but left to join the United States Navy where he attained the rank of rear admiral. In 1854 he fitted out the famous naval expedition to Japan. His father, Charles, Sr., had been a student at St. Omer's with Bishop Carroll. He was a devoted member of the faculty of Georgetown from 1797 to 1819.

[61] "In concert with Bishop Neale I provided means for the reception of education of her two sons for at least some years, and trusted that in the meantime providence would open other resources." Bishop Carroll to James Barry, Esq. April 8, 1806. MS BCA, 9 C 6. See also Thomas Kelly to Mrs. Seton, April 8, 1806. MS Seton Papers, Archives of Mt. St. Joseph's College, Emmitsburg, Maryland, II, 54. Kelly, at the time a part-time teacher at Georgetown, wrote an interesting plea to Mrs. Seton to send her sons to Georgetown.

[62] It should be recalled that the debt was very high at the time of Bishop Neale's ascending to the presidency. See *supra.* p. 98.

[63] "An Account of the Reestablishment of the Society in the United States," *The Woodstock Letters*, XVI, 162.

wanting." The year, Neale added, had been financially one of
the most trying of his college experience, due to the high cost
of the necessary articles as well as to the delayed payments of
many parents.[64]

Lack of students and lack of money were trying enough
problems. But to add to these, Bishop Neale also faced a lack
of teachers. In order to meet this problem, a leaf was taken
from the book of Liége and Stonyhurst, and the device of the
clerical oath was introduced. This meant, as phrased in
the words of the directors' resolution of July 2, 1800:

> . . . that all those who are educated at the College of Geo-Town on
> free places shall when of competent age, bind themselves by oath
> to serve said College, on the salary of clerical professors employed
> therein if required by the Directors, during six years from the time
> of finishing their studies in said college. Provided their studies have
> not been interrupted in which case a proportionate length of time
> shall be deducted from the said six years.[65]

Coming as it did in the tense years following DuBourg's
difficulties with the directors, and at the time of the introduction
of the philosophy course into the Georgetown curriculum, this
resolution was at first looked upon by Bishop Carroll as an
attempt to circumvent his authority in the "locating or fixing"
of professors in the college. He did not question the legitimacy
of the move. It had been employed, he knew, at Liége and was
not an uncommon practice. The time of the resolution, however,
seemed to place it, along with the introduction of philosophy,
into a single pattern of an attempt to by-pass the authority of
the bishop, and to disregard any course of action outlined by
him. Doubtless, too, the necessary delay in the ordination of the
clerical students as a result of this device of the clerical oath,

---

[64] L. Neale to Carroll, March 17, 1805. MS BCA, 5 P 6.

[65] Meeting of the Board of Directors, July 1-2, 1800. *Minutes of the Directors,
Georgetown College, 1797-1815.* GUA, 398.

was not to Carroll's liking. Bishop Neale hastened to assure the
founder of Georgetown that disrespect or suspicion of Carroll
had been far from their minds. If the words of the resolution
appeared to be disrespectful to the bishop, they solemnly dis-
avowed any such intention. They further declared that they
fully intended to submit to the bishop for his approval the form
of the oath, once it had been drawn up by the president. Influenced by the example of Liége and Stonyhurst (which required
eight years' service), they had concluded that the oath was the
only course open to the college, if it were "to be perpetuated
in its proper line of tendency [with] steady good characters for
professors and prefects."[66] The college, it was pointed out, was
contributing at least one hundred dollars a year to each one
enrolled as a clerical student and, consequently, seemed to the
directors to possess a natural claim to their service, if such
service was necessary for the perpetuation of the college.[67]

Bishop Carroll eventually gave his approval, but the problem of a steady source of professors for the college was not
even partially solved until 1806. Bishop Neale had long
desired two things—the restoration of the Society of Jesus in
America, and relief from his post of president of Georgetown.
While waiting to hear from Russia that the American ex-Jesuits
might be aggregated to the canonically recognized Society there,
he had written to Father Stone that "were it the will of heaven
that the Society be speedily re-established here, I should be
happy to deliver my presidency to their happyer [sic] guidance."[68] Both of Neale's desires were realized. On June 21,
1805, by authority of the letter of aggregation from Reverend
Father Gabriel Gruber, General of the Society of Jesus in

---

[66] L. Neale to Carroll, July 21, 1800. MS BCA, 5 O 1.
[67] *Ibid.*
[68] Bishop L. Neale to Father Marmaduke Stone, June 25, 1803. Hughes, *History of the Society of Jesus, Documents*, Vol. 1, Part II, p. 798.

Russia, Bishop Carroll, acting for Father Gruber, appointed
Father Robert Molyneux superior of those Jesuits in the United
States who had become affiliated with the Society in Russia.[69]
In the following year Bishop Neale resigned from the presidency of Georgetown and Father Molyneux was again called
to head the institution.[70] The college at the same time passed
into full possession of the partially restored Society of Jesus.

---

[69] The Society of Jesus had not as yet been restored throughout the world. The
restoration of 1805 was an "approved affiliation with the canonically recognized Society in Russia." See Chapter VI.

[70] Carroll looked on Molyneux's appointment to the presidency as temporary. "He
[Bishop Neale] is no longer president of the college which he resigned about
a week ago and is replaced by Mr. Molyneux who is too old and inactive but
who will hold it for a time till something better can be done." Carroll to
James Barry, September 19, 1806. MS BCA, 9 D 1.

Georgetown and the
Restoration of the Society of Jesus

On March 7, 1801, the pontifical brief *Catholicae Fidei* granted canonical status to the small band of Jesuits who had continued to exist as a body in Russia, and permitted the Society there to aggregate to itself members from any part of the world.[1] On April 21, 1802, Bishop Neale, whose anxiety for the restoration had increased day by day as he saw the blessings it would bring to Georgetown College, wrote to Father Stone in England. He had heard of the reestablishment of the Society of Jesus from Father Strickland, but apparently had learned none of the details. "You," Neale wrote, "who are near the sun, should not refuse to communicate its benign rays."[2] He would take all the members of the Society that could be spared. "Any-

---

[1] The power to admit foreign ex-Jesuits was not immediately evident in the brief. In answer to the requests of the general, Cardinal Consalvi, Secretary of State to Pius VII, declared that the brief did not forbid the aggregation of foreign members. Hughes, *History of the Society of Jesus, Documents*, Vol. 1, Part II, p. 816.

[2] Bishop Neale to Father Marmaduke Stone, April 21, 1802. *Woodstock Letters*, XII (1883), 81. See Molyneux to Carroll, September 16, 1805. MS BCA, 5 L 7. "I am anxious to know what arrangements have been made or making for our poor college at George Town."

thing genuine," he said, "from our ancient body would be highly gratifying." He was certain that Stonyhurst, if the restoration there had already taken place, would not refuse to send assistance to "our poor Georgetown College."[3] Communications were painfully slow between England and America, and Father Stone was not a very prompt correspondent. In June of 1802 Bishop Neale pleaded again for an answer. His fellow ex-Jesuits were continually asking if he had received any response, and he implored Father Stone "for God's sake relieve me of my distressing situation."[4] The college was in dire need of professors[5] and, further, if the restoration did not occur soon, the members of the old Society would be gone, and the Society, though reestablished, would not succeed to the property which the clergy had been studiously preserving against the day of restoration.[6] In the meantime, the clergy had met, and had sent a petition to Bishop Carroll to be forwarded to the general of the Society in Russia, asking to be restored and united with the Society existing there.[7] At long last, Father Stone's pen, in Neale's phrase, "was set at liberty" or some "mighty control" was removed.[8] Having heard of the authority of the general in Russia to aggregate members to the Society from other lands under the *"vivae vocis oraculum"* forwarded by Cardinal Consalvi, and of the general's desire to know the names, ages, employment, etc., of the applicants, the clergy of Charles and St. Mary's counties again made application to Bishop Carroll. They desired to enter the Society and wished that their petition,

---

[3] *Ibid.*

[4] Bishop Neale to Father Stone, June 30, 1802. *Woodstock Letters*, XII (1883),81.

[5] The report was current at this time that Father Emery, Superior General of the Sulpicians, was about to recall the Sulpician Fathers to France.

[6] Bishop Neale to Father Stone, June 30, 1802. *Woodstock Letters*, XII (1883), 81.

[7] The Jesuits of Maryland to Bishop Carroll, August 30, 1802. MS BCA, 11 G 2.

[8] Bishop Neale to Father Stone, June 25, 1803. *Woodstock Letters*, XII (1883), 81.

with entire confidence, should be forwarded to the general through Carroll's hands.[9] Accordingly, Bishops Neale and Carroll wrote a joint letter of petition to the general of the Society in Russia, in which they declared that "there were thirteen ex-Jesuits in the United States and other priests, who asked for affiliation."[10] The original letter apparently miscarried, for, six months later, Carroll sent duplicates of the original petition to be forwarded from London. At last, under date of March 12, 1804, the general of the Society of Jesus in Russia admitted the American ex-Jesuits to affiliation. It is not known just when the reply reached the United States, but it was at least early in 1805 before a copy finally reached Carroll through the agency of Father Stone in England.[11] In accord with the power granted him by the letter of Father Gruber, Bishop Carroll on June 21, 1805, appointed Father Robert Molyneux as superior of the Jesuits who were affiliated with the Society in Russia.[12] On August 10, 1805, Father Molyneux, along with Fathers Charles Sewall, Charles Neale, John Bolton, and Sylvester Boarman, entered into a retreat of eight days, after which Father Molyneux renewed his vows in the presence of Fathers Sewall and Charles Neale at St. Thomas Manor, Charles County, Maryland. On the same day and at the same place, Father Sewall renewed the simple vows, and Father

---

[9] Jesuits of Charles and St. Mary's Counties, Maryland, to Bishop Carroll, April 25, 1803. MS BCA, 11 G 3.

[10] Shea, *Life and Times of the Most Reverend John Carroll*, p. 517.

[11] Father Stone to Bishop Carroll, February 24, 1805. MS BCA, 4 C 7. That Carroll had some misgivings is evidenced in Father Stone's regret "that you seemed to differ from us in opinion respecting the congruity of the ancient members of the Society availing themselves of the Pope's private approbation or *vivae vocis oraculum* to reenter into the order."

[12] Bishop Carroll had met in May, 1805, with the ex-Jesuits who desired readmission. Those unable to meet sent certificates of their desire. "The whole number of them was as follows — Messrs. Robert Molyneux, John Bolton, Charles Sewall, Sylvester Boarman, Charles Neale, and Ignatius Baker Brooke." Carroll to Father Stone, —— 1805, *Woodstock Letters*, XXXIV, 224.

Neale, who had been only a novice in the old Society, pronounced the simple vows for the first time.[13]

The history of the restoration of the Society of Jesus in the
United States, and the history of Georgetown College are
intimately connected. The restoration, as we have seen, could
provide for the college the only answer to the problem of a
steady succession of teachers, imbued with one and the same
spirit. It was, in fact, to spell the difference between success
and failure for Carroll's beloved academy.

On the other hand, the move toward restoration was to
affect in an important way the relationship between the ex-
Jesuits, and one of their former brethren, Bishop Carroll.
Carroll and the ecclesiastical organization of the Church in
America; Carroll and the restoration of the Society of Jesus
in America; these were parallel operations crossing lines at
many points, with Georgetown often a focal one. Add to this
the facts that Carroll loved Georgetown, that Carroll was an
ex-Jesuit, and that Carroll was now charged with the care of the
entire Church in America. How could he discharge all his
obligations, fulfill all his desires and maintain the peace and
harmony necessary, if the cause of religion was to prosper?
To cite but one problem: Carroll was the representative of
Rome in the United States, charged with duly carrying out the
decrees of the Roman Catholic Church. Grieved as he was by
the suppression, it had been, he insisted, canonically and legally
put into effect. He would never be satisfied until a brief of
restoration, as inclusive as that of suppression, had been issued.
Only thus would there be a restoration worthy of the name.[14]

Carroll loved the Society of Jesus. He had been at Rome

---

[13] Edward I. Devitt, S.J., "The Suppression and Restoration of the Society in
Maryland," *The Woodstock Letters* XXXIV, No. 2 (December, 1905), 222,
citing *The Register of the Novitiate.*

[14] See *supra*, p. 26, n. 41; p. 29.

when it was being suppressed, and when finally the news reached him at Bruges, he had declared that he would never recover from the shock of "this dreadful intelligence."[15] He could not bear to see its possible rebirth jeopardized by imprudent haste. But the ardor of his brethren often misinterpreted this caution and prudence as disfavor, and even enmity.[16] Dear as the interests of the Society of Jesus were to Carroll, he was charged with higher, even dearer interests. He had to consult his head as well as his heart and, while aiding his brethren to effect that restoration which would mean so much to the cause of religion, he was bound to safeguard also the interests of ecclesiastical organization in general for the present and the future.

The effect of this interplay of interests and forces on Georgetown College and its administration is evident. The scarcity of manpower demanded that the priests be deployed for the greatest good. On occasion this would mean that the bishop would ask or demand that a priest be assigned by his religious superior to a parish rather than to a teaching post in the college; or one of the Jesuits, a member of an exempt religious order, would be recalled from a parish which he was administering for the bishop, and assigned to the college. Suspicions naturally arose. Old doubts received new life. The bishop, it was charged, was an enemy of the Jesuits. The Jesuits, it was said in rebuttal, wished none but their own, and cared more for the success of their own establishments than they did for the cause of religion. That these conflicting strains were

---

[15] See *supra*, p. 19.

[16] Late in 1800 a meeting had been held of the ex-Jesuits. Carroll had not been invited, for, as Father Sewall wrote: ". . . it appeared to me that your affection for us was much cooled, that your heart was now fixed on the Sulpicians of Baltimore in preference to all others." Father Charles Sewall to Carroll, December 15, 1800. MS BCA, 705. See also Sewall to Carroll, March 23, 1801. MS BCA, 606.

finally blended together into harmony, speaks well for all the great figures involved in these important years. Frictions, serious and sharp, would arise, but the high motivation which prompted each to champion his own side, could not help but be a certain omen of a future resolution of all differences for the success of religion.

Bishop Carroll had earnestly longed for the reestablishment of the Society. As early as 1783 he had written, "God grant that the little beginning in White Russia may prove a foundation for erecting the Society once again."[17] The continued success of "the Russian brethren" led Carroll to say, despite an habitual distrust, as he put it, of "his own hopes and expectations," that he owned on this occasion that it would be too great diffidence not to believe that "God has an extraordinary and salutary purpose in this."[18] His next years had naturally been too much taken up with the foundation of Georgetown and the establishing of the seminary at Baltimore to devote much time to the question of the restoration. In 1796, however, he had been requested by his brethren in Maryland and Pennsylvania to make application to His Holiness for a grant in their favor of the same status as was enjoyed in White Russia by their Jesuit brethren. He was embarrassed. Naturally he wished to do all that he could to fulfill the wishes of the Maryland and Pennsylvania ex-Jesuits, but he could summon little enthusiasm for the task. He wished the Society of Jesus to be restored, but he wished it restored with the same constitution, government, and functions it had enjoyed prior to 1773. If it did not have these, it would not be, he thought, the Society of Jesus, but some other organization. Again, were the brethren living here to choose their own superior and have but a connection of brotherhood with the Society in White Russia, it could hardly be said

[17] Carroll to Plowden, September 26, 1783. MS WCA, 202 B 5.
[18] Carroll to Plowden, January 22, 1787. MS WCA, 202 B 13.

The Observatory

to be the same body instituted by St. Ignatius. A more real unity
was precluded by the difficulty of communication as well as by
the fact that the vicar general's power, on his own assertion,
was limited to White Russia. The political situation in Russia,
furthermore, offered little encouragement. Catherine was dying
and her successor was less likely to show favor to the Jesuits.
For all these reasons, Carroll could see little stability in the
prospect of a union of the American ex-Jesuits with the remnant
of the Society still existing in White Russia.[19]

Neither Bishop Carroll nor Bishop Neale ever reentered
the Society. Their failure to do so was often discussed in the
first decade of the nineteenth century, and has often been discussed since. Oddly enough, in the case of Bishop Carroll,
his decision not to reenter has been offered on occasion as a
proof of his enmity to the Society, while Bishop Neale has
generally been exonerated of any such feeling.[20] The founder
of Georgetown and its fourth president both ardently desired the
restoration, and would, it can safely be said, have reentered
the ranks of the Society of Jesus had they not been raised to the
episcopacy. Both had considered long, before coming to their
decisions. Carroll, particularly, feared to take action on the
vivae vocis oraculum. He saw, too, that he might help the
Society avert the danger that could menace those who acted
on any such basis. They had signed the brief of suppression
and their names were on file. What if the next pope were to
"deny the authenticity of the verbal permission, of which the
Archives could afford no official record, and treat as rebels
to the Church those who in defiance of the brief of Clement XIV
had resumed the habit . . .?"[21] In a letter to Father Stone in

---

[19] Carroll to Plowden, May 23, 1796. MS WCA, 202 B 48.
[20] Although on one occasion, at least, Bishop Neale to his great distress had been
  cited as "unfriendly." Bishop Neale to Father J. Grassi, S.J., September 12,
  1812. MS WCA, 203 C 11.
[21] Shea, *Life and Times of the Most Reverend John Carroll*, p. 522.

England shortly after he had assisted Father Molyneux to put "the engine in motion," Carroll wrote:

> The example of the good Bishop of Verona is a lesson for Bishop Neale and myself to meditate on; and it has, indeed, before and since the receipt of your letter, been often a subject for consideration with me whether I ought not to petition the Pope to resign and resume my former state. My bishopric, as you know, gives me no worldly advantages, and is very burthensome [sic]. Can I promote the honor of God more by relinquishing, than by retaining it? Into whose hands could the Diocese be committed who would not, perhaps thwart the establishment in it of the Society, and oppose a reinvestment in it of the property formerly possessed, and still so providentially retained? These considerations have hitherto withheld my Coadjutor and myself from coming to a resolution of reentering the Society.[22]

In 1814, after the solemn re-establishment of the Society throughout the world, Father Marmaduke Stone expressed a wish that all the former members of the Society might now return to the "embrace of their beloved Mother."[23]

Archbishop Carroll and Bishop Neale replying early in 1815, again considered the question of re-entering, but felt that until more was known of "the mind of our rulers" regarding the restoration, although no opposition had as yet appeared, it might not be for the best interests of the Society if they were to vacate their Sees. There was, as Carroll saw it, the danger of exposing the concerns of the Society to successors who might be unfriendly or, more dangerous still, "liable to be imposed on by malicious representations." He did not close the matter, however, declaring that it had not yet received his full con-

---

[22] Carroll to Father Stone, August, 1805. Hughes, *History of the Society of Jesus, Documents*, Vol. 1, Part II, p. 822.

[23] Shea, *Life and Times of the Most Reverend John Carroll*, p. 521, is of the opinion that had the "restoration" of 1805 been a canonical one, Carroll and Neale would have resigned their bishoprics and re-entered the Society. There is some evidence for this in the letter to Father Stone cited above.

sideration.[24] By the end of that same year Carroll had died
without re-entering the Society, and Neale had decided to
remain outside of the order and carry on the work begun
by Carroll as Archbishop of Baltimore.

Although Carroll continued after 1805 to have misgivings
about the "restoration" and would continue to be dissatisfied
until the hoped-for-brief had been issued, he strove to do all in
his power to assist the "affiliated Jesuits." He considered
it imperative, if the infant Society were to progress, that a
supply of able members should augment the aging group in the
United States. Above all, he hoped that "a man of learning
and conciliating character" would be sent to take the presidency
of Georgetown College. Two others were needed, as well, for
the higher classes in order to save the college from falling into
insignificance. On the "must" list should be placed, too, a
professor of divinity and, if possible, a superior or master of
novices well versed in the spirit and customs of the Society.[25]

The general of the Order was faithful to the promise he had
given of sending aid, and in 1805 sent Fathers Adam Britt
and John Henry to America. These were not to find places in the
college but were welcomed by Bishop Carroll as vital replacements in the missions,[26] and as indirect aids to the college in
releasing others who could take places in the classroom. Very
Reverend Thaddeus Brzozowski, S.J., who had succeeded to
the generalate upon the death of Father Gruber,[27] attempted

[24] Carroll to Father Stone, January 5, 1815. *Woodstock Letters*, X, 122-133.
[25] Carroll to Father Stone, August-December, 1805. Hughes, *History of the Society of Jesus, Documents*, Vol. 1, Part II, p. 822. This letter was begun in late July or early August. In December Carroll added some thoughts and posted it. There is a copy also in the Shea Transcripts, GUA, 255.1.
[26] Father Britt was sent to the Church of the Holy Trinity in Philadelphia, then in vital need of a zealous priest. Past scandals, trusteeism, etc., had dealt a serious blow to the congregation there.
[27] Father Gruber had died on April 7, 1805. Father Brzozowski to Bishop Carroll, November 17, 1805. MS BCA, 2 C 1.

to fill minutely the requisition suggested by Bishop Carroll, but he was unable to supply anyone for the higher classes as Carroll had desired, since there were none among the members who could speak English. He sent, however, in 1806, Fathers Francis Malevé, Anthony Kohlmann, and Peter Epinette. The latter, a Frenchman who was also fluent in German, was to act as the professor of philosophy. For the present, at least, it would be necessary that Father Neale assume the post of Master of Novices, but with the assistance of Father Molyneux, who could acquaint him with the customs of the Society and the novitiate.[28] Carroll was delighted with the general's fulfillment of his promise to send the assistance, which had been solicited for the "expiring College of Georgetown."[29] The crisis had been passed. On October 10, 1806, Father Molyneux proceeded "to set the engine in motion"[30] with the foundation of a novitiate in a house opposite Trinity Church, Georgetown.[31] The novitiate, when the customary thirty days retreat was completed, was moved to the college campus, and occupied the second floor of the Old South Building.[32] Vocations were not lacking from the Catholic families of Maryland. By 1808 four novices, Enoch Fenwick, Benedict Fenwick, James Spinck, and Leonard Edelen, were completing their second year of theology, and "four others were employed in teaching classes of Latin, Greek, French, writing, arithmetic, and mathematics."

---

[28] Father T. Brzozowski to Bishop Carroll, February 22, 1806. MS BCA, 2 C 2. In this same letter Father Brzozowski approved formally the appointment by Carroll of Father Molyneux as Superior.

[29] Carroll to Molyneux, July 9, 1806. MS WCA, 203 S 4.

[30] Father Molyneux to Bishop Carroll, August 24, 1805. MS BCA, 5 L 6.

[31] Trinity Church was then the present convent on N Street between 35th and 36th Streets. The novitiate hence occupied the present site of the N Street entrance to the Georgetown University Graduate School.

[32] "Reminiscences of Father John McElroy," *Woodstock Letters*, XVI (July, 1887), 161-168. Father McElroy was one of the first novices. He entered originally as a brother. Later he was advanced to the priesthood.

Besides these there were five in the first year of the noviceship, and strictly confined to its exercises under the care of
Father Francis Neale, now assisted by Father Kohlmann.[33] In
October, Bishop Neale had resigned his position as president
of Georgetown College and was succeeded, as we have seen,
by Father Robert Molyneux. Georgetown, from its foundation
under the direction of ex-Jesuits, henceforth was, formally, a
college of the Society of Jesus. With Father Molyneux as
superior of the Jesuits in America, and at the same time president of Georgetown, and with the opening there of the novitiate,
Georgetown became the center of the new life of the Society of
Jesus in the United States.

Grateful as Bishop Carroll was for the new source of supply
for his college and diocese, he could not rid himself of the
uneasy feeling that possessed him at the position of the Jesuits
of America. From the first, he had steadfastly clung to his
view. The *vivae vocis oraculum* was too weak a foundation
for his liking. Another pope could declare such "reestablishment, in virtue of mere verbal grants, void and contrary to
ecclesiastical constitutions."[34] Carroll's correspondence with
Plowden enters into long discussions on the subject, and is
a manifestation of how dear the reestablishment of the Society
was to his heart. To him, the situation would ever remain
"unsatisfactory," although he would never blame another who
might regard the matter otherwise, and rely on the *"viva voce"*
restoration for "renewing [his] engagement."[35] He could not
trust to such a guarantee himself, nor could he advise others
to do so. He urged Father Molyneux to present to candidates
for the Society a clear picture of its situation so that no one

---

[33] Molyneux to Rev. Mother Dickinson, February 23, 1808. Shea Transcripts, GUA,
105.3.

[34] Carroll to Father Strickland, August 4, 1804. *Woodstock Letters*, X, 97.

[35] Carroll to Plowden, December 7, 1804. *Woodstock Letters*, X, 98.

would be misled.[36] If they then still wished to enter, they were to be received joyfully. "The magnanimous reliance of many young men on the protection of heaven" was very inspiring to him. He rejoiced at the courage of the young hearts, but Rome of 1773 was "yet fresh in [his] remembrance," and he had seen so many young men (of whom he had been one) upset and disappointed in their plans for their whole lives, that he earnestly begged of heaven that there would not be a renewal of those bitter days. It was because of these impressions on his mind, and for this reason alone, that he dared not encourage any one who consulted him, to enter into the obligations of religious life while as yet in America it enjoyed "no other canonical sanction (if it ever be canonical) than a verbal one."[37]

Bishop Carroll, with the concurrence of Bishop Neale, repeatedly made efforts to secure the complete and canonical reestablishment of the Society of America.[38] In 1808 it seemed that his efforts might meet with success. The Reverend Luke Concanen, O.P., Bishop-elect of New York, was at Rome for the purpose of securing his necessary credentials before sailing for America. Carroll requested him to "feel the pulse there and see if a brief might not be obtained, granting to this country authenticity and solidity to that establishment" for which the Jesuits had labored so long without obtaining the desired sanc-

---

[36] Carroll to Molyneux, March 27, 1807. MS WCA, 203 R 3. This request was complied with, as Carroll himself testifies, and one can detect a note of pride when he writes to Strickland "but there is no instance of any one having recoiled on that account." Carroll to Strickland, April 2, 1808. *Woodstock Letters*, X, p. 105.

[37] Carroll to Father Strickland, April 2, 1808. Stonyhurst Transcripts, CUA. Father Brzozowski had assured Carroll in a letter of June 9, 1806; "Sufficit nobis S. Pontificis assensus verus, quamquam ob temporis circumstantias duras scripto non declaratus." MS BCA, 2 C 3.

[38] Father Molyneux was in complete accord. "Forget not," he wrote, "to solicit a brief from Rome granting the reestablishment of the Society of Jesus in yr. Diocese." Molyneux to Carroll, October 18, 1805. MS BCA, 5 L 8. At the time of writing the novitiate had just been opened .

tion.[39] From Leghorn, Bishop-elect Concanen wrote that he had in his possession, besides the documents for the new bishoprics in America, some special communications to make to Carroll. But Bishop Concanen never reached New York. The French authorities then in possession of Naples, on the pretext that his passport was not in order, demanded that he remain there until authorization was given him to disembark. The bishop, not long recovered from a serious illness, was so severely shocked by this unexpected delay that he suffered a relapse and died on June 19, 1810. His effects were seized by the civil authorities, and the documents of great interest, as well as the special communication—presumably the reply of Pius VII to the request for canonical reestablishment of the Society of Jesus in America—never reached Carroll.[40]

Historians, amateur and professional, however much they try to limit themselves to an objective presentation of the facts, must all at some time or other have mused over an ironical "if." There arises an opportunity for such speculation as we study the attitude of Bishop Carroll to the restoration of the Society of Jesus. Due to the difficulty of communications, the impossibility of checking vague suspicions, and the natural proclivity for reading actions of the present against those of a past long faded away, the mind of Carroll was not known to his ex-Jesuit brethren. What was, on his part, an attitude of caution ruled by reason against the promptings of his affections, was looked upon by some of them as a calculated decision to hold the Society of Jesus in disfavor.

A circumstance which added to the misunderstanding between Carroll and the Georgetown Jesuits, was the precarious

---

[39] Carroll to Father Strickland, December 3, 1808. Stonyhurst Transcripts, CUA.

[40] Shea, *The Life and Times of the Most Reverend John Carroll*, pp. 622-627. See Grassi to Plowden, January 10, 1811. Trans. from the Italian by Plowden. Hughes, *History of the Society of Jesus, Documents*, Vol. 1, Part II, p. 978 f.

state of the college during the period, 1806-1808. By the same token, however, Carroll's solicitude for the college's welfare during this trying period should have allayed any fears on the part of the Jesuits.

While the formalities of their status were being ironed out, and while the problems of jurisdiction were long discussed after 1805, the Jesuits affiliated to the Society in White Russia, began in that year and the succeeding one, what was to be the long task of reviving Georgetown College. The prospects were anything but bright. Financially the college was at a very low, if not at its lowest, point since its foundation. The new building had remained unfinished for lack of funds, and the entire college was in such a "state of depression"[41] that Bishop Carroll reluctantly made the motion, which was not adopted, that the school be suspended.[42] What Carroll planned was a period of recuperation, for it was at that time "draining the estates, and all the resources of the corporation and must finally overwhelm them."[43]

Father Molyneux misunderstood the bishop's intent, and was deeply chagrined at the thought of closing Georgetown. He had been the outstanding advocate of Carroll in the days of its foundation, and could hardly believe that the founder had given up what had been once his prime hope for the permanency and success of religion in the United States. Carroll quickly assured him that a "wish to put an end to the College" never entered his heart.[44] His only desire was to see the college first in character and merit in America. The condition of the institution in 1806 augured little for such a hope. Parents "of tender feelings for their children" would hardly, wrote Carroll, send them

---

[41] Carroll to Molyneux, December 19, 1806. MS WCA, 203 S 10.
[42] Carroll to Molyneux, December 19, 1806. MS WCA, 203 S 10.
[43] *Ibid.*
[44] *Ibid.* February 15, 1807. MS WCA, 203 R 1.

to "lodge and study in unplastered and cold apartments."[45] It was true that the building was not as bad as it seemed, but, unfortunately, people judged by appearances. Carroll's plan, then, was to suspend the college for a time and to arrange that the expenses generally allocated to finishing the "new" building would be used for the forwarding of the education of the novices and the ecclesiastical students, and, "after forming from the latter who are certainly possessed of sufficient talents, an able and even distinguished list of professors, to recommence a general plan of education."[46] The closing lines of this letter reveal as much of the history of Georgetown of 1806 as they do of Georgetown's warmhearted and clearheaded founder: "As things are now going we are exhausting our funds and sinking the reputation of the Society. Disagreeable as this truth is, we cannot shut it from our minds. No one feels more pain from the reflection than, Revd. and dear Sir, your most humble servant, John, Bishop of Baltimore."[47] But the enthusiasm he had communicated to Molyneux in 1784 had remained.

Father Molyneux did not close the college; such a decision would have been a mistake. But each succeeding day made the closing seem imminent. When Father Anthony Kohlmann arrived at Georgetown in the fall of 1806, he found less than thirty students at the college.[48] By the following April, Father Molyneux was obliged to borrow money to meet the running expenses of the house.[49] Father Kohlmann, however, had been deeply impressed with the spirit at the college now that the link has been made with the Society in White Russia, and he was

---

[45] *Ibid.*

[46] *Ibid.*

[47] *Ibid.*

[48] Father Anthony Kohlmann, S.J., to R. F. Thaddeus Brzozowski, S.J., November 25, 1806. *Woodstock Letters*, XXXV, 1-10. This letter was copied from the Archives of the Galician Province, S.J.

[49] Notley Young to Carroll, April 13, 1807. MS BCA, 8 R 3.

confident that the number of students would soon increase.[50] Father Molyneux seems to have shared this hope. The start would be slow, but if he could hold on until the "engine were put in motion," the crisis might be passed. Bishop Carroll, to whom he might have looked for encouragement, was heavy with disappointment, and very pessimistic over the future of the college. His spirits reached their low point in May of 1807, when there seemed to be no relief in sight for Georgetown. Difficulties he had known, but the distresses of the college now were incessant, and it seemed hopeless to look to their ending. There must be, thought Carroll, some radical defect in the constitutions of the college, at least in regard to their adaptability to the inclinations of American youth. Molyneux, its president, enjoyed the love and respect of everyone who came in contact with him, and if he were not successful, judged Carroll, the fault must lie in the rules and regulations hitherto in effect in the college. It was a source of great shame to him to realize that, whereas the excellence of his former brethren was universally acknowledged in the field of education, their college in this country should be, "I do not say, deservedly," he wrote, "eclipsed by that of the Sulpicians."[51]

Father Molyneux had hoped to obtain assistance in the administration of the college from his brethren at Stonyhurst. Father Plowden, however, had been forced to admit that he was totally unable to send out any men qualified to assist in such a college.[52] For this reason, Father Molyneux, with unaccustomed

---

[50] Kohlmann to Brzozowski, November 25, 1806. See *supra*, p. 136.

[51] Carroll to Molyneux, May 22, 1806. MS WCA, 203 R 2.

[52] Molyneux to Father Francis Neale, May 23, 1806. MS WCA, 203 S 2. "For this reason," wrote Molyneux, "it is therefore high time to begin seriously to make the best provision possible for ourselves. . . . to arrange some plan suitable to our circumstances, of making a beginning of forming a novitiate with ever so small a number of postulants of such talents and qualifications as the Institute requires." *Ibid.*

haste, decided to begin the novitiate immediately in order that a supply of teachers might be obtained. Whatever traits of indolence might have been attributed to Molyneux at other times, they were certainly absent in the fall of 1806. It was a courageous and bold step to open the novitiate at a time of financial distress, but he saw it as necessary, and carried it through. Georgetown and the Society of Jesus in America both owe much to Father Robert Molyneux. The novitiate was to prosper amid many vicissitudes, but it would be years before it could hope to supply teachers in any large numbers. The difficulties of the interval were alleviated, as we have seen, by the assistance afforded by the general of the Society in White Russia. In 1806 Fathers Anthony Kohlmann and Peter Epinette arrived at Georgetown. The former had been sent to be professor of philosophy, while the latter was to teach theology. As there were no pupils as yet to occupy them, Father Kohlmann was appointed to be assistant to the master of novices, Father Francis Neale, while Father Epinette was engaged in teaching Sacred Scripture to the novices, and Latin to future candidates for the Society.[53] Bishop Carroll, more acutely conscious of the need of careful distribution of the available priests than Father Molyneux, considered these appointments as ill-advised. If Father Kohlmann was necessary for the novices, why not appoint him outright as master of novices, and thus leave Father Neale free to attend to the congregation of Trinity Church, his procuratorship at the college, and his post as agent of the corporation? Carroll cautioned Father Molyneux about permitting "titular offices in the Society, the holders of which cannot perform the duties belonging to them."[54]

---

[53] Kohlmann to Rev. Father Thaddeus Brzozowski, November 25, 1806. See p. 136; Carroll to Plowden, January 10, 1808. Stonyhurst Transcripts, CUA; Carroll to Molyneux, November 24, 1808. MS WCA, 203 S 12.

[54] Carroll to Molyneux, December 19, 1806. MS WCA, 203 S 10.

From his vantage point, viewing the needs of the infant Church in America, and on the basis of his long friendship with Molyneux, Carroll presumed to review the recent appointments.

Father Epinette surely could assume the duties of assistant to the master of novices, as well as teach his scripture class. When he noted that Father Kohlmann was also engaged in teaching German to the novices, Carroll was outspoken in his criticism of this misuse of talent:

> Bless me! What need is there for keeping a man of his talents and acquirements as the companion of a master of a few novices, a man who is able to render such important services elsewhere, if not wanted as professor of philosophy? And as to the German lesson, *cui bono?* How many of the novices will learn or have occasion to use it? Allow me to offer one piece of advice, suggested by a more ardent wish not only for the restoration of the Society, but the restoration of it with all that energy and enterprise for promoting the divine honor and exertion in the service of religion, which characterized it, even to the downfall, especially there where its spirit was best preserved. Now nothing will damp more this spirit and therefore nothing was guarded more against in the best provinces of the Society than to restrain the vigor and zealous exercises of those who might do credit to their body, and wonderfully benefit the faithful, by confining their abilities and allowing them no theatre for exerting them to their full extent.[55]

Father Kohlmann, reasoned Carroll, could be used to great advantage in the German congregations until such time as Georgetown would have again a class in philosophy for him to teach. This missionary experience, too, would serve him in good stead as a means of learning the "habits, management and best methods of serving religion here . . . this I earnestly recommend and earnestly entreat for the glory of God above all things and next for the honour of the Society."[56] Previously

---

[55] *Ibid.*, November 24, 1808. MS WCA, 203 S 12.
[56] *Ibid.*

Carroll had requested one of the Fenwicks for New York.[57] For, though he considered the Society in America as being very unstable until it should receive a more authentic authorization, "yet every use should be made of it, as it now exists, to diffuse its usefulness and encourage its propagation by making its spirit and services known in the most populous parts of the United States."[58] Either of the Fenwicks would be invaluable, and would be the means, as well, for widening the Society's sphere of activity.[59] Although the college had begun "to raise itself from that state of degradation to which it was reduced," there was still no need of Father Kohlmann's services as professor of philosophy.[60] Most of the activity at the college was centered around the completion of the "new" building, since a donation of four hundred dollars from a postulant for the Society had made it possible to finish the structure.[61] Accordingly, Father Molyneux not only sent Father Benedict Fenwick to New York, but Father Kohlmann and four scholastics as well to assist with the congregation, and to open a school.[62] This was the beginning of the New York Literary Institute, which was to have a successful, but brief, career. It would be closed in September, 1813,

[57] Fathers Benedict and Enoch Fenwick. Both had been students of Georgetown. Later they were to head the college — Benedict as ninth and twelfth president, Enoch as eleventh president. Benedict was consecrated Bishop of Boston on November 1, 1825. Enoch was of invaluable assistance to Archbishop Carroll as rector of the Baltimore Cathedral.

[58] Carroll to Kohlmann, August 15, 1808. MS WCA, 203 P 5.

[59] Carroll to Molyneux, July 1, 1808. MS WCA, 203 P 3.

[60] Kohlmann to Father Strickland, March 9, 1808. *Woodstock Letters*, XII, 89.

[61] "Reminiscences of Father John McElroy," *Woodstock Letters*, XVI, 163. Father Kohlmann in his letter to Father Strickland above, gave the figure as five hundred dollars.

[62] Fathers Benedict and Enoch Fenwick had been ordained by Bishop Neale in June, 1808, along with James Spinck and Leonard Edelen. Two others had also been ordained by Archbishop Carroll in Baltimore. The acquisition of these "six priests . . . . happy day for the Diocese" made it possible to spare two for New York. Carroll to Neale, June 15, 1808. MS BCA, 9 Q 6; Carroll to Plowden, December 5, 1808. Stonyhurst Transcripts, CUA.

over the long and ardent protests of Father Kohlmann, when it was found impossible to supply teachers for both it and Georgetown College.

The decision to accede to Bishop Carroll's wishes, and expand the activities of the newly, though yet partially, restored Society into New York, was one of Father Molyneux's last acts. He died on December 9, 1808, "after being prepared," wrote Carroll, "by a life of candour, virtue and innocence."[63] There was none of the spectacular about Father Robert Molyneux, but he deserves a prominent place in Georgetown's history. John Carroll had opened the doors of Georgetown. Robert Molyneux, at a very crucial period in its history, had kept them open.

Previous to his death, and in consequence of powers granted to him by the general of the Society in Russia, Father Molyneux had designated Father Charles Neale as his successor. In giving notice of his appointment to Bishop Carroll, Father Neale hoped that the change of superiors would make no change in the bishop's attitude towards the Society.[64] The note of suspicion that there might be a change, or that any good will shown had been contingent on Father Molyneux being the superior, caused Carroll in his reply to object to such an implication. Father Neale assured him that it was not personal on his part, but as he was about to write to the general he did not wish to include the "little suspicions of others."[65] He insisted that there never would be any lack of harmony on his part, but hoped that Carroll would never let any non-Jesuit members of the Select Clergy take colleges away from the Society.[66] Father Kohlmann, writing to one of the Society in England, expressed his fear that

---

[63] Carroll to Plowden, February 21, 1809. Shea Transcripts, GUA, 255.3. Published in *Woodstock Letters*, X, p. 106.
[64] Father Charles Neale to Bishop Carroll, January 2, 1809. MS BCA, 5 N 7.
[65] Father Charles Neale to Bishop Carroll, January 16, 1809. MS BCA, 5 N 7.
[66] *Ibid.*

Bishop Carroll was unfavorable, and calamitously added
that some even said the new Bishop Concanen was "inimical
to the Society; that he is charged by the propaganda to keep an
eye over us."[67] The occasion for this suspicion arose from two
actions of Bishop Carroll. The first was his declaration that until
the canonical reestablishment, the bishop, in his opinion, could
not ordain the members *sub titulo paupertatis*. The second
action was a circular letter in which Carroll requested Father
Neale to admonish the members who had been affiliated to the
Society in Russia, to "abstain from all such exterior marks
that could distinguish them from secular priests, acknowledging
however the obligation of our vows to the Society."[68]

Due to the scarcity of priests and the necessity of employing
those available in stations where they would accomplish most,
the problem of appointments and jurisdiction arose often to
endanger good relations between the bishop and the Jesuit
superior. As early as 1807, Carroll reminded Molyneux that
"we Bishops though we allow you to keep a control over the
members of the Society must not admit of your assigning them
their congregations."[69] The problem became much more acute
during the superiorship of Father Charles Neale. Bishop Carroll
on one occasion deemed it necessary to call Father Enoch
Fenwick from the college to assist him at Baltimore. He sincerely regretted the necessity, but judged that, due to the small
number of students at Georgetown, Father Fenwick could easily
leave his post of vice president for more important work. What-

---

[67] Kohlmann to someone in England, July 26, 1809. MS WCA, 203 N 4. Father
   Kohlmann, as is evident from his letter, did not know of or understand the
   doubts that assailed Bishop Carroll. He looked on this action of Carroll's as
   another manifestation of a persecution of the Society, listing Carroll among
   its newest adversaries.

[68] Carroll explained numerous times in his correspondence why he thought it best
   that the Society make no pretensions until it had received the full and
   canonical reestablishment. If he erred, it was on the side of caution.

[69] Carroll to Molyneux, December 11, 1807. MS WCA, 203 R S.

ever functions remained for a vice president could be filled by
Father Matthews. In his request Carroll pointed out that he had
been given such power by the general of the Society in Russia,
and that the state of the Society outside of Russia did not
warrant its enjoyment of that freedom from episcopal jurisdiction that might be its right in a canonically recognized
restoration.[70] Father Neale replied that the power of appointment must reside in the superior, if he were to merit the name.
Again he construed Carroll's action as flowing from some
personal animus toward his former brethren. He expressed his
"hope in God" that Carroll "from a friend will never turn into
a persecutor of the Society."[71] Father Fenwick was not sent to
Baltimore until after a delay of more than two months when,
as Father Neale expressed it, the arrival of Father John Grassi
put it in his power to send Father Fenwick "for your consolation." He remained adamant as to his rights as superior:

> . . . Be it, however, Most Reverend Sir, positively understood that I
> mean not thereby to give up any control over any individual subject
> of our congregation (that being absolutely necessary for the well-
> being thereof).[72]

The friction that developed between these two zealous men,
both conscientiously maintaining and defending the rights of
their respective offices in the Church, arose from a definite
misunderstanding, apparently on the part of Carroll. He maintained again and again that the general had given him power to

---

[70] Carroll to Father Charles Neale, September 11, 1810. MS WCA (not numbered).
Carroll certainly understood that he had the power to make such changes.
"I presume the more on this [using Father Kohlmann for the German congre-
gations before assigning him to Georgetown] because the general of the
Society has granted me a power which however will never be used to the
prejudice of your authority for neither of us will, as I firmly persuade myself,
be unreasonable." Carroll to Molyneux, April 7, 1807. MS WCA, 203 R 4.
Other instances could be cited.

[71] Father Charles Neale to Carroll, September 18, 1810. MS BCA, 5 N 8.

[72] Father Charles Neale to Carroll, November 28, 1810. MS BCA, 5 N 9.

change and remove men from office, even against the will of the superior of the Jesuits. Father Brzozowski denied that such a power had ever been granted by him.[73] Eventually, in order to create harmony, Father Brzozowski removed Father Neale from office at the close of his three-year term, and appointed in his place Father John Grassi, who was again to combine the offices of superior of the Jesuits and president of Georgetown.[74] He was to have a brilliant career in both offices, but the problem of jurisdiction continued, and even increased, during his term of office. Again, it should be noted, bitter and acrimonious as the arguments would wax, it can be said, to the credit of the disputants, that the debates were always on a high plane. Neale, Grassi, Carroll were great men. They were conscious in the exercise of their respective offices that they were pioneers, and that each agreement, each concession, was important. Each fought hard *"pro domo sua"*, but because he thought that in such wise would the task common to all be best accomplished.

It was the view of Bishop Carroll that until the Society had attained its complete restoration by a papal brief, the affiliated ex-Jesuits could have no corporate rights in ecclesiastical property.[75] This led him, while not opposing the move, to declare that the general had made a mistake in appointing Father Grassi as president of Georgetown, since the general had had no authority to do so.[76] Again, Carroll was afraid that

---

[73] Extract of the general's letter given in C. Neale to F. Neale, September 11, 1811. MS WCA, 203 H 2. ". . . . se habere potestatem a me sibi datam mittendi nostros quocumque velit inconsulto et invito superiore, hoc totum gratis asserit."

[74] In view of the fact that Kohlmann at this time considered Carroll as an adversary of the Society, it is interesting to note that Carroll in his letter to the general recommended that Father Kohlmann succeed Neale. It is another instance of a want of knowledge of each other's views. Father Grassi's career as president will be treated in detail in Chapters VII and VIII.

[75] Carroll to Grassi, October 16, 1813. MS WCA, 204 T 14.

[76] *Ibid.*, July 9, 1812. MS WCA, 203 C 1.

haste would bring ruin. "I see," he wrote to Grassi, "a cloud gathering and raised up by some anti-Jesuitical clergymen of different nations amongst us, which is irritated by the premature pretensions of some of yours."[77]

Carroll warned Grassi himself not to be too covetous for immediate management of temporalities, which patience would restore to the Society.[78] Father Neale had apparently reviewed the situation with Father Grassi upon leaving office, and the picture he drew of Carroll was felt by the latter to be a definite misrepresentation. The bishop was indignant. He could account for it, he said sharply, only on the "supposition that my authority and obligation to obey orders which I have sworn to obey, might prevent him [Neale] from exercising episcopal jurisdiction more than myself."[79]

Throughout the entire period of strained relations in 1808, Carroll continued to seek for the brief of restoration. At the close of a beautiful eulogy on the constitutions of the Society, occasioned by a charge by Father Charles Neale that the bishop was requiring him to violate those constitutions, Carroll summed up his own personal position. He was waiting, he declared, at that very moment for some answer from Rome about the brief he had requested:

> . . . and I know that my delicacy and embarrassment between inclination and attachment on one side and duty confirmed by oath on the other, has induced some and perhaps yourself to impute to me disaffection to the society, which I am confident that I love more than you do, because I knew it much better.[80]

---

[77] *Ibid.*, October 16, 1813. MS WCA, 204 T 14.

[78] *Ibid.*

[79] Carroll to Grassi, October 27, 1811, MS WCA, 202 H 4.

[80] Carroll to Father Charles Neale, November 5, 1811. MS WCA, 203 H 5. Father Neale did not change his opinion. Almost a year later he counseled Father Grassi: "You must not wonder if you find the archbishop more inclined to favour others than the Society. He has always been so." October 12, 1813. MS WCA, 204 T 11.

At the close of 1812, Carroll showed that the debates over jurisdiction had not lessened his affection for his former brethren. In a New Year's greeting to Father John Grassi, he sent his cordial and sincere wishes for health and happiness in the year to come, and many more.[81] The same were to be extended, he requested, to Bishop Leonard Neale. In typical fashion he informed Grassi, lest he think his greeting rather brusque, that Italian and French etiquette, he knew, would demand mutual letters between the bishops, but "American rusticity contents itself with the expression of the heart."[82] Since this was so, and since he knew that the greeting would be accepted in like vein, he asked Grassi to convey his good wishes to the "Rev. companions and cooperators in the college" and to assure them that he took "a lively interest in their welfare, spiritual and temporal." In closing, he commended Father Grassi for the improvements made in the college during the past year. Important as they were in themselves to the good name of the college, they were even more significant as pledges of others to "be successively expected." The one fear he had, was for the "solicitude of the Society in Russia at this time." This could only be removed if his wish were fulfilled, and "we had here a solemn authentic restoration to repeal effectually and destroy the effects of the Ganganellian Brief."[83] He continued his efforts to obtain that brief throughout the ensuing year, but by October of 1813, although he had made three applications, he had received no answer. He was determined to beseech Rome, for, as he wrote to Grassi, "the flame was kindled. We must seek canonical reestablishment.[84] It was not until the fol-

---

[81] Carroll to Grassi, December 31, 1812. MS WCAA, 203 B 12.

[82] *Ibid.*

[83] *Ibid.*

[84] Carroll to Grassi, October 25, 1813. MS WCA, 204 T 17. The war, as he learned later, had blocked all communication. Carroll to Father Stone, January 31, 1814. Stonyhurst Transcripts. CUA.

lowing year that rumors began to trickle through that Pope Pius VII was considering restoring the Society of Jesus throughout the world. Father Simon Bruté at the seminary in Baltimore had received word from Prince Rohan de Chabot that the pope had assured him that one of the means of healing the wounds of the Church would be the reestablishment of the Society; and he was "warmly occupied with the reestablishment"[85] Carroll was more than pleased to send on this report to Grassi, for it "was the most interesting part of the letter to us."[86] The report was apparently true, since, on December 7, 1814, Archbishop Carroll received a copy of the Bull *Sollicitudo Omnium Ecclesiarum* of August 7, 1814, which restored the Society of Jesus throughout the world. On that very evening, not having as yet read the entire bull, he had instructed Father Enoch Fenwick to send it on to Father John Grassi "with all possible dispatch."[87] A few days later Carroll, writing to Grassi, referred to himself as "having contributed to your greatest happiness on earth by sending the miraculous bull of restoration."[88] Practical even in a moment of great enthusiasm, he proposed a conference, now that the Society was fully restored, in order to settle the knotty problem of appointments and other matters, "at least in this diocese."[89]

He also intended, he informed Grassi, to issue a pastoral to the Catholics of the United States on the subject of the restoration.[90] Later in the same month he returned to the subject of the proposed conference, for in it he saw the solution to the problem

[85] Carroll to Grassi, October 14, 1814. MS WCA, 204 M 2. Carroll also enclosed a letter from Plowden, "knowing that you [Grassi] will gladly pay postage for such a treat." *Ibid.*

[86] *Ibid.*

[87] Father Enoch Fenwick to Father John Grassi, December 7, 1814. MS WCA, 204 M 15. Fenwick's letter is a joyous expression of thanksgiving.

[88] Carroll to Grassi, December 10, 1814. MS WCA, 204 M 16.

[89] *Ibid.* He closes his letter with "Laudemus Dmum et exaltemus in eo."

[90] *Ibid.*

which had vexed him so often, and a solution, too, that he recognized as so necessary not only for the present but for the future. John Carroll was ever conscious that he was a pioneer. Every step was a precedent, and the relationship between the regular clergy and the bishops must be placed on a firm foundation. He desired, as soon as it would be convenient to both parties, that a conference be held to effect a perfect understanding for future conduct between the ordinaries and the superior of the Society in the United States, "so that there may be no conflict of jurisdiction and source of dissension hereafter."[91] In the meantime, it would be best to await the arrival of the formal communication of the news from the Reverend Father General of the Society, who would doubtless suggest some considerations on the subject of the relations that should exist "between the bishops of the various dioceses and the members of the Society."[92] Carroll reminded Grassi that Bishop Neale and himself were the only prelates in the country who had ever been Jesuits, and doubtless would be the only such who would ever be called on to govern any of the churches in this country. Theirs, then, could be a two-fold opportunity. They could establish a precedent which would convince their successors "of its being for the advantage of their dioceses to live in perfect intelligence with the regular clergy and especially our Brethren." And this *modus vivendi* could be worked out to the mutual advantage of the parties, in such wise that the regular clergy could "exercise the functions of the ministry, both in due subordination to episcopal authority, and likewise in compliance with the obedience due to their religious superiors."[93]

Universal as was the joy at the restoration of the Society, the *modus vivendi* of the preceding years could not be abrogated

[91] Carroll to Grassi, December, 1814. MS WCA, 204 M 17.
[92] *Ibid.*
[93] *Ibid.*

immediately. Certain restraints to complete freedom of action for the Society's members had, due to its non-canonical status since 1805, been necessary; and these could not be removed "otherwise than gradually, without irritating certain passions."[94]

Father Grassi, meanwhile, was a pioneer, too, who just as clearly recognized that every step of his would be a precedent for future superiors of the Society of Jesus in the United States. He was just as anxious that these restraints be removed from the Society lest the Society be hampered in its work. He allowed himself to be influenced, however, in Carroll's opinion, "chiefly, if not exclusively [by] foreigners, that is, his brethren from Russia, Germany, Flanders, etc., all of them good religious men but not one of them possessing an expansed [sic] mind, discerning enough to estimate the difference between the American character and that of the countries which they left."[95] Carroll, now a venerable old man of eighty, felt keenly the insinuations in some of Grassi's letters that he was an enemy of the Society, and that he was unjust or unfair, etc., but he bore Grassi no ill will. He continued with his project of the pastoral on the restoration, but he was hindered by the pressure of "so many urgent affairs" and there were but few hours of the day now during which his mind was "fit for any serious application."[96] He was, however, wearied with the attacks regarding his attitude towards the Society and its missions, and he determined that Father Grassi should be brought up to date

---

[94] Carroll to Grassi, February 21, 1815. MS WCA, 204 K 6. Grassi had apparently echoed some of the old complaints and insinuations that "Carroll was lax in forwarding the interests of the Society and helping to reinvest the order with its old property." Hughes, *History of the Society of Jesus, Documents*, Vol 1, Part II, p. 850.

[95] Carroll to Plowden, June 25, 1815. Stonyhurst Transcripts, CUA.

[96] Carroll to Grassi, March 16, 1815. Hughes, *History of the Society of Jesus, Documents*, Vol. 1, Part II, p. 853.

on the subject of Archbishop John Carroll. The venerable old
prelate found it hard to write of himself, and he was ashamed
to defend himself so vigorously, but the good estate of the
Church and of Georgetown demanded that he pen his apologia.
Carroll's biographer was correct when he declared that Grassi
needed to see the record.[97] The same biographer goes beyond the
evidence, however, in declaring that "it is evident that death
alone saved Carroll from the misery of an open break with the
Jesuit superior."[98] What might have been the future relations
of Carroll and Grassi is outside the realm of history, and, if
one wishes to deal in conjectures, the signs we do possess all
point in the opposite direction. Preferable is the same author's
judgment in another place, that "Archbishop Carroll could not
bear anyone ill-will.[99] The record sustains this estimate.

Carroll's apologia of February 21, 1815, was addressed to
Grassi, but "Grassi" should not be used to designate any one
man. The letter could well have been addressed "To whom
it may concern." The fact that it was addressed to Grassi was
occasioned by reproaches in the superior's letters to Carroll
for not having immediately concurred with Grassi's view relative to the affairs of the Corporation. Grassi seemed to "distrust
[Carroll's] zeal for the full and entire reestablishment of the
said Society."[100] As the venerable father of the American
hierarchy looked back over the difficult years, his feelings rose
"almost to indignation" when he conceived that he was being
accused of coldness or apathy toward the Society. He felt that
he must do himself "the justice" of declaring that if "ever any
measures were taken to organize a system for the preservation
of the property, which formerly did and now again does belong

---

[97] Guilday, *The Life and Times of John Carroll*, p. 564.
[98] *Ibid.*, p. 563.
[99] *Loc. cit.* See also pp. 197, 198.
[100] Carroll to Grassi, February 21, 1815. MS WCA, 204 K 6.

to the Society; [and] to prevent it from becoming liable to waste and individual usurpation," the credit belonged to him and to him alone. In fact, the existence of the college over which Father Grassi now presided, its legal capacity to acquire property and to receive donations, the "very spot on which it stands" and the fact that the Church[101] was now vested "in the representatives of the college," all were due to his acts, and to his acts alone. "They were performed without the smallest expense to those who have ever since enjoyed the property."[102] He could list as well his "journeys year after year," his "attendance on the general assemblies," his "sollicitations, care and watchfullness over the wording of the different acts of the legislature, which were necessary to erect corporations for the clergy and the college so that they might not be a bar against the Society in case of its revival."[103] Alone, he had effected all this without any assistance, in fact, against the opposition of "those who have enjoyed the possession and administration of all which was acquired for them." Far, then, from being unfavorable to the Society, he could claim, contrary to his usual custom, "to be in an humble degree, *de Societate bene meritus*."[104] As far as the charge of being an enemy of the Society was concerned, he was at a loss to see how that could be sustained; indeed, he could say:

> . . . whilst all others were remaining with folded arms, without moving a step to prepare the way for the return of the Society, I alone opened and continued the correspondence with the General in Russia, and with his concurrence gave all that existence to it which it could receive without a full and authentic repeal of the destructive Brief of Clement XIV.[105]

---

[101] The "Church" was Holy Trinity parish church in Georgetown.
[102] *Ibid.*
[103] *Ibid.*
[104] *Ibid.*
[105] *Ibid.*

He was ashamed, he repeated, for having said so much of himself; but the undeserved insinuations of unfriendliness had "extorted" it from him. He realized that the charges had their source in zeal for the Society, but he had ever felt that it was a zeal which was so "precipitate as to endanger the harmony of our fellow labourers, to hurt the interests of the Society, and to embarrass my conscience, as long as the Ganganellian Brief remained unrepealed."[106]

The difficulties between the superior of the Society of Jesus in America and the archbishop had too long a history, and were too complicated to be solved at a stroke. But, throughout, Archbishop Carroll never lost his sincere admiration and appreciation for Grassi. He looked on him as the rebuilder of Georgetown. Similarly, Father Grassi recognized in Archbishop Carroll the outstanding churchman in America.[107] When the news came that the venerable prelate was dying, Grassi wrote to Plowden that his death would be a heavy blow to the Church in America. It is more than probable that no one's presence at the bedside of Carroll, as he lay dying, was of more comfort than Grassi's. Grassi records in his diary:

> November 28, 1815. News of the imminent death of the archbishop determined me to leave [Georgetown]. November 30. Went about with (Rev.) Mr. Dubuisson. The Archbishop called me to speak with him about various matters. December 1. Watched at night with the Archbishop. December 2. Passed the night with the Archbishop. December 3, 1815. At 5 past Archbishop Carroll died holily.[108]

It was in the writings of Grassi that Carroll's biographer, Monsignor Peter Guilday, found the felicitous phrase that

---

[106] *Ibid.*
[107] Gilbert J. Garraghan, S.J., "John Anthony Grassi, S.J., 1775-1849," *The Catholic Historical Review*, XXIII, 284.
[108] Diario of Rev. John Grassi, S.J. MS JGA (Photostatic copy of the portions relative to America in possession of the author.)

summed up Carroll's character: "rare goodness of heart."[109]
This sincere tribute from a man who had crossed swords with
Carroll often, but who had kept his fighting to the battlefield,
would have embarrassed but would not have surprised John
Carroll. Grassi, like Carroll, was a man of greatness who could
engage in a sharp and keen struggle for a cause that he felt
was just, without permitting the struggle to influence his judgment of the character of his opponent.

In a word of advice to Father Charles Neale, Carroll had
phrased the attitude thus: ". . . you will find by experience,
that men may think very differently even on subjects interesting
to the conduct of religious affairs, without therefore deserving to
be utterly distrusted."[110] John Grassi, too, might well have been
the author of those words.

---

[109] Guilday, *Life and Times of John Carroll*, p. 830. Guilday cites from the
*Memorie sulla Compagnia di Gesu ristabilita negli Stati Uniti dell' America
Settentrionale dal 1810 al 1817* compiled in 1836 by Father Grassi at the
instance of the Father General, John Roothaan. Father Grassi had had many
occasions to form this judgment. The "apologia" letter, for example, of
February 21, 1815, *loc. cit.*, concludes: "But I pretend not to dictate. I transmit a letter from Mr. Pl. [Plowden] of an old date, received yesterday, and
being much tired must conclude with my best respects to and hearty congratulations to Bp. Neale and compliments to your esteemed companions."

[110] Carroll to Father Charles Neale, January 19, 1790. MS WCA, 202 B 25.

CHAPTER VII

The Struggle
for Survival

Upon the death of Father Molyneux, the position of
president of Georgetown was separated from that of superior
of the Jesuits in America. Father Charles Neale was appointed
to the post of superior, but for the presidency, the directors of
the college chose the Reverend William Matthews, for many
years a professor in the college, who had but recently entered
the novitiate of the Society of Jesus.[1]

Father Matthews was one of the most outstanding maintenance men with whom the college was ever blessed. Lest that
seem to be but little recommendation, it must be recalled that it
fell to the lot of Father Matthews to be called to the presidency
of Georgetown at a time when survival spelled success. His
presidency was brief and unmarked with epoch making events.

---

[1] Father Matthews did not remain in the Society. Born in Charles County,
Maryland, in 1770, after ecclesiastical studies at St. Mary's Seminary in
Baltimore he had been ordained by Bishop Carroll in 1800. He was the first
native of the country to be raised to the priesthood in the diocese of Baltimore.
In 1796 and 1797 he had served as professor of rhetoric in the college and
tradition has it that he first greeted George Washington on the latter's visit
to the college. In later years Father Matthews became pastor of St. Patrick's
Church, Washington, and served at a very difficult time as vicar apostolic and
administrator of Philadelphia. He was a nephew of the Fathers Neale.

Great educators, brilliant leaders, skillful planners Georgetown
has seen, but in Father Matthews it knew also a president who
felt called upon to roll up his sleeves and mix mortar. And he
was equal to the task, as succeeding presidents have been equal
to their more glorious functions. The new building, which had
never been completed due to a lack of funds, seemed destined
to become a ruin before it was finished. Curriculum, expansion
of faculty, community service, and all other functions of a
college had to be forgotten. The new building clamored for
first place in the new president's attention. The improvements
begun in Father Molyneux's last year with the aid of the anony-
mous donor's gift of four hundred dollars were continued, with
every effort being made to make the benefaction stretch as far
as possible. It was an inspiring scene. Father McElroy recalls
that a plasterer was engaged but that his helpers were members
of the faculty "who attended him . . . made mortar, etc."[2] Father
Matthews is said to have been one of these academic appren-
tices. Apparently they tried their hand at other trades besides
plastering, for Father McElroy continues: "After this we had
the windows glazed and the house painted inside and outside,
without, however, employing a painter."[3] The college towers,
too, were completed, and due recognition was officially given to
Father Matthews for the improved picture of the college by the
directors who passed the resolution: "That the Directors of
Georgetown College have viewed with pleasure the improvements made in said college."[4] A reading of the minutes of the
board of directors for this period substantiates Father Stonestreet's judgment that this resolution should be considered as
being very high praise, for the "directors were used to speaking
to the president with the same freedom the Colonies had used

[2] "Reminiscences of Father John McElroy," *Woodstock Letters*, XVI (1887), 163.
[3] *Ibid.*
[4] *Minutes of the Directors, Georgetown College, 1797-1815.* GUA. 398.

in speaking to the Mother Country and . . . they took note of the debit as well as of the credit side of facts and fame."[5]

It was, however, during Father Matthews' administration that Georgetown's first offshoot came into being. Shortly before his death, Father Molyneux had acceded to Bishop Carroll's request, and in the fall of 1808 had permitted Father Kohlmann and Benedict Fenwick to be assigned to New York. They brought along with them four scholastics, with the intention of beginning a college there. Upon their arrival they found a large and urgent field for their pastoral labors, and the school project had to be postponed for a while. Father Kohlmann declared that they found the parish—one might rather say city—"so neglected in every respect that it goes beyond all conception."[6] But the zealous missionaries to New York (they could hardly be called less) did not forget that they had come to found a school. Archbishop Carroll in a letter to his friend Father Plowden on September 19, 1809, after declaring his joy at the "most happy fruits" effected in the diocese by the introduction of exercises of piety and sodalities, states also that they had established "an extensive academy."[7]

The new academy, called the New York Literary Institute, was begun by Father Kohlmann in a house rented in Mulberry Street, opposite the site on which Kohlmann was also raising St. Patrick's Church.[8] With the scholastics, Michael White, James Redmond, Adam Marshall, and James Wallace, doing the bulk of the teaching, the school was opened. James Wallace,

---

[5] Rev. Charles H. Stonestreet, S.J., "Georgetown College," *The Philadelphia Catholic Instructor*, February, 1854.

[6] Henry DeCourcy and John G. Shea, *History of the Catholic Church in the United States* (New York: Kenedy Co., 1875), p. 366.

[7] Carroll to Plowden, September 19, 1809. See also Carroll to Plowden, December 3, 1808. Stonyhurst Transcripts. CUA.

[8] J. Wilfrid Parsons, S.J. "Rev. Anthony Kohlmann, S.J.," *The Catholic Historical Review*, IV, 44.

S.J., was considered by many the best astronomer of his day in this country, and later won renown by winning the prize offered by the French government for solving a mathematical problem.[9] Mr. White, S.J., was professor of "the English, Latin and Greek tongues," with which, says Kohlmann he was "well acquainted."[10]

Shortly after Christmas of 1808, the school already numbered seventeen students, and by July this number had risen to thirty-five "of the most respectable children of the city, Catholic as well as Protestant."[11] Four students were boarding at the residence, and it was expected that by August there would be seven or eight boarders.[12] Father Kohlmann, as Carroll had done in the early days of Georgetown, looked to his English brethren for assistance in obtaining equipment, but on a more ambitious scale. He wished to know from Father Strickland what the price would be for "a good electrifying machine, a *machina pneumatica* or air pump, a good telescope and a machine for surveying, and the most essential instruments for navigation."[13] These, more than anything else, he was sure, would impress the American people. They already had at the Institute "the finest set of globes in America, which cost . . . $160."[14] The school continued to prosper, and in September of 1809 it was moved to a new site on Broadway, only to be moved again in March, 1810, to a new site "far out in the country"[15] on which there already was a building to which additions were made. This site, declared to be the "most healthy and delightful

9 *Ibid.*
10 Kohlmann to Strickland, September 14, 1810. *Woodstock Letters*, IV (1875), 147.
11 DeCourcy-Shea, *op. cit.*, p. 367.
12 *Ibid.*
13 Kohlmann to Strickland, September 14, 1810. *Woodstock Letters*, IV (1875), 148.
14 *Ibid.*
15 Parsons, *op. cit.*, p. 44. Father Kohlmann described it as "four small miles from the city, and of half a mile from the East and North rivers, both of which are seen from the house." Kohlmann to Strickland, September 14, 1810, *loc. cit.*

spot on the whole island,"[16] was located where St. Patrick's Cathedral now stands.

Father Benedick Fenwick, of an old Maryland family, alumnus of Georgetown, and later administrator of Charleston and bishop of Boston, was head of the college. It attracted public notice and the public examination of August, 1810, was advertised in the papers and "gave great satisfaction to the respectable audience of ladies and gentlemen who attended the occasion."[17] Father Kohlmann thought that since New York was, and always would be, the first city in America due to its advantageous situation for commerce, the college would in a short time "rivalize" [sic] any in the country.[18] Friendly relations were established with "the professors of the State's, or Columbia College." The directors of the latter institution had invited the faculty to attend the annual commencements of 1809 and 1810. "They had never," noted Father Kohlmann, "paid that attention to the Catholic Clergy before."[19] Among the students was a son of the late Governor Livingston, and a son of Governor Thompkins, later vice president of the United States.[20] In its first eight months, the school had received thirty-six pupils, and later the attendance rose to nearly one hundred.[21] Father Fenwick wrote in December of 1810 that they had then enrolled sixty students, and could have three times that many if space could be secured. He was then considering a trip to Albany to secure the legislature's approval for a lottery in order to raise funds for a new building.[22]

---

[16] Kohlmann to Strickland, September 14, 1810, *loc. cit.*

[17] *Ibid.*

[18] *Ibid.*

[19] *Ibid.*, p. 147.

[20] *Ibid.*, p. 149.

[21] *Ibid.*

[22] Father Benedict Fenwick to Mr. George Fenwick, December 4, 1810. MS WCA, 203 M 9.

It was while the New York school was in process of formation, that Father John Grassi was sent from White Russia by the general of the Society. Father Kohlmann, who announced this arrival with "inexpressible joy," would have been more pleased had the newcomer been assigned to New York; but he was sent to Georgetown. New York's loss was Georgetown's gain. Father Grassi was to merit the title of second founder of Georgetown.

John Anthony Grassi was born at Bergamo, Italy, September 10, 1775, and entered the Society of Jesus at Colorno in northern Italy on November 21, 1799.[23] Still a novice, he was sent to Russia where the Society of Jesus possessed at that time canonical existence. All of Grassi's higher academic training was obtained in Russia, where, also he was ordained to the priesthood. He was a brilliant student, particularly in the natural sciences. No less gifted with administrative ability, he had been named rector of the college at Polotsk as early as 1804 when he was but twenty-nine years of age. While at Polotsk he was assigned by his superiors to the mission of Astrakhan on the Caspian Sea, and set himself to the study of Armenian.[24] At this time, at the request of the Russian government, he was made part of a mission to China.[25] After a sorely disappointing odyssey of five years, the project was abandoned, and Father Grassi was at length assigned to the United States.[26]

---

[23] This novitiate at Colorno was the first opened in Italy since the suppression of the order in 1773. "It was a significant step in the movement then under way which was to issue in 1814 in the complete reestablishment. . . ." Garraghan, *op. cit.*, p. 273. The master of novices at Colorno was Father Joseph Pignatelli, S.J., who was canonized by Pope Pius XII.

[24] Garraghan, *op. cit.*, p. 275.

[25] "Voyage of the Very Rev. Father John Grassi, S.J., from Russia to America. January 1805-October, 1810," *Woodstock Letters*, IV (1875), 115-136.

[26] *Ibid.* Father Grassi's odyssey is given in almost diary fashion in this fascinating account. See also Garraghan, *op. cit.*

On August 31, 1810, he sailed on the *Leda* for Baltimore, where he arrived on October 21.[27] Father Strickland, in announcing Grassi's departure from England, informed Carroll that he knew not whether the priest was assigned to Halifax or to the United States. He was sure, however, that he would be a great acquisition to either mission. He considered him a pious, laborious, and zealous young man, "of more information in natural philosophy than any he left behind him at Stonyhurst." Stonyhurst deeply regretted his departure.[28] Carroll's English friend, Father Charles Plowden, wrote to Grassi shortly after the latter's arrival in the United States, congratulating him on his appointment. He himself would almost wish, he wrote, to be on the same mission, "if it were not for the odious prevalence of French politics and principles" in America.[29]

Arrived at Baltimore, Grassi notes in his diary under the date of October 21: "Dined at the Globe Tavern and then presented myself to Archbishop Carroll."[30] The next day, he was in Philadelphia, where he had dinner with Bishop Egan; and four days later, on October 26, he arrived at Georgetown, where he was welcomed warmly by Bishop Neale and the community. As Archbishop Carroll had long requested the services of Father Enoch Fenwick at Baltimore, his wish was granted, since the arrival of Father Grassi had made it possible.[31] It is more than likely, although the appointment does not appear

---

[27] Garraghan, *op. cit.*

[28] Strickland to Carroll, September, 1810. MS BCA, 8 E 7.

[29] Plowden to Grassi, December 26, 1810. MC WCA, 203 M 10. Father Plowden hoped that "the good archbishop will find you a station untainted by Frenchmen; but alas it seems they were destined by Almighty God to punish mankind in every country for having followed their lessons." *Ibid.*

[30] Diario of Father John Grassi, S.J. Archives of the General of the Society of Jesus in Rome (hereafter, JGA). The original is in Italian with a few words in English. The first English words occur for the novices. He notes that later that day they had a "good dinner."

[31] Father Charles Neale to Archbishop Carroll, November 28, 1810. MS BCA, 5 N 9.

in the minutes of the board of directors, that Father Grassi, as Father Kohlmann expected he would do, assumed the post of vice president vacated by Father Enoch Fenwick.[32]

Upon the resignation of Father Matthews on September 12, 1809, effective November 1 of the same year, Father Francis Neale had been chosen to succeed him. Father Neale had served for many years as vice president, which office, it may be recalled, chiefly concerned itself with the temporal affairs of the college. At this point, however, the directors resolved to re-define the respective duties of the president and vice president, and declared that it should now be the duty of the vice president, to "superintend the literary department, correspond with the parents and guardians with the approbation and concurrence of the president, any resolve to the contrary notwithstanding."[33] At this same meeting, Father Enoch Fenwick was named vice president to assume these duties.[34] It was this post, a combination of dean and vice president, which Father Grassi in all likelihood assumed almost immediately upon his arrival at Georgetown. He was of incalculable assistance to Father Francis Neale, for the latter was more than occupied with his other positions as master of novices and as pastor of the parish of Holy Trinity. Neale had, moreover, neither the qualities necessary for the position nor the inclination to act as president of the college. He busied himself zealously in his other tasks and was often, Grassi informs us, away from the college from morning till night on parish business.[35] Father Neale seems to have been fitted for the task of temporal administrator, having often been chosen for that post, both in the corporation of the clergy

---

[32] Kohlmann to Strickland, November 28, 1810. *Woodstock Letters*, IV (1875), 148.
[33] Meeting of Board of Directors, September 11-12, 1809. *Minutes of the Board of Directors, Georgetown College, 1789-1815.* GUA, 398.
[34] *Ibid.*
[35] Transcript and translation of an Italian letter of Father Grassi, October 8, 1811, GUA, 257.14.

and in the college; but for the office of president, according to
the prescriptions laid down by Carroll, he was unfitted. Carroll
must have given evidence of his dissatisfaction in a letter to
Father Strickland, for the latter in his reply, declared that
he had little acquaintance with the Neales, except Francis.
"They were said to be," he wrote, "and I believe are very holy
men, tho they were never considered to have talents peculiarly
adapted for government."[36] Carroll himself a few years later
expressed the judgment that Father Neale had "good inten-
tions" but "no ability for his station and was nominated by a
strange combination."[37] Neale's administration would seem
to have been marked by but two important events; the arrival of
John Grassi at Georgetown, and the organizing there of the
sodality of the Blessed Virgin Mary in 1810.

The date, 1810, is generally assigned to the establishment
of this important phase of Georgetown college life—as of every
Jesuit college—but there is some evidence to show that the
sodality existed at Georgetown before 1800. Brother Joseph
Mobberly records in his diary his admittance into the sodality
at Georgetown by Father DuBourg in 1802.[38] Father DuBourg,
however, had left Georgetown in 1799, so that Brother Mobberly, if we trust his memory as more faithful with regard to
the person receiving him than in respect to the date of his
reception, was admitted into the sodality prior to 1800. The
formal and complete establishment of 1810 was probably due
to the efforts of Father Neale. He had long been interested in,
and associated with, sodalities. In 1805, when Bishop Carroll
feared that Neale's appointment as master of novices might be
a risk since the latter had never himself passed through the
novitiate, Father Molyneux assured the bishop that there was no

[36] Strickland to Carroll, November 8, 1811. MS BCA, 8 E 10.
[37] Carroll to Plowden, December 12, 1813. Stonyhurst Transcripts. CUA.
[38] Diary of Brother Mobberly, S.J., Diary #4, p. 5. MS GUA, 4.4.

need for fear. Neale, declared Molyneux, had passed a regular juniorship course under a regular master of the Society, and had followed the same spiritual exercises and practices of the novitiate. Besides, Molyneux reminded Carroll, Francis Neale had later been "employed as Father Prefect of the sodality and gave the Sp. exercises of St. Ignatius to the sodales and others for several years."[39]

The college records of the sodality contain the earliest rules of that organization at Georgetown, and indeed, they reflect high spiritual ideals. Members of the sodality were expected to attend daily Mass, to give one hour on Sundays to spiritual reading, and to confess and receive Holy Communion once a month and on important feasts. At this time, everyone at the college was expected to use each day a little book, *Practical Reflections for Every Day of the Year,* which had been edited by Father Francis Neale.[40] In the list of the first members is to be found the name of "Edwd Kavanagh" who later was governor of Maine in 1843-1844.[41]

The sodality was devoted explicitly to the Immaculate Conception of the Blessed Virgin Mary, and on that feast day, December 8, each year, it was customary for old members to renew their act of consecration. On that day, also, the new candidates were admitted. After the service a breakfast of "an elaborate nature" was served. No pains were spared to add

---

[39] Molyneux to Carroll, September 16, 1805, MS BCA, 5 L 7.

[40] The book was published by Bernard Dornin, New York, 1808, pp. ii, 426. Wilfrid Parsons, S.J., *Early Catholic Americana* (New York: Macmillan, 1939), p. 74.

[41] *Records of the Sodality B.V.M. Georgetown College, 1810.* GUA, 333.1. Others listed in the first year of the formal establishment were "George Boarman, William Brent, John Cottrill, Thoms Downing, Robert Durkee, John Kelly, Geo King of Chas., Wm. Llewellin, Richd. McSherry, Henry Quinn, Ignatius Newton, Thos. Richardson, and Aloysius Young." *Ibid.* Kavanagh's career has been well treated in William Leo Lucey, S.J., *Edward Kavanagh* (New Hampshire: Marshall Jones Company, 1946).

to the solemnity of the occasion. Poems were usually recited in honor of the Blessed Virgin, and addresses delivered on her virtues. On one occasion, in 1814, the Mass of the reception of candidates was celebrated by Bishop Leonard Neale, who gave also a brief exhortation following the Mass.[42] The sodality of Georgetown is also said to enjoy the distinction of having held the first May devotions celebrated in America. This was in 1830, when Father George Fenwick, having learned the custom in Rome, introduced it into the Georgetown sodality.[43] The practice is still a feature of Georgetown College life.

During Father Neale's presidency the college went through some of its leanest years. The war with England had, it is true, hurt commerce and business, and college enrollments, as a consequence, suffered. But this can not be declared to be the only, or even the principal, cause. The fact was that the college had lost credit. Neale felt that the New York Literary Institution was harmful to the school at Georgetown, and even suspected that a plan had been deliberately contrived to supplant Georgetown by the New York college.[44] This dispute was to carry over the next few years until the closing of the New York Literary Institute. The truth was that there was a definite need for a complete reorganization of the college administration.[45] In a letter of October 8, 1811, Father Grassi undertook to give a "succinct account of this house" [Georgetown College].[46] He considered that he had been placed in a "melancholy situation, compelled to be a sorrowful spectator of the miserable state of this college, and still more of the novitiate of our dearest

---

[42] Father McElroy's Diary, December 8, 1814. MS GUA, 256.
[43] H. F. Pease, "History of the Sodality," *Georgetown College Journal*, XXXIII, No. 3 (December, 1904), 103.
[44] Benedict Fenwick to Francis Neale, June 10, 1811. MS WCA, 203 K 14.
[45] Carroll to Enoch Fenwick, June 19, 1811. MS WCA, 203 K 16.
[46] Italian letter of Father John Grassi to......................, October 8, 1811. Transcript and translation in GUA, 257.5.

mother, the Society."[47] He gave a summary sketch of the presidents who had headed the college, and was particularly harsh
on Bishop Leonard Neale and Father William DuBourg. The
former, he found, had "succeeded in nothing but in giving
universal dissatisfaction, probably by indiscreet stiffness and
untimely rigor." Father DuBourg, he complained, had left
"very heavy debts." Father Matthews had failed as a discipli-
narian: "By his weak indulgence to the boys, and neglecting to
control their prefects [he had] brought the whole establishment
into the most horrible confusion and disorder."[48] The novitiate,
due to Fr. Francis Neale's preoccupation with the parish and
his lack of familiarity with Jesuit customs and manner of life,
was in an even worse state. Little hope could be found from the
superior of the Society, for he "dwells thirty-six miles from
the college and is confessor to more than twenty Carmelite
Nuns." All these things, Grassi reported, displeased the archbishop very much, and some very wrongly imputed his
displeasure to a feeling of alienation from the Society.[49] As for
Grassi himself, it had been a dismal change "from dear
Stonyhurst to this college, which, with exception of very few,
contains nothing but a crew of blackguard youths and boys."[50]
With feeling he concluded, "I cannot and never will suffer it to
be said that such a college belongs to the Society; it belongs
to the Body of the Clergy of Maryland."[51] In fairness to the
administration at Georgetown, it should be noted that this
account must have been written when Father Grassi's spirits

---

[47] *Ibid.* In his diary Father Grassi records that on May 8, 1811, he had received
from Brother McElroy the "stato del collegio."

[48] Father Grassi to Plowden, October 8, 1811, *loc. cit.*

[49] *Ibid.*

[50] *Ibid.*

[51] *Ibid.* In the light of his later debates with Archbishop Carroll over jurisdiction,
etc., it is interesting to note the rash disowning of Georgetown made by Grassi
at this period of despair.

were at a very low ebb. In later letters he was more hopeful, particularly after he had taken charge of the college.

Father Grassi had every reason to deplore the situation at Georgetown. When he arrived at the college in the autumn of 1810, there were but ten boarders and prospects for any improvement were very small. Carroll felt that the institution had sunk "to the lowest degree of discredit" although Father Grassi was "doing all the good that is to be done under its actual administration."[52]

Grassi, indeed, while apparently despairing of the college, which he in a rash moment had disowned, busied himself, even before assuming the office of president, in recovering for the college the public esteem it had lost. He made use of his attainments in the field of science much as he had wished he might have done at the Imperial Court of China. He had one of the Jesuit brothers at Georgetown construct out of wood, since the college could not afford to supply brass for their construction, a number of mechanical devices for illustrating the Copernican system, the motion of the planets, the annual and diurnal movements of the earth, the succession of the seasons, and like phenomena. He is said to have fashioned a globe and geometrical figures, composed a dialogue on the Copernican system which the students recited very successfully at a public function, and finally fitted up a museum in which he displayed his home-made apparatus, together with the optical and astronomical instruments which he had brought with him from Europe. A large number of visitors, including senators and congressmen, came to see the exhibits, than which, Grassi proudly asserted, "there were none better in these parts of the country."[53] The general examinations of 1813 were attended by "several strangers." Grassi seized the opportunity to have

[52] Carroll to Plowden, January 27, 1812. Stonyhurst Transcripts, CUA.
[53] Garraghan, *op. cit.*, p. 280.

"several chemical experiments . . . performed [and] the vicissitudes of the seasons explained."[54] He continued to add to the
display from time to time, and the museum grew to be a regular
and popular feature of the Georgetown campus. Father Grassi
missed no chance to draw visitors to the college.

Someone had relegated to an obscure corner of a building a
set of Piranesi's etchings of Roman antiquities. These Grassi
recovered, and placed in a prominent spot in the museum.[55]
Gradually Georgetown came to be better known, and more and
more students were attracted to the college. All the while, too,
Grassi was continuing his scientific studies and experiments.
He calculated the eclipse of September 15, 1811; on another
occasion he took the altitude of the sun, which he found to be
85° 30', and at another time measured the perpendicular height
of the ground level of the old Georgetown building above the
garden gate. Frequently he visited the Patent Office and
the Navy Yard, and on occasion paid visits to Congress.[56] On a
visit to New York in 1811, he was an interested reader of the
manuscript recently completed by the Jesuit scholastic, James
Wallace of the New York Literary Institute, on the use of the
globes.[57] A few years later, it was Grassi's lot as superior of
the Jesuits in America to recall his subjects from New York
with the consequent closing of the institute. On this occasion he
made sure to request its director, Father Benedict Fenwick,
to send to Georgetown the set of terrestrial globes acquired by
Father Kohlmann, and which he had proudly boasted were the
finest in America.[58]

---

[54] Diary of Father John McElroy, August 12, 1813. MS GUA, 256.
[55] *Ibid.*
[56] Diario of Father John Grassi, S.J., *passim.*
[57] James Wallace, S.J., *A New Treatise on the Use of the Globes and Practical
    Astronomy, etc.* (New York: Smith and Forman, 1812.) There is a copy in the
    Riggs Library, Georgetown University.
[58] Kohlmann to Strickland, September 14, 1810. *Woodstock Letters,* IV (1875), 148.

On April 21, Father Grassi noted in his diary the receipt of a letter from Father Strickland dated February 12, 1812.[59] This epistle contained the news that the general of the Society in Russia had named Grassi as rector of Georgetown and provincial of what was termed the Province of North America. Just how soon Father Grassi made this known, is not certain. Perhaps he wished to have the actual communication from the general at hand before attempting to assume office, or perhaps he surmised what proved to be correct—that Carroll would not approve of any appointment of a rector for Georgetown until the Society should be restored fully throughout the world.[60] The appointment of Grassi as president of Georgetown, however, to the surprise of no one, to the great joy of Carroll, and to their own credit, the directors of Georgetown College unanimously made their own on August 11, 1812, less than two years since Grassi's arrival at Georgetown.[61] Four days later, August 15, 1812, he took office also as the superior of the "Society in North America."[62]

---

[59] Diario of Father John Grassi, S.J.

[60] Carroll to Grassi, July 9, 1812. MS WCA, 203 C 1.

[61] Meeting of the Board of Directors, August 11, 1812. *Minutes of the Board of Directors, Georgetown College, 1789-1815.* GUA, 398. At this same meeting Father Francis Neale was named vice president again with "control over and management of the temporal concerns of the College."

[62] Diario of Father John Grassi, S.J. August 15, 1812.

CHAPTER VIII

Father John Grassi
Second Founder of Georgetown

When the energetic Father Grassi was appointed president of Georgetown, he was just thirty-seven years of age. Forceful, vigorous, a man of action, he, too, unfortunately viewed non-Jesuit clergymen with some, at least, of that suspicion which was so prevalent among not a few of his Jesuit contemporaries. At the very beginning of his presidency, he evidenced a bit of a "chip on shoulder" attitude which stemmed from a suspicion that the non-Jesuit members of the board of directors were endeavoring to limit the authority and duties of the new Jesuit president.

At the same meeting at which Father Grassi had been elected president, Father Francis Neale, the almost perennial vice president, was again chosen to the latter office "with controul [sic] over and management of the temporal concerns of the College."[1] Father Grassi took vigorous exception to this, and after a meeting of the consultors of the superior of the Society in North America he wrote to each of the directors a strong letter of protest. The replies of two of them are on record.

---

[1] Meeting of the Board of Directors, August 11, 1812. *Minutes of the Board of Directors, Georgetown College, 1789-1815.* GUA, 398.

169

Bishop Leonard Neale, in equally unyielding terms, declared
his displeasure at being "summoned to answer for [his] past
proceedings whilst a director of George Town College at the bar
of [the superior] and [the] consultors' tribunal."² In a thinly
veiled *praeteritio*, Neale declared that he would not enter into
the question of the right of Father Grassi or his consultors to
investigate his actions, but would answer the letter in that spirit
of mildness and simplicity of truth which he had been taught to
follow in those days when it was his happy privilege to be a
member of the Society of Jesus.³ The protest, he declared,
evidenced "suspicious intemperateness and agitation of mind"
on the part of Grassi and his consultors, rather than "cool,
calm, and deliberate discussion."⁴ They had, out of suspicion,
seen an action against them where there was none, and they
were equivalently making a mountain out of a molehill. Had
they investigated, Bishop Neale continued, they would have
learned that, for example, he himself when president of Georgetown stood in the same position then as Grassi did now. The
vice president then "had the controul [sic] over the management of the temporal concerns." At that time Neale had not felt
any cause for indignation or alarm at the appointment of a vice
president with such powers. He considered it neither a "mark
of distrust", nor a "diminution of that confidence" which he
might have thought himself "entitled to at the hands of the
Directors."⁵ In the protest of Grassi and his consultors sentiments of unfriendliness to the Society were imputed to Neale,
and he deeply resented the charge. He closed his reply on a
very solemn note, declaring that he could with all truth and
calmness of soul assert that nothing but the honor and true

2 Bishop L. Neale to Father J. Grassi, September 12, 1812. MS WCA, 203 C 11.
3 *Ibid.*
4 *Ibid.*
5 *Ibid.*

interests of the Society had led him to vote on the motion in question, and with the true spirit of charity, his sincerest wish was for prosperity for the Society of Jesus.[6]

Father Matthews, whose answer is also on record, gave the same explanation in greater detail. It had always been the duty of the vice president to manage the temporal details of the college under the supervision of the president.[7] This had been the custom since the various duties had been defined in 1796. On occasion, however, the directors had found it necessary to change the duties of the president and vice president. The most recent case was that of Father Francis Neale. When he assumed office, the duties of the respective offices "were inverted . . . giving to the president the control over the temporal department."[8]

Upon Grassi's accession to the presidency, then, it had been necessary for the directors to designate the duties of the vice president; otherwise Father Neale would be in charge of the literary department of the college—the very thing neither Grassi nor the directors desired.

There was, continued Father Matthews, no reason for Grassi or his consultors to consider that the directors had been actuated by "improper or unfriendly motives toward him."[9] They had merely defined the offices as they had existed originally, and had placed the vice president in "his original sphere."[10] As Father Matthews pointed out, the same situation had existed at Stonyhurst, so recently the home of Father Grassi.[11]

---

6 *Ibid.*

7 Father Wm. Matthews to Father J. Grassi, September 14, 1812. MS WCA, 203 C 15.

8 *Ibid.*

9 *Ibid.*

10 *Ibid.*

11 "Mr. Neale stands precisely in the same relation to you, as Mr. Wright does to the Prest. of Stonyhurst College—Mr. Wright you know has the complete control over the temporal concerns of that college, and yet he is subordinate to the Prest. and it is thus with Mr. Neale to you." *Ibid.*

Happily, Father Grassi was satisfied. He noted on the margin of the letter from Bishop Neale that his complaint had been based on the "obvious sense of *control* and [its] having never been expressed for any other than for me."[12] In this judgment, of course, he was wrong. The office of vice president had been defined in precisely those terms from the time of the presidency of Father DuBourg. When the procedure had been explained to him, Grassi realized that he had been rash, and he ends his notation on Neale's letter with the words, "if the same with other Pres. I cannot complain."[13]

Upon his accession to the presidency, Grassi continued to make use of his scientific equipment and various exhibits in order to make the college better known to the general public. He had found, too, that Georgetown lacked more than students. The curriculum, discipline, and college life in general needed an over-all plan and organization. This had become known even as far away as England, for Father Strickland wrote to Grassi that it was to be hoped that he had already begun at the very outset of his presidency to "introduce a regular system of education into the college of Georgetown upon the plan usually practiced in the Society."[14] Evidently the task would not be an easy one, since it was a much more difficult matter "to reform abuses than to institute a new college upon a regular plan."[15] Father Grassi, too, would be "at a loss for subjects proper to carry a plan of regular education into execution."[16] Father Strickland closed his suggestions with a recommendation that perhaps the solution for the problem of an adequate staff of professors would be to unite the colleges of George-

---

[12] Notations made by Father Grassi on Bp. Neale's letter of September 12, 1812, *loc. cit.*

[13] *Ibid.*

[14] Father Strickland to Father Grassi, April 6, 1812. MS WCA, 203 D 4.

[15] *Ibid.*

[16] *Ibid.*

The Healy Building

town and New York.[17] This last suggestion was to receive greater currency throughout the mission; but for the present, at least, Father Grassi was determined to attempt the work of Georgetown's restoration without resorting to such an important step. Paradoxically, however, the very success that he had in rebuilding Georgetown, and in increasing the number of students, was to demand more and more teachers, so that finally the choice between New York and Georgetown had to be made, since it was impossible to staff both institutions adequately. By December, 1813, Carroll could write approvingly that "Grassi has revived the college of Georgetown, which has received great improvement in the number of students and courses of study."[18] At the same time he noted that the college in New York was also very promising "if it could be supplied with teachers."[19] Unfortunately, Father Kohlmann had been unwilling to "receive any but members of his body and these are too few to supply that place and Georgetown," with the consequence that if he persisted in his resolution, it would become necessary to close the institution for lack of teachers.[20]

As is evident, there was never any hesitation in Carroll's attitude as to which of the institutions must yield. The year before this report to Plowden, apparently in answer to a letter of Grassi's containing Father Strickland's suggestion to combine the two colleges, Carroll had made his decision: "If either the College of Georgetown is to be discontinued or the littarary [sic] institution near New York, undoubtedly it must be the latter."[21] He realized that this would be a disagreeable step

---

[17] *Ibid.*

[18] Carroll to Plowden, December 12, 1813. Stonyhurst Transcripts. CUA.

[19] *Ibid.*

[20] *Ibid.* Apparently Archbishop Carroll did not know that Father Grassi had already made his decision to close the N.Y. Institute. Father Kohlmann continued to represent the matter and to hope for a change in the decision but to no avail.

[21] Carroll to Grassi, November 11, 1812. MS WCA, 203 B 2.

to take, but justice to the scholars and their parents demanded it. If competent teachers could not be supplied, then the "most frank and honest proceeding" would be likewise "the most beneficial."[22] It was his wish, which agreed with Grassi's own in the matter, that "there should be no hurrying to this extremity" of closing the New York college, but "it should be kept in view and when it must be resorted to, Mr. Kohlmann and his friends ought to be prepared for the manner of doing it."[23]

The constantly expanding duties of Carroll as "Father of the American Church"[24] left him little time for his beloved college, but when opportunity afforded, he never missed the chance to visit Georgetown. The improvement effected by Grassi naturally made the archbishop's visits at this time doubly pleasurable. On April 22, 1812, he visited the college and treated the students to a special dinner. The check for this banquet amounted to (it was the year 1812!) fifteen dollars and eleven cents.[25] Later that same year he sent a young man to the college, Matthew Deagle, who had been his Mass server in Baltimore. In a letter of introduction he recommended Matthew to Father Grassi's care, and then took the occasion to offer a few suggestions which hark back to the plan he had drawn up in 1788. He exhorted the president to make it his "constant endeavor to awake in your masters a passion for study, reading and literary improvement, an acquaintance with the ancient and modern elementary books of literature and sound criticisms, for many useful methods and instructions are to be gathered from the latter as well as from the former."[26]

---

[22] *Ibid.*

[23] *Ibid.*

[24] The title was given to Archbishop Carroll by Bishop Cheverus. Bishop Cheverus to Archbishop Carroll, May 9, 1815. Shea Transcripts, GUA, 92.7.

[25] *Cash Book of the Agent of the Corporation of Roman Catholic Clergymen.* WCA, 190 B 5.

[26] Carroll to Grassi, October 30, 1812, MS WCA, 203 C 25.

This appreciation of the contribution of the modern authors to the tradition of great teaching was characteristic of Carroll. He would certainly have nodded his head in silent confirmation when a twentieth century Jesuit declared to his brethren: "We would not be in the tradition of those who have gone before us, if we were content simply to conserve the heritage they have left us. Rather our primary duty must be to enrich it. Then only will they acknowledge us as their worthy successors if we . . . do the work that they did better than they did it."[27] No one can give what he does not himself possess, reasoned Carroll, and hence he urged that first attention should be given to improving the masters. For, "the Masters having once caught a passion for improvement by reading and comparing, they will infuse the same insensibly into their pupils, and teach them to emulate the most distinguished pupils of other institutions."[28] As proof that the years had not dulled his keenness, the venerable archbishop exhorted Grassi: "Never relax in your attention to the neatness and cleanliness of the College and the personal neatness of your scholars, and to their diet."[29] Was he recalling the dinner of April 22 when he remarked that the diet "was good in substance but I fear your cook is deficient"?[30]

The difficulty of supplying both Georgetown and the New York Literary Institute continued, and the "extremity" which both Archbishop Carroll and Father Grassi had hoped to postpone, seemed to be inevitable. Father Kohlmann sent an urgent call for teachers in September of 1812, but Grassi was unable to fill the request.[31] Not many months later it seemed futile to continue to hope any longer. Archbishop Carroll suggested that

---

[27] John Courtney Murray, S.J., "Woodstock's Wisdom," *Woodstock Letters*, LXXIII (1944), 280-281.
[28] *Ibid.*
[29] *Ibid.*
[30] *Ibid.*
[31] Kohlmann to Grassi, September 11, 1812. MS WCA, 203 C 10.

tne Literary Institute be closed and the Father General of the Society of Jesus, Thaddeus Brzozowski, had already directed Father Grassi to follow the advice of the archbishop.[32] Grassi had offered to turn over the Institute to Father Maréchal who was expected to be the new bishop of New York, but the Sulpician superior said "no! no!"[33] The faculty of the Institute resigned themselves to the closing of the college. Wallace, for example, wrote to Grassi that he was ready to come to Georgetown, and wished to know if Grassi desired him to bring the globes, maps, and mathematical books along with him.[34]

Father Kohlmann, who was convinced of the superiority of New York to any other location in the United States, was not inclined to abide by the decision without making sure that the situation was fully understood. Although informed by Grassi that no priests would be forthcoming, and that the Institute must be closed,[35] he wrote, some time in 1813, his brief for its continuance. Wallace, who informed Grassi that Kohlmann was writing to Russia in defense of his position, felt that Kohlmann was hoping for a change "in the cabinet at Georgetown."[36] Kohlmann's brief consisted of a "plan of converting the College of G Town into a house of noviceship and transferring the College of G Town to New York," a move which, he felt, would be "highly beneficial to the Society in America."[37] In support of his plan he pointed out that "New York was acknowledged at all hands to be the Emborium [sic] of the commerce of America."[38] He was certain that it would increase in extent and population above any other city of the union on account of its

---

[32] Grassi to Kohlmann, August 31, 1813. MS WCA, 204 W 18.
[33] *Ibid.*
[34] Wallace to Grassi, September 21, 1813. MS WCA, 204 T 1.
[35] Grassi to Kohlmann, August 31, 1813, *loc. cit.*
[36] Wallace to Grassi, September 21, 1813, *loc. cit.*
[37] Kohlmann's Plan for Moving Georgetown to N.Y. n.d. MS GUA, 6.2.
[38] *Ibid.*

local situation. In fact, he pointed out, expert opinion predicted that in fifteen years New York would rival London. Was it not Ignatian to concentrate the labors of his men in the large cities?[39] Financially, Kohlmann reasoned, the venture was bound to be a success, for an enrollment of two hundred or three hundred students was almost a certainty. The experience at the New York Literary Institute had proved to him that if a tuition fee of two hundred and twenty dollars was charged, it would be possible to spare half of the amount received, and apply it to the education of future priests. In fact, he could see little reason for hesitation. The Catholic population was greater in New York than in any other city, and consequently there was an "ampler field" for their labors.

A further reason was not likely to be received favorably by the citizens of either the Keystone State of Pennsylvania, or the Free State of Maryland. Kohlmann contended that "a college in the State of New York will furnish the Society with a greater number and of more respectable subjects than any other state."[40] A consideration, too, that should not be overlooked was the fact that due to New York's situation, affording "easiest land and speediest communication with all the quarters of the world, everything may be bought for half price in New York by a skillful procurator."[41] Were the Jesuits to be excluded from New York, he was sure that it "would grieve and damp the spirits of those who by living out of the State of Maryland had had a full opportunity of making the comparison between the State of New York and that of Maryland."[42] Lest he be

<hr>

[39] "Magnas Ignatius Urbes." At the entrance to the City Hall Building of Fordham University, New York City, may be read a Latin inscription to the effect that St. Bernard loved the valleys, Benedict the hills, Francis the little towns, but Ignatius sought the great cities.
[40] *Ibid.*
[41] *Ibid.*
[42] *Ibid.*

considered to be arguing *"pro domo sua,"* he was ready to make a vow to his superior "never to do or say or write anything either to [his] Supr. or any other, which may insinuate either directly or indirectly even a distant desire ever to be sent to New York." He added succinctly: "I wish the Society there— but not myself."[43]

Archbishop Carroll acknowledged that he had been impressed by Kohlmann's brief for New York, but that if only one of them could be chosen—Georgetown or the Literary Institute—there must be no hesitation.[44] Georgetown must be selected. It was already completely set up, and if the mistakes of the past were not repeated, it would continue to grow and prosper. The prime mistake at Georgetown, as Carroll saw it (and the obvious implication was an exhortation to Father Grassi not to repeat the error) was "a narrow jealousy against admitting others than old or new Jesuits to a participation of its direction." He felt that the same mistake had been made by Father Benedict Fenwick at New York. He should not have hesitated, when he found that he did not have a sufficient number of Jesuits to staff the college, to call upon the assistance of others.[45]

On October 20, 1813, Mr. Wallace wrote to Father Grassi that the school would be definitely closed on November 1, although Father Kohlmann was still "holding out," hoping that there would be a change of heart among the superiors.[46] Wallace was hopeful of obtaining the famous globes, but Fenwick could not let them go until he was able to ascertain whether he could pay the debts of the Institute without relying on the sale of the globes.[47] Eventually, to Grassi's disappointment, they had to be

---

[43] *Ibid.*

[44] Carroll to Grassi, September 24, 1813. MS WCA, 204 T 3.

[45] *Ibid.*

[46] Mr. James Wallace to Father Grassi, October 20, 1813. MS WCA, 204 T 15.

[47] *Ibid.*

sold. He would have been more than pleased to exhibit them in his museum. In December, Kohlmann was still clinging for dear life to the Institute, although by now nothing remained but the building. In April of 1814, the building was sold to the Trappists who had recently come to America: "Domn. Augustin, the general of the order . . . agreed to pay $1000 dollars cash, $1000 more in one year and the ballance [sic] of 10,000 dollars to be left on mortgage."[48] At last, in May, even Father Kohlmann had to realize that the New York Literary Institute was no more. He wrote to Father Grassi in very solemn words that "next Saturday we leave the college and thus put an end to the Literary Institute."[49]

Kohlmann did not give up easily. After his departure from New York he was assigned to the post of master of novices at the White Marsh. Feeling that now he could speak more freely and with greater expectation of being heard more objectively, early in 1815 he again opened the question. He realized that the issue had been settled, but wished for the peace of his conscience to be sure that the situation had been clearly understood, and that no mistake could be laid to his silence. Again he had no kind words for Maryland. He thought that "to be confined to Maryland the poorest and most beggarly of the whole union, would be a true misfortune for the Society and would deprive it of any prospect of success."[50] Little good, as he saw it, could be accomplished in Maryland, and even that little called for "infinite labour on account of the local situation of the country and the moral dispositions of its inhabitants."[51] He was of the opinion that "the state of New York is of greater importance to the Society than all the other states

---

[48] Father Benedict Fenwick to Father Grassi, April 5, 1814. MS WCA, 204 P 1.
[49] Father Kohlmann to Father Grassi, April 26, 1814. MS WCA, 204 P 6.
[50] Kohlmann to Grassi, April 24, 1815. MS WCA, 204 H 3.
[51] *Ibid.*

together"[52] because it would supply more subjects for the Society. For these and other reasons, he deemed that it would be the wisest course for the Society to fix the noviceship permanently in the college of Georgetown and to "transfer yr. college and with all yr. professors, apparatus, library and brothers to the house of N.Y."[53] His conscience was now at rest, but the college stayed at Georgetown.

As a result of the closing of the New York Literary Institute, Georgetown gained the services of Mr. James Wallace as professor of mathematics as well as a small number of scholars.[54] In later years it was to acquire as well two former members of the Literary Institute—Father Anthony Kohlmann and Father Benedict Fenwick.

The decision not to close Georgetown and move to New York, had not been an easy one to make. Carroll (for Grassi acknowledged that the Jesuit general had told him to abide by the archbishop's choice) did not make the choice blindly. He owned to being impressed with the arguments, and weighty they were, of Kohlmann in behalf of New York, but Georgetown was his choice. It would be an injustice to lay his decision to sentimental considerations, beloved as the academy on the Potomac was to him. It is a tribute to his remarkable vision and foresight that he chose Georgetown, and provincial (even though it was the capital) Washington over New York, the "emporium of commerce." He seemed to feel that New York and other cities would have their day later. But at Georgetown, as the nation would rise, a center of Catholic learning would rise, too. Did he envision that it would be the "Alma Mater" of other colleges and universities? Documentary evidence we do not have but it would certainly have been in character.

---

[52] *Ibid.*
[53] *Ibid.*
[54] Diary of Father John McElroy, 1814, *passim.*

At the beginning of the year 1814, Father McElroy prefaced his diary with a summary of the state of the college. At that time he noted that there were residing in the college 102 persons; five priests, two scholastics, nine brothers, nine seculars (masters and tradesmen), sixty-five scholars[55] and twelve servants. There had been in the past year an increase of thirty-three, twenty-three of whom were students; and only one student had left the college during the preceding year. Due to the increased enrollment a number of improvements were made. In the large dormitory sixty small apartments were constructed "of the best materials," and in the lower dormitory sixteen apartments were erected. New bedsteads were obtained for the new quarters, and a new recreation room and a guest room were added in Old North. In Old South a "room was painted and furnished for a parlour as it now stands." Besides these improvements, the laundry was completely refitted and "a small bath house with bathing tub, etc." was erected. On the farm had been erected a new hen house, slaughter house, and a cow stable. There was also, now, "a permanent gravel road from the new college door to the gate."[56] Modest as these improvements may seem, they were of great magnitude to the officials and students, as well as to the well-wishers of Georgetown. They can best be appreciated by noting that they cost close to $2,500, when, but a few years before, the completion of Old North had to be delayed due to the impossibility of raising $400. Father McElroy was able to say that "now for the first time, for many years, we are (nearly) clear of debts."[57] Father Grassi had revived Georgetown College.[58]

---

[55] *Ibid.* Under date of January 1, 1813, McElroy noted that there were in the college 43 boarders as compared with "16 in Jany. 1812—in 1811-24—in 1810-30."

[56] *Ibid.*

[57] *Ibid.*

[58] See Carroll to Plowden, December 12, 1813, *supra.* p. 174.

About this time the historian Warden was preparing his *Description of the District of Columbia,* and on his visit to the college to obtain information for his volume, was welcomed by "An Italian from Milan who gives lessons in natural philosophy."[59] Naturally Grassi showed him his exhibit of scientific curiosities, "among which is a species of orrery and armillary sphere executed by his own hand." The details given to Warden, and also contained in the prospectus issued in 1814 by Father Grassi, reflect some of the changes introduced into the Georgetown regime by the progressive president. The long arm of inflation had extended to college tuition. Students over twelve years of age now paid two hundred and fifty dollars, and those under that age two hundred dollars. Warden noted that those who attended the classes of philosophy paid two hundred and fifty dollars; this, he added cryptically, "owing to extraordinary expenses and some particular indulgences."[60] Those parents and guardians who supplied the scholars with clothes, were at this time allowed a deduction of fifty per cent; but the uniform must be the same, still the striking one of Father DuBourg's time, "a plain coat . . . pantaloons of blue cloth . . . and a waistcoat of red cloth or kerseymere."[61] The house for non-Catholic boarders established by Father DuBourg was still maintained. The curriculum now included English, French, Latin, and Greek, as well as geography, arithmetic, algebra, and "the different branches of classical education." Public examinations were scheduled four times a year and "the idle" were again punished by "confining them to their rooms and studies during the period of vacation." An elementary class had been

---

[59] D. B. Warden, *A Description of the District of Columbia* (Paris: 1816), pp. 106-108.

[60] *Ibid.* The same is contained in Warden's *Account of the United States of North America* (Edinburgh: Archibald Constable and Co., 1819), Vol. 3, p. 209.

[61] *Ibid.*

instituted wherein, if necessary, the scholar was "taught to read and write, and prepared for a classical education."[62]

In May of 1813, Father Grassi fell ill and was forced to leave Georgetown for a time "for a change of air and the recovery of his health" which Carroll described as being "in a precarious condition."[63] Before leaving, the president presented the directors of the college with a petition asking "the total and independent direction both spiritual and temporal" of the college be given over to the Jesuits. He declared that Father General, though he was "full of reverence for those who desired to employ his Subjects in this Country and of desire to render every service in his power to this College," felt that this was imperative. In fact, he had declared his opinion that it would be better for all of his religious to abandon entirely the care of the college unless some such arrangement could be made.[64] This was not immediately granted, since Grassi, in a letter to Father Plowden in November of 1815, declared that "this concession was at last made."[65] It would seem logical to assume that the request was not acceded to until after the restoration of the Society of Jesus throughout the world in August of 1814.

Grassi's presidency of Georgetown covered the period of the War of 1812. In order to reassure the students and their parents, Father Grassi inserted the following announcement in the *National Intelligencer* for September 6, 1813:

---

[62] *Ibid.*

[63] Carroll to E. Fenwick, May 28, 1813. MS WCA, 204 Z 7. Grassi's health had been failing for some time. Carroll told him that the change of climate often affected foreigners thus but that he had "much confidence in the salubrious air of Georgetown." His confidence was evidently not rewarded. Carroll to Grassi, March 8, 1813. MS WCA, 204 Z 8.

[64] Petition of Father John A. Grassi, S.J., to the Directors of Georgetown College, May 24, 1813. MS GUA.

[65] Grassi to Plowden, November 23, 1815. Hughes, *History of the Society of Jesus, Documents*, Vol. 1, Part II, 866.

The public are respectfully informed that schools have commenced the 1st inst. and will continue as usual; the existing state of affairs leaving no apprehension of any further disturbances.[66]

His calculations proved to be inaccurate. About a year later, on August 24, 1814, the British troops entered Washington, and from the college grounds Father Grassi witnessed the burning of the Capitol and other buildings by the British troops. Father McElroy records in his diary that the flames from the burning buildings "were so great that a person could read at the College."[67]

The inhabitants of Georgetown, then a municipality distinct from Washington, were "in consternation."[68] The women and children and principal possessions were moved to the country districts.[69] On the morning of the 25th, Father Grassi went into Washington to inspect the damage, and on his return met the deputies from Georgetown who had been to see the British commissioners. They had been assured, he learned, that the inhabitants of Georgetown would be respected provided they remained quiet in their homes.[70] All that day the British were "momentarily expected in Geo:T."[71] At the college everyone "remained quiet" and nothing was removed from the place; but the precaution was taken of concealing the sacred vessels and "other articles of plate."[72] Throughout that week the citizens of Georgetown prepared for the British attack.[73] The attack never came, and school commenced promptly on September 1.[74]

---

[66] Quoted from James S. Easby-Smith, *Georgetown University* (New York: The Lewis Publishing Co., 1907), Vol. 2, p. 48.

[67] Diary of Father John McElroy, August 24, 1814. MS GUA, 257.

[68] *Ibid.*

[69] *Ibid.*

[70] Grassi Diario, August 25, 1814., *loc. cit.*

[71] McElroy Diary, August 25, 1814, *loc. cit.*

[72] *Ibid.*

[73] *Ibid.*, August 30, 1814.

[74] *Ibid.*, September 1, 1814.

Due to the burning of the public buildings, there was some thought of housing Congress in the Georgetown College buildings. This would have been a great blow to the college, then "reviving," and one which it probably could not have survived. Father Grassi consulted Archbishop Carroll as to what course of action he should pursue in the event that he should be so called upon by the government.[75] The archbishop set himself against the proposal, and advised Father Grassi to refuse, if he could do so without "giving general offence to the people of America."[76] He saw fully the painful consequences for the college that such a move would bring. If Congress came to Georgetown, the only alternative to closing the college would be to rent houses in the town and attempt to conduct classes there. As Carroll saw it, this would mean a "destruction of the excellent discipline now established, prevent their literary improvement and render impracticable the same attention at their moral conduct."[77] It would doubtless do harm, too, to the masters not yet priests, who would of necessity have to carry "additional burthen" [sic] which would deprive them of all time for study and their own improvement.[78] His reluctant conclusion was that if it did become necessary to cede the college, "painful as it is," the scholars should be dismissed, and the scholastics of the Society should be retained in a part of the old college, there to carry on their studies under the direction of perhaps Father Grassi and Father Kohlmann, until "circumstances change."[79] Although he outlined this plan with his usual thoroughness in the event that Congress should request the buildings, it was his belief that the request would not be made. Were the British to receive reinforcements, the government

---

[75] Grassi Diario, September 27, 1814, loc. cit.
[76] Carroll to Grassi, September 30, 1814. MS WCA, 204 N 22.
[77] Ibid.
[78] Ibid.
[79] Ibid.

would be "so little more safe there than at Washington that they will seek some safer refuge."[80] Contrary to Carroll's expectations, the college authorities were formally requested to offer the facilities of the college, and John Peter, the Mayor of Georgetown, was appointed by the aldermen and council to make the offer to the committee of Congress appointed to "enquire into the expediency of removing the seat of the general government to a place of greater security and convenience."[81] The offer was not accepted, and the college was able to continue without interruption.

The war naturally had its effect on the enrollment in the scholastic year of 1814-1815, but, with the news that the British had departed from the Potomac, students gradually returned, and by the end of October nearly eighty were in attendance.

On December 9, 1814, Father Grassi and Brother McElroy were more than usually busy with their diaries. On that day Father Grassi received from Archbishop Carroll[82] the news so long but confidently, patiently and heroically expected.[83] His Holiness, Pope Pius VII by the Bull, *Sollicitudo omnium Ecclesiarum* had reestablished the Society of Jesus throughout the world. The war, classes, studies, and even discipline, perhaps, were soon forgotten as Father Grassi assembled the community in the domestic chapel for the recitation of the *Te Deum* and *Veni Creator* in thanksgiving. It was a simple ceremony but there must have been many of those present whose thoughts went back to that heroic band who had sadly signed their acceptance of the brief of suppression, but who had never doubted that this day would come. After the ceremony Grassi hastened to spread the good news to Bishop Neale and to invite

---

[80] *Ibid.*
[81] Resolution of the Board of Aldermen and Board of Common Council of the Corporation of Georgetown. *National Intelligencer*, October 5, 1814.
[82] See *supra*, Chap. VI, p. 147.
[83] Grassi Diario, December 9, 1814, *loc. cit.*

him to the college for the solemn *Te Deum* on the following morning.[84] The bishop was a stalwart among those who had never wavered in the confident expectation of this event, and he gladly complied with the request. The ceremony was held at 11 o'clock, attended by the entire faculty and the student body.[85]

Carroll related to Plowden that the news had "diffused the greatest sensation of joy and thanksgiving not only amongst the surviving and new members of the society, but also all good Christians, who have any remembrance of their services, or heard of the unjust and cruel treatment and have witnessed the consequences of their suppression."[86] In New York, Father Benedict Fenwick was beside himself with joy. "The Society of Jesus is then completely reestablished," he wrote to Grassi, "That long-injured, long-insulted Society! That Society which has been denounced as the corrupter of youth, the inculcator of unsound, unchristian and lax morality." It would have been hard enough to bear if the impious had so judged, but "that Society [had] been degraded by the Church herself, rejected by her ministers, outlawed by her kings, and insulted by her laity!" And now the Society could proudly boast that it was "restored throughout the whole world, and restored by a public Bull of the Sovereign Pontiff!!" "Cooped up" as the Society had been in a small corner of the uncivilized world, to Fenwick she was now being called forth as the "only plank left for the salvation of a shipwrecked, philosophized world, the only restorator [sic] of ecclesiastical discipline and sound morality, the only dependence of Christianity for the renewal of correct principles and the diffusion of piety." His enthusiasm grew as he wrote: "What a triumph! How glorious to the Society! How confounding to her enemies! *Gaudeamus in Domino, diem*

---

84 *Ibid.* See Carroll to Plowden, March 20, 1815. Stonyhurst Transcripts, CUA.
85 McElroy Diary, December 10, 1814, *loc. cit.*
86 Carroll to Plowden, January 5, 1815. Stonyhurst Transcripts, CUA.

festum celebrantes, etc. If any man will say after this that God is not a friend of the Society, I shall pronounce him, without hesitation, a liar."[87]

With the complete restoration of the Society of Jesus a fact, and with the consequent clarification of the status of the Jesuits at Georgetown and with the college itself now "revived," Father Grassi felt that the time had come to seek a charter for the school comparable to any then in existence in America. He had enlisted the aid of Georgetown's first student, William Gaston, now a member of Congress, a few weeks before.[88] After the joyful news of the restoration of the Society, he was more determined than ever to obtain the charter. Upon the advice of Father Benedict Fenwick, the application was made "in the name of and with the signatures of the Directors of [the] College."[89] Lest Grassi should fear that there would be a recurrence of the difficulty which had marked the beginning of his presidency, Fenwick assured him that he need have no such apprehension. The directors from this time on would be Jesuits who would be exercising only the post of consultors to the president. They should be given the office, however, of director, for "it will be extremely difficult not to say impossible to obtain that grant of the legislature without such a measure as those wise legislators cannot form other than suspicious ideas of a college that has no directors."[90]

On Friday, January 27, Representative Gaston presented the "petition of the President and Directors of the College of Georgetown . . . to be invested with authority and power to confer the usual academical honors on those who by their proficiency in the liberal arts may be judged deserving of such

---

[87] Father Benedict Fenwick to Father Grassi, December 23, 1814. MS WCA, 204 M 20.

[88] Grassi Diario, November 16, 17, 1814, *loc. cit.*

[89] Father B. Fenwick to Father Grassi, December 23, 1814, *loc. cit.*

[90] *Ibid.*

distinctions."[91] The bill was referred to the committee on the District of Columbia and when a favorable reply was received from this committee, the bill was passed in the House of Representatives on Saturday, February 4.[92] The bill was sent to the Senate, and after the committee appointed had returned the bill without amendment, it passed the Senate on Monday, February 27, 1815.[93] During this same month had come the news of the conclusion of the treaty of peace between the United States and Great Britain. On the very day when the Senate ratified this treaty, the president of the United States added to the joy of the Georgetown faculty and students by signing the act granting to Georgetown its charter. The document reads thus:

> *Be it enacted by the Senate and the House of Representatives of the United States of America, in Congress assembled,* That it shall and may be lawful for such persons as now are, or from time to time may be, the President and Directors of the College of Georgetown, within the District of Columbia, to admit any of the Students belonging to said College, or other persons meriting academical honors, to any degree in the faculties, arts, sciences, and liberal professions, to which persons are usually admitted in other Colleges or Universities of the United States and to issue in an appropriate form the diplomas or certificates which may be requisite to testify the admission to such degrees.

LANGDON CHEVES,
Speaker of the House of Representatives.

JOHN GAILLARD,
President pro tempore of the Senate.

March 1, 1815.   Approved,
                        JAMES MADISON[94]

---

[91] *Annals of the Congress of the United States. Thirteenth Congress, Third Session, September 19, 1814-March 3, 1815* (Washington: Gales and Seaton, 1854), Vol. 3, Col. 1106.

[92] *Ibid.,* Col. 1122.

[93] *Ibid.,* Vol. 4, Col. 277.

[94] Original in GUA.

The news of the granting of the charter was naturally most pleasing to Georgetown's venerable founder, Archbishop Carroll. He had maintained his lively interest in the college, and had been more than pleased to be able to write to England that Georgetown now numbered "nearly one hundred pupils" and that that number could hardly be exceeded without additional building.[95] As the end of his life drew near, Carroll could view with satisfaction the revived state of his beloved college, as well as the rapidly expanding American Church. To him, however, it seemed, that "the excellent bishops of Boston and Bardstown, and Fr. Kohlmann, administrator of New York, are doing wonders in their respective dioceses. I am the only sluggard, and do no good."[96] He visited Georgetown rather frequently during the year 1814-1815,[97] his last visit being on June 21, 1815, the feast of St. Aloysius Gonzaga, the patron of youth, on which occasion the archbishop was a guest at dinner with the community.[98] He had been taken to Georgetown at this time, in the hope that the change would benefit his health, but early in July of 1815, he had returned to Baltimore. Towards the end of November, he became so weak that his recovery was despaired of. On November 22, 1815, Bishop Leonard Neale was summoned, and on the day following, at six in the evening, the archbishop received the last sacraments.[99] His mind remained vigorous to the end. Father Grassi, on hearing of the imminent death of the archbishop, had hastened to Baltimore,

---

[95] Carroll to Plowden, January 5, 1815. Stonyhurst Transcripts. CUA.

[96] *Ibid.*

[97] From the diaries of Father McElroy and Father Grassi we note that he was a visitor on May 24, June 10, June 21, September 19, 1814, and June 14 and 21 of 1815.

[98] Grassi Diario, June 21, 1815. MS JGA.

[99] For an account of this scene as well as the short but very moving address by Carroll to a group of seminarians assembled in the sick room, see Guilday, *Life and Times of John Carroll*, p. 826, quoting from a paper in Maréchal's handwriting preserved in the Baltimore Cathedral Archives, 12 V 1.

and conversed with him for quite a while just a few days before his death.[100] Here was Georgetown's founder on his death-bed in conversation with the beloved academy's second founder. What did they talk about? Is it mere conjecture to imagine that the words "Georgetown" and "my hopes" could have been over-heard? Did he tell Grassi about the chance he took in raising the building before he possessed the deed for the ground? Did he tell him of his begging tours for the college? Did he ask him if he had followed his suggestion and obtained a new col-lege cook? Did he smile and say, "Now, don't be a Neale with the boys"? One thing we know he did say. He confided to Grassi that "of those things which give me most consolation at the present moment is, that I have always been attached to the prac-tice of devotion to the Blessed Virgin Mary, that I have established it among the people under my care, and placed my diocese under her protection."[101] We can be certain that George-town's founder had placed the college also under her protection. On December 3, 1815, John Carroll died. Grassi, as we have noted earlier, characterized him as endowed with "rare good-ness of heart." The phrases "Father of the American Church" and "Founder of Georgetown" are better known but "rare goodness of heart" reveals the secret of John Carroll.

When the will of Archbishop Carroll was read, it was found that he had not forgotten the college he had labored so hard and under such adversity to found.[102] He bequeathed to "the Revd.

---

[100] See *supra*, p. 152.

[101] "Reminiscences of Father John McElroy, S.J.," *Woodstock Letters*, XVI (1887), 167-168. Father Grassi repeated these words of Carroll's in a sermon delivered to the students the Sunday following the Archbishop's death.

[102] Among the bequests he directed that "some special tokens of my tender and paternal regard and gratitude may be distributed at my funeral to each of the vocal and instrumental performers who by their voluntary exertions con-tribute much to the decency and dignity of divine service in the Catholick [sic] Church of St. Peter and likewise a suitable memorial of my sincere good will to the Clerk or sacristan of the Church and to the boys who attend about the altar." Will of Archbishop Carroll, November 22, 1815. MS BCA, 11 I 4.

John Grassi now president of the Colledge [sic] of Georgetown, Columbia and his heirs four hundred pounds sterling in five percent stock."[103] He had intended earlier that one of his shares in "the Potowmack [sic] Company" should go to the college, but he changed that disposition in this will. He further directed that the president of the college could dispose of the stock and invest the money in some other way, using the interest as a fund "for augmenting the library thereof" or he could dispose of the capital "if he can employ it advantageously in the purchase of valuable works of real learning and utility suitable to the course of studies pursued in the Colledge [sic]."[104] Besides this general bequest, there was a personal one to the "Revd. Enoch Fenwick and the Revd. John Grassi all those books which have lately been sent to me by a priest at Louvain in Flanders and which are expected soon to arrive in this Country."[105]

---

[103] *Ibid.*

[104] *Ibid.*, Bequest No. 7.

[105] *Ibid.*, Bequest No. 13. Grassi wrote to Fenwick: "I expect that I shall be obliged to present a petition to Congress to obtain that the library sent to the late Archbishop and by him left for this college may be free from duties." Grassi to Fenwick, n.d., MS WCA, 204 F 12.

CHAPTER IX

Matters
Are Not So Bad...

Georgetown meanwhile continued to prosper under Grassi's able direction. On his faculty for 1816-1817, he had the very capable assistance of the Reverend James Wallace as professor of mathematics, natural philosophy, and chemistry, and the Reverend Roger Baxter as professor of languages and polite literature.[1] Having weathered the difficult war years, blessed with a very gifted president, and endowed with a fully empowered academic charter, the college seemed well on the way to success.

The year 1816, it would seem, marked the initial steps toward Georgetown's second offshoot, the Washington Seminary,

---

[1] Father Baxter had been obtained from England not without some difficulty as he had been educated at the expense of Bishop Walmesley who regarded him highly and was naturally very reluctant to part with him. Father Plowden in a letter to Grassi praised Baxter highly as "possessing great ability and knowledge and an easy style in writing." Under his direction the class of rhetoric in 1817 presented to Archbishop Maréchal a very creditable volume of verses in English, French, Latin, and Greek, which bears witness to Plowden's estimate of Father Baxter's ability. Father Nicholas Sewall to Father J. Grassi, October 14, 1816. MS WCA, 205 W 14; Father C. Plowden to Father Grassi, January 10, 1817. MS WCA, 205 T 1.; *Reverendissimo Domino Domino Ambrosio Maréchal Arch. Baltimorensi Neoconsecrato Haec Qualiacumque Carmina Rhetores Georgiopolitano.* MS BCA, 17 D 27.

in later years to become Gonzaga High School.[2] This venture
was to become, for two reasons, an important factor in the
Georgetown story. In the first place, its success, like that of
the New York Literary Institute earlier, was to lead to a reopening of the old question. Ought Georgetown to be set aside for a
Jesuit house of studies, and college efforts for lay-students
concentrated elsewhere? In the first decade of the nineteenth
century New York seemed tempting. In the second decade it was
the city of Washington which seemed the better place for the
college. Secondly, the Washington Seminary was to pin-point
the question of tuition money in Jesuit schools in the United
States, Georgetown included.

Father Grassi had desired that the novitiate of the Society be
established in the city of Washington, and Archbishop Carroll
had given his approval.[3] The way seemed open for the carrying
out of the plan when, after the final restoration of the Society in
1814, Father Matthews had requested the assistance of the
Jesuit fathers for the congregation in Washington.[4] The foundation stone of the new building was laid on Wednesday, May 24,
1815, by Bishop Neale.[5] The building—to become in time one
of the landmarks of Washington—on the north side of F Street
between Ninth and Tenth Streets was planned as a novitiate,[6]
but shortly after its completion was converted into a school. In
referring to it in 1818, Father Grassi did not even mention its

---

[2] The year 1816 marked the beginning of the move. The school did not get under
way until September 8, 1821. Gilbert J. Garraghan, S.J., *The Jesuits of the
Middle United States*, (New York: The America Press, 1938), Vol. 1, p. 303.

[3] Carroll to Grassi, March 16, 1815. Hughes, *History of the Society of Jesus,
Documents*, Vol. 1, Part II, p. 944.

[4] Hughes, *History of the Society of Jesus, Documents*, Vol. 1, Part II, p. 947.

[5] Grassi Diario, May 24, 1815.

[6] The novices, it would seem, did not occupy the building until 1818. Father C. F.
Van Quickenborne to ...., January 16, 1818. *The
Woodstock Letters*, XXX (1901), 85, speaks of the novices as soon to occupy
the new building in Washington.

original designation, but listed it as "a house near St. Patrick's Church, erected for the education of youth."[7] The school seems to have prospered from the beginning, since, in 1821 Father Kohlmann was busy at an old task—the suppression of Georgetown.[8] He suggested to the Father General of the Jesuits, Aloysius Fortis, that Georgetown be suppressed as a college for lay-students, and converted into a philosophate and theologate for the Jesuit students. The city seminary would supplant Georgetown, but would be operated only as a day-college.[9] This brought him face to face with the problem of tuition money, and to his credit Father Kohlmann did not evade the issue. He was to be unsuccessful, but his efforts were to contribute to the successful solution later of this vexing problem of American Jesuit education—should the Society's schools be reimbursed for their services to the public?

According to the letter of its rule, the Society of Jesus may not assume the direction of a school unless the latter has been endowed sufficiently to meet all the necessary expenses, so that tuition fees will be unnecessary.[10] St. Ignatius had thus sought

---

[7] Father John Grassi, "The Catholic Religion in the United States in 1818," *The Woodstock Letters*, XI (1882), 234. This article is a translation of Grassi's *Notizie sullo stato presente della Republica degli Stati Unit i dell' America Settentrionale, scritte al principio del 1818* (Edizione-Seconda; Milano: MDCCCXIX). The money for the house had been given by Alexander Divoff, a Russian nobleman who had been converted in Russia. After being assigned to the Russian Legation at Washington he had declared himself a Catholic and later entered the Society of Jesus. Hughes, *History of the Society of Jesus, Documents*, Vol 1, Part I, p. 538; McElroy Diary, February 14, 1813, March 29, 1818.

[8] In the meantime, from 1820-1823, the Washington Seminary also housed the theological students of the Society. Here they were completing their studies while at the same time assisting with the teaching in the school. See e.g., *The Laity's Directory to the Church Service for the Year of Our Lord M, DCCC, XXII*, revised and corrected by the Rev. John Power of New York (New York: Wm. H. Creagh, 1822), p. 81.

[9] Father Kohlmann to Father Aloysius Fortis, December 5, 1821. Hughes, *History of the Society of Jesus, Documents*, Vol 1, Part 1, p. 457.

[10] Garraghan, *Jesuits of the Middle United States.* Vol 1, p. 303.

to provide free instruction in all the educational institutions of
the Society. In Europe, at least in the pre-suppression period
of the Society, adequate endowments from wealthy benefactors
made it possible to carry the principle into practice. The newly-
restored Society, however, particularly in the English-speaking
countries, found the situation quite otherwise. The endowed
school was the exception and not the rule. The only course
open was to require the students to pay for their education, or,
more correctly, that they should aid the school in meeting its
current expenses. The problem was more vital in day-schools,
since there was no objection to a boarding school asking payment for the support of the boarders. Tuition money became,
eventually, as we shall see, a recognized means of support for
Jesuit schools in English-speaking lands; but the general of the
Society resisted the innovation vigorously, and it was permitted
only after all other means had failed.

It was this problem which Father Kohlmann met head-on.
He wrote to the general insisting that the regulations of the
Society regarding colleges should be relaxed in America. It
was imperative that the American Jesuits be allowed to receive
from boarding college students, a fee which would exceed the
bare cost of maintenance, since the faculty had to be supported
and the scholasticate maintained as a seminary for future
faculty members. With respect to day-scholars, he argued that
the rule against receiving tuition should be abrogated in
America. Here colleges were not endowed, and the public were
accustomed to paying tuition. A *minervale*, or payment for
tuition, seemed perfectly reasonable.[11] His request was not

---

[11] Father Kohlmann to Father Aloysius Fortis, February 19, 1822. Hughes, *History
of the Society of Jesus, Documents*, Vol 1, Part I, p. 546. Father Grassi had
obtained a dispensation for the Jesuits of America to receive Mass stipends,
stole fees, and salaries as it had been the custom in England before the
suppression. He had not obtained the dispensation for tuition. Father Charles
Neale to Father Dzierozynski, February 19, 1822. MS WCA, 206 Z 4.

granted, and repeated representations brought no relaxation of the rule.[12] The Washington seminary prospered for a few years, and had the distinction on one occasion of having its scholars examined in Greek and Latin by the president of the United States, John Quincy Adams.[13] Eventually, however, on September 25, 1827, it was found necessary to close the institution for lack of funds.[14]

Although Georgetown College was prospering with eighty students in 1816, ninety-eight in 1817, and one hundred and one in 1818, there were still some difficulties to be considered. The sea was not completely calm. An old document in the archives of the University reveals that, at least in one quarter, some consideration was given to the possibility of a temporary closing of the school. The proposal does not seem to have received any official status, but its content points out a problem that still faced the president and directors. The author of the document suggests that it might be expedient to "shut up the college for a certain number of years say 3 or 4 or 5 years."[15] He reasons thus: due to the shortage of priests, it had

---

[12] In a document preserved in the office of Very Rev. Father Provincial, S.J., Maryland Province, and signed by Father Aloysius Fortis, the results of a General Consultation for America held on August 2, 1824, are given. The first item is the negative decision rendered on the request to receive tuition for day-students. "De Stipendio pro scholis tertio repetita est in Consultatione eadem Decisio Negativa." Father Kohlmann was unsuccessful again in 1826. Kohlmann to Fortis, February 19, 1826. JGA. Cited from Garraghan, *Jesuits of the Middle United States*, Vol. 1, p. 304.

[13] *Truth Teller*, New York, August 6, 1825, in *The Woodstock Letters*, XXVII, 47.

[14] The dispensation to receive tuition money was finally granted in 1833. In 1848 the Washington school was reopened and later moved to its present site at North Capitol and I Streets. The building on F St. was torn down in 1882. "The Catholic Seminary, Washington," *The Woodstock Letters*, XI (1882), 90-91. Garraghan, *Jesuits of the Middle United States*, Vol. 1, p. 304.

[15] Various Subjects to be Proposed to the Trustees of the Corporation and Consultors. MS GUA, 398.1. No date is given but a letter from Father General, Thaddeus Brzozowski, S.J., of 1817 is referred to as well as a letter of Father Grassi's. It would seem to be about 1818 or 1819.

been found necessary to employ as teachers in the college aspirants for the priesthood who were still engaged in their philosophical or theological studies. These, naturally, were unable to give the attention to their studies that they might have given if unencumbered with teaching duties. Such a program would result in poorly formed priests and educators. Would it not be wiser to call a halt to the college for a few years, until the ecclesiastical students could be properly trained, and a backlog of teachers obtained? Otherwise, would it not be a case of attempting to meet the manpower shortage by a temporary remedy which would, in the end, prove too costly?[16] The objections to this plan are also fairly reviewed: "What will the world say if the college be shut up? How will it be possible afterwards to open it? Where will the Catholic youth in the interim be educated? How shall the Novices and Scholasticks [sic] in the College be supported? Whence in the interim shall the subjects of the Society come from?"[17]

These reasons clearly indicate why no action could be taken on the proposal at the time, but the whole discussion must have served to point very clearly a problem that had to be faced. The dilemma could be solved only when it would be possible to set up the complete course of Jesuit training, which contains a "regency" or teaching period when the seminarian interrupts his studies for a few years to gain experience in the classroom, and then returns for his theological studies preparatory to ordination to the priesthood. Until such time as the numbers had increased sufficiently to allow completion of the studies "in the proper manner,"[18] the problem could only be met with more careful supervision, and by a distribution of

---

[16] *Ibid.* The author mentions five young men who left the society who had they "been separated from the distractions of the college and compleated [sic] their studies in a proper manner . . . would probably have persevered."

[17] *Ibid.*

[18] *Ibid.*

assignments calculated to leave the young teachers as much time as possible for study.

On June 7, 1817, Father Grassi was again at the deathbed of a man prominent in Georgetown's founding. He administered the last sacraments to Archbishop Leonard Neale who died, after an illness of but thirty-six hours, between one and two o'clock on the morning of June 18.[19] Carroll gone, Neale gone, and in but ten days Grassi would be leaving Georgetown never to return. An era at Georgetown was passing.

Father Grassi's relations with Archbishop Neale had been most cordial and friendly. On April 3, 1816, in accord with an earlier intention of Archbishop Carroll, Neale signed a concordat with Grassi relative to the stations or mission to be assigned permanently to the care of the Society of Jesus.[20] Georgetown College was one of these.[21] It was an important event in the history of the college and the mission. Legal formalities now confirmed an existing *de facto* status. The problem of jurisdiction, we have seen, arose often in Archbishop Carroll's time, and in Neale's time it arose again. The college was, and would continue to be, the center of that problem. The archbishop, in need of a priest for a congregation, would suddenly call for one of the college professors and on one occasion, at least, for its president. If the college were unable to comply and the Jesuit superior claimed his right of exemption, difficulties were inevitable. The Neale-Grassi concordat was not the complete answer but it marked a notable step in the solution.

---

[19] Father McElroy wrote of Neale: "To him under God I am indebted for my vocation to the Society of Jesus; . . . I had the consolation of being present when he departed, and of saying for him the next morning the first Mass I had offered for the dead." "Reminiscences of Father John McElroy," *The Woodstock Letters*, XVI (1887), 163.

[20] Hughes, *History of the Society of Jesus, Documents*, Vol. 1, Part II, p. 952. For a complete treatment of the question with the pertinent documents, see *Ibid.*, pp. 888 ff.

[21] Carroll to Grassi, March 31, 1815. *Ibid.*, p. 856.

Father Grassi felt that a major source of friction had been removed by this concordat.[22] He was grateful to Neale and, hence, when the archbishop needed his services in a matter vital to the Church in America, he could not refuse. The so-called Charleston schism had been completely misrepresented at Rome, with the result that Archbishop Neale had been directed by Propaganda to reinstate in the ministry men whom he knew would be detrimental to the cause of religion. This he would not do. He could not, however, go against the directives of higher superiors without explaining his actions. The issue had to be presented at Rome and by a competent legate. He was reluctant to ask Georgetown to make the sacrifice but he must. On April 9, 1817, after conferring with Father Maréchal, Neale asked Grassi to come to Baltimore. "I make no calculations," he wrote, "for disappointments in the case, the importance of which suggests pressing necessity."[23] Grassi's diary for April 12 records: "Yesterday I went and today I returned from Baltimore, where it was proposed to me to go to Rome."[24] He at first hesitated. There was an old dread of a sea-crossing which always left him violently sick. But more important was the doubt he had of the propriety of a Jesuit undertaking the mission at this time. The affair, he wrote, could not be put in its proper light without descending into full particulars. To do this "would hurt the feelings of the Irish nation and cause many reflections and constructions on me not as a simple individual but they would be extended to the very body to which I have the

---

[22] Difficulties were later to arise, particularly during the episcopate of Archbishop Maréchal. He ignored the concordat, declared it to be null, and refused to grant faculties to Jesuits except for the parishes, etc., where he wished them to be assigned. Hughes, *History of the Society of Jesus, Documents*, Vol 1, Part II, p. 954.

[23] Archbishop Neale to Grassi, April 9, 1817. JGA, *Marilandia*, 1-VIII-1. Cited by Garraghan, "John Anthony Grassi, S.J.," *Catholic Historical Review*, XXIII, 285.

[24] Grassi Diario, April 12, 1817.

happiness to belong."[25] Finally his consultors, although they knew what a great loss Georgetown would suffer by his absence, prevailed upon him to undertake the mission. He wrote to Father Maréchal that he realized there were "sufficient reasons for me to undertake such a journey and that I will do it, if I can make arrangements in the college that in my absence things may not suffer more than they do when I am here."[26] After assuring himself, Father Grassi agreed to go to Rome.

Georgetown and Georgetown's president made a great sacrifice to the greater cause so immediately and pressingly vital to the Church in America.[27] To do otherwise, would, he said, be unfaithful to the idea of Ignatius.[28] In July, Grassi sailed for Europe, leaving behind him a widely known and respected name. "Probably no other ecclesiastic of the day enjoyed in greater measure the esteem and confidence of the hierarchy."[29] Carroll's regard for him has been noted more than once. Bishop Flaget proposed his name for the new See of Detroit. Bishops DuBourg, Connolly, and Maréchal sought his assistance in matters touching their dioceses.[30] Although his return was anxiously expected (it was hoped that he would bring recruits for the mission back with him), Grassi was never to see America

---

[25] Grassi to Abbé Maréchal, April 17, 1817. MS BCA, 17 G 9. It seemed to Grassi that propaganda was "preposessed in favor of the Irish clergy" and that it was necessary for him to "be extremely cautious to avoid all occasion or danger of misrepresentation . . . since the Society is just reestablished, our Father General is like a prisoner in Russia and a conspiracy against the Jesuits is prevailing more perhaps than we are aware of." *Ibid.*

[26] Grassi to Abbé Maréchal, May 3, 1817. MS BCA, 17 G 10.

[27] Grassi had become an American citizen on December 27, 1815. See Grassi Diario.

[28] *Ibid.* "It has always been the practice of the Society highly recommended in the Institute to proffer every respect and render every possible service to the various Bishops where ours are residing."

[29] Garraghan, "John Anthony Grassi, S.J., 1775-1849," *Catholic Historical Review* XXIII. 288.

[30] *Ibid.* See Hughes, *History of the Society of Jesus, Documents*, Vol. 1, Part I, p. 584.

or Georgetown again. Georgetown had made an even greater sacrifice than she knew.[31]

It would be difficult to overestimate the loss that the college sustained when its "reviver," its "second founder," left Georgetown for Rome. It was not to know another president of his stature for twelve years, when the Reverend Thomas Mulledy would take office. During those intervening years, 1817-1829, no less than seven presidents would attempt to carry on the work of John Anthony Grassi. Brilliant in other fields of endeavor, they lacked the genius that Carroll long before had seen was necessary to mark the successful college president. The lack of a steadying hand was reflected in the successively declining rolls of the college. A low point of thirty students was reached in 1825, after which there was a small recovery; but when Father Mulledy took office in 1829 there were but forty-five students in the college.[32]

Before his departure for Rome, Father Grassi had named as his successor Father Benedict Fenwick, who had had experience as head of the New York Literary Institute until that institution had been forced to close for lack of teachers to staff

---

[31] On his arrival in Rome Grassi was told by the Father General that he was to remain permanently in Italy. Later, when it was clear that he was needed, the general appointed him to America. This, however, was subject to medical approval which was not given. The doctors felt that he would be placing his life in great danger if he were to attempt another sea voyage. Finally, at the beginning of 1819 the question was closed and Grassi spent the remaining thirty years of his life in Italy. Garraghan, "John Anthony Grassi, S.J." *Catholic Historical Review*, XXIII, 288.

[32] While the financial "panic" of 1819 must have affected registration considerably and the fault may not justly be laid entirely at the door of the president, the steady decline in registration was remarkable. In 1818 the number was 101. The roster of the succeeding years was:

1819—80	1824—40
1820—64	1825—30
1821—53	1826—41
1822—46	1827—33
1823—34	1828—45

it.[33] The new president, who had first entered Georgetown as a student in April of 1793,[34] gave every promise of being a worthy successor to Father Grassi, but his term was to be brief. Archbishop Maréchal, who had succeeded Archbishop Neale, asked that Father Fenwick be permitted, along with Father James Wallace, to be sent to Charleston in 1818 in order that that trouble spot might be served by worthy priests.[35] His request was granted.

It was during Father Fenwick's brief presidency that Georgetown, in virtue of its charter, conferred its first degrees. The recipients were Charles and George Dinnies. At this exhibition, or commencement, the orators of the day delivered extracts from speeches which had been made in Congress on the Compensation Bill. This bill had held more than usual interest for the Georgetown students, since William Gaston had spoken so brilliantly in the debates on the question. The youthful orators reenacted the debate in part, and William Gaston's role was played by his son, Alexander.[36] The "Speaker of the House" was Peter Menard of Kaskaskia, Illinois.[37]

---

[33] Father Benedict Fenwick to Archbishop Maréchal, July 1, 1817. MS BCA, 16 N 1. Father Kohlmann was named to succeed Father Grassi as superior of the Society of Jesus in North America. He did not expect his term "to be long." Kohlmann to Archbishop Maréchal, September 21, 1817. MS BCA, 17 S 1.

[34] Benedict Fenwick was born near Leonardtown, Md., on September 3, 1782. His father later changed his residence to Georgetown in order, says Father Stonestreet, that his sons might attend the college. Rev. Charles H. Stonestreet, S.J., *Discourse on the Right Revd. Benedict J. Fenwick, D.D., pronounced in St. John's Church, Frederick, Md., September 11, 1846,* (Frederick: J. W. Baughman, 1846).

[35] The Charleston Schism was like the earlier one in New York—the outgrowth of trusteeism. The Rev. Simon Felix Gallagher and the Rev. Robert Browne, O.S.A., assisted by the trustees were determined to oust the Rev. Joseph Picot de Cloriviere from the pastorate in Charleston. See Rev. Peter Guilday, *The Catholic Church in Virginia, 1815-1833* (New York: The United States Catholic Historical Society, 1924), p. 279.

[36] Commencement Program, 1817. Commencement File, GUA.

[37] *Ibid.*

On the 19th of November, 1817, the usual routine of the day for both the president and the students was given a welcome variation. Seven or eight Indian chiefs who had come to Washington to present land claims to President Monroe, visited the college and expressed their appreciation for the ministry of the Jesuit fathers among the tribes of the Indian nations. The following Wednesday, the chiefs were the guests of the president and faculty at dinner.[38]

In October, 1818, Father Fenwick left Georgetown for the delicate post at Charleston, taking with him Father James Wallace, Georgetown's famed mathematician.[39] The great needs of Charleston had made great demands on Georgetown—first Grassi, then Fenwick and Wallace. The college could ill spare these men, but the greater good demanded the sacrifice.

Father Fenwick was succeeded as president by Father Anthony Kohlmann who had been named superior of the mission on Father Grassi's departure for Rome. Father Kohlmann thought to hold the position of president himself rather than to appoint another, since he "daily expected" the return of Father Grassi to his post.[40] But Kohlmann was to be disappointed. Throughout 1818, and well into the midsummer of 1819, it was still hoped in America, and in reality it was planned in Rome, that Grassi should return. He had written often of his projected return, and heartened many with the news that he was not re-

---

[38] Shea, *History of Georgetown*, p. 52.

[39] Father Wallace was later dismissed from the Society for disobedience and accepted the post of professor of mathematics in Columbia College, Charleston, South Carolina, until "an anti-Catholic feeling forced him from the chair." *Ibid.*, p. 53.

[40] On September 15, 1818, he had the following item placed in the local paper. "The exercises of the college will recommence on Wednesday the 16th inst. The different departments being filled with competent professors, the classes will proceed as usual. The Rev. Dr. Grassi being daily expected from Europe to resume the presidency, the subscriber will, in the meantime, supply his place," *Commencement File—1818.* GUA.

turning alone.[41] Many had desired to come to America with him,
and the Father General had promised Archbishop Maréchal
that when Grassi returned he would have a few companions.[42]
On the last day of Lent, 1819, however, Father Grassi suffered
an accident, a very bad fall which resulted in a rupture. The
physicians, knowing that he would always be a victim of very
violent seasickness, "positively declared that [he] must not be
exposed to the danger of a sea-voyage," and the general of the
Jesuits ordered him to remain in Italy.[43] It was a blow to Father
Grassi, who declared that he could but "say *fiat voluntas tua*
and assure yr. Lordship [Archbishop Maréchal] that I shall
at least be at your service in America and I shall endeavour to
do for the American missions all that is in my power."[44] As a
result, what Father Kohlmann thought would be but a few
weeks' substitution as president became a two-year term. He did
not find the office to his liking, nor did he have the qualities
necessary to cope with the demands it made on him. The college
enrollment fell considerably during his two-year term as president, and while it is true that the economic and financial
difficulties consequent on the panic of 1819 were in large
measure the cause of the decrease, Kohlmann was not the Grassi
of 1812, who could initiate a revival. The heroic strains (one
might be tempted to say mock-heroic posture if his sincerity
were not so apparent) in which he recounted to Archbishop
Maréchal a projected "riot" among the students, gave evidence
of his inability to cultivate the Grassian large view:

> The late projected riot and the writing of so many letters which it
> rendered indispensable took up all my thoughts and leisure to such
> a degree that it was scarce in my power to forward er [sic] this to

---

[41] Grassi to Archbishop Maréchal, n.d., MS BCA, 17 G 7. See also Grassi to
Father Enoch Fenwick, June 29, 1819. MS WCA, 205 N 14.
[42] Father Aloysius Fortis to Archbishop Maréchal, April 17, 1819. MS BCA, 16 S 4.
[43] Grassi to Archbishop Maréchal, July 15, 1819. MS BCA, 17 G 13.
[44] *Ibid.*

Yr. Grace this short account of the above scheme. It was contemplated to assail the amiable Mr. Dubuisson on the 24th inst. in the evening recreation. Of this I was most providentially informed by some good friend at the very time the students went to supper and of course we were on the watch. The thing came actually on, the candles were put out in one of the recreation rooms and a noise raised. At the very minute we were on the spot and order was not so much restored than preserved; those whom we had most reason to suspect of being at the head of the business were called up and examined and in a few hours time we came nearly to the bottom of the whole affair. The ringleaders were expelled early in the morning, some others less guilty were dismissed without the disgrace of a formal expulsion, the smallest otherwise punished. The scheme was contrived by some or other of the largest boys, who wished to keep behind the curtain, whilst they commited the execution to smaller boys.

In reflecting in my mind what could possibly have led to such a black design against Mr. Dubuisson, I cannot conceive any other cause than the publication of the rules which were framed by the RR. Messrs. Fenwick, Wallace and Baxter, and which it would appear the students ascribed chiefly to the framing of Mr. Dubuisson. Upon the whole we have reason to admire divine providence in sending me his angel to apprise me of the intended riot, and in furnishing me with a plausible reason for dismissing those, who would not have failed to perpetuate a bad spirit among their fellow students.[45]

In announcing the disappointing news that he would not be returning to America, Father Grassi relayed the information that the Father General of the Society had appointed the Reverend Peter Kenney of Ireland as Visitor of the Society in America. Father Kenney was twice to fulfill the office of Visitor, and he was to play an important role in Georgetown's history. He had had experience as an educator at Clongowes Wood in Ireland, and was to introduce many important changes into the Georgetown curriculum and discipline. With tact and courtesy,

---

[45] Kohlmann to Archbishop Maréchal, October 28, 1818. MS BCA, 17 T 17.

but lacking nothing in firmness, he was to make very clear the Society's position in the jurisdictional disputes with the Archbishop of Baltimore. He was a man of virtue and abilities, and Grassi was certain that his mission would meet with success. Grassi's interest in America, it may be noted, never flagged, and in this letter he expressed the hope, which was later realized, that it might be possible, when finances would warrant it, to send the "best young men after their novitiate or even after philosophy to finish their studies in Rome."[46]

In his account of his diocese sent to Propaganda under date of October 16, 1818, Archbishop Maréchal was proud to list Georgetown College as an institution of his diocese, but he felt that it was a source of wonder to all that the Jesuit superiors had not sent six or eight outstanding men to lend prestige to the college.[47] He was most anxious to see English Jesuits sent to the aid of Georgetown, but Father Plowden informed him that it would be impossible to send anyone for quite a few years, as the situation of the newly restored Society of Jesus in England, was still in great jeopardy.[48] Father Kenney, he was sure, would prove equal to the task of so reorganizing the mission that the

[46] Grassi to Archbishop Maréchal, July 15, 1819. MS BCA, 17 G 13. Father Kenney wrote to Father McElroy from Liverpool on September 4, 1823, that "Grassi is doing much good in Rome in correcting misconceptions about America." MS WCA, 206 R 11a. Grassi's own *Notizie* already referred to he explained was written to "try to give Europeans a better idea of America. They had the wrong idea entirely." Grassi to Archbishop Maréchal, n.d., MS BCA, 17 G 7. He was anxious, too, to receive clippings, statistics, etc., of the missions. Grassi to McElroy, July 14, 1819. McElroy Papers, MS WCA.
[47] *Archbishop Maréchal's Account to Propaganda. October 16, 1818. The Catholic Historical Review,* I (April, 1915-January, 1916), 439. Printed from photographed copy in the Dominican Archives, Immaculate Conception College, Washington, D.C. The original is in the Archivio della S.C. de Prop. Fide—America centrale. Del Canada all' istmo di Panama. Vol. 4. Scritture originali. Vol. 922.
[48] Archbishop Maréchal to Father Charles Plowden, October 24, 1818. MS WCA (not numbered); Father Charles Plowden to Archbishop Maréchal, July 24, 1819. MS BCA, 19 W 9.

best possible use would be made of the men available, and would, in due course, establish a system whereby successors would be supplied.[49]

On September 16, 1819, Father Kenney announced his arrival to Archbishop Maréchal. He had been sent as "Visitor of Georgetown College and of the American mission of the Society." Unity, "so necessary and so commended by [the Jesuit] institute" was to be his goal.[50] After a few weeks devoted to surveying the scene, Father Kenney found that the reports that had gone to Rome were highly exaggerated: "Matters are not so bad as they were made to appear." The "poor general has been more plagued then he ought to have been."[51] He found that those who had been most loud in their complaints, could not be acquitted of having had a large share in creating the difficulties they were reporting.[52] It was true that some of the young priests wished to be independent, "to live in the college their own way," and that some of the trustees had made regulations which would interfere with the authority of the superior; but Kohlmann had acted courageously against them, and the difficulty had been avoided. The discipline in the college he found to be good, but the studies were deficient for lack of system. The proper formation of the scholastics must be effected, and a long-range view taken, if the standard of the teachers was to be kept at a high level. Great good had certainly been done by the college, and it was accomplishing much at present, but not certainly a fourth of what it could do if the financial picture could be brightened, and a steady supply of teachers could be sufficiently maintained.

---

[49] Plowden to Archbishop Maréchal, July 24, 1819. MS BCA, 19 W 11.
[50] Father Peter Kenney to Archbishop Maréchal, September 16, 1819. MS BCA, 17 R 1.
[51] Kenney to Father Charles Aylmer (Clongowes Wood, Ireland), October 5, 1819. MS WCA, 205 M 6a.
[52] Ibid.

Father Kenney was not long in the mission before he was involved in a jurisdictional dispute. Father Roger Baxter had been assigned by Archbishop Maréchal to the congregation at Richmond, Virginia, although he had been quite successful as a teacher at Georgetown. Father Kohlmann wished him to return to the college, and Baxter, preferring the pastoral work to a teaching post at Georgetown, appealed to the archbishop on the supposition that the superior would not risk the archbishop's displeasure.[53] Eventually the case led to friction between the archbishop and Fathers Kohlmann and Kenney, Kohlmann insisting that Baxter was needed at the college as professor of philosophy, and that Baxter needed the college as a place to "recruit his spiritual strength."[54] Father Baxter eventually returned to the college, and served later very successfully as prefect of studies.

Toward the close of the scholastic year of 1820, Father Kenney had reached the conclusion that Georgetown's ills could not be cured as long as Father Kohlmann remained president. He was "amiable, venerable etc.," and had accomplished great things on the mission, but *"non omnia possumus omnes . . .* in no circumstance is the Rectorship of a college the place for Mr. K and in the present case he is peculiarly ill-adapted for it." For a college president, you must have "a man of high estimation," and, whereas Grassi had been held in great esteem, Kohlmann was a man of whom "the public have not an high opinion and in whom the Jesuits themselves have no confidence."[55] This lack of confidence on their part had been of necessity reflected and transmitted to those outside the Society.[56]

---

[53] Father Roger Baxter to Archbishop Maréchal, March 2, 1819. MS BCA, 13 E 12.

[54] Kohlmann to Archbishop Maréchal, September 28, 1819. MS BCA, 17 V 32; Kenney to Archbishop Maréchal, October 6, 1819. MS BCA, 17 R 2; Kenney to Father Esmonde (Ireland), March 20, 1820, MS WCA, 205 K 16.

[55] Kenney to Archbishop Maréchal, June 11, 1820. MS BCA, 17 R S.

[56] *Ibid.*

The reason for it, Kenney informed Grassi, was Kohlmann's habit of frequent changes whereby he had "ruined the college."[57] It seemed to Kenney that, far from being disappointed by the archbishop's request for Fathers Benedict Fenwick and James Wallace, Kohlmann had welcomed it. He seemed to be "glad to get rid of B. Fenwick and Baxter and Wallace; in fact he put them out and requested Archbishop Maréchal to give the congregation of Charleston to B. Fenwick to keep him there."[58] Whatever Kohlmann's personal feelings may have been, this judgment of Kenney's is too severe. Fenwick and Wallace were asked for and needed in Charleston. In Baxter's case, as noted, Kohlmann more than once protested to the archbishop that he was needed at the college. At all events, Kenney's solution was that Kohlmann, who still retained his post as superior of the mission, should live at the seminary in Washington, and that a new president should be appointed for the college.[59]

The change projected by Father Kenney would naturally be but the first in a series, inasmuch as some post in the mission would have to yield to the good of the college. Kenney took this opportunity to open the discussion of the problem of appointments with Archbishop Maréchal. He had earlier given his opinion "on the importance of supporting effectually an establishment so intimately connected with the good of Religion in this vastly extensive but deeply afflicted mission."[60] He was confident that the archbishop had the good of the college at heart, and had seen "often, too often alas! the sad effects of a neglect of religious education and collegiate discipline in those men who so horribly scandalized Yr. Gr. flock and so unfeelingly increased the anxieties of pastoral solicitude."[61] The college must

[57] Kenney to Father Grassi, May 31, 1820. Transcript. GUA, 257.2.
[58] Ibid.
[59] Ibid.
[60] Kenney to Archbishop Maréchal, October 6, 1819. MS BCA, 17 R 2.
[61] Ibid.

have assistance if it were to survive. A change must be made in the administration of Georgetown, for "if matters go on . . . there will not be twenty scholars in the house this year." It would be impossible to find "an easy and effectual remedy by which no risk would be incurred."[62] A remedy would have been applied sooner "had the subjects of the Society been wholly under the government of the Society, [for] Messrs. Ben. Fenwick and Wallace would have been recalled had not a fear of distressing and displeasing the Archbishop suspended the authority of the Superior."[63] It was Father Kenney's idea that either of the Fenwicks or Wallace should be appointed rector.[64] The change of Father Kohlmann along with Father Rantzau to the Washington seminary would make it possible for them to be of assistance to Father Matthews at St. Patrick's. Father Kenney realized fully the need for men, but he insisted that "if the College be not better supported it will sink and yr. Grace will consider who it is that withholds the only desirable [sic] remedy."[65]

On July 7, 1820, Archbishop Maréchal dined at the college and had as table companions three Indian chiefs. "The principal one," he wrote to Father Fenwick, "made me a fine speech, as being his Great Father."[66] It would seem to have been on this visit that the archbishop was greeted with another speech. Father Kenney insisted that Father Enoch Fenwick be freed of his duties at the cathedral in Baltimore in order to take the post of president of Georgetown. Archbishop Maréchal objected that the execution of this plan would cause great difficulties in the congregation at Baltimore, but Father Kenney would not yield.

---

[62] Kenney to Archbishop Maréchal, June 11, 1820. MS BCA, 17 R 3.

[63] *Ibid.* It would seem that Kenney had changed his ideas, expressed to Grassi a month earlier, regarding Kohlmann's attitude toward Fenwick and Wallace.

[64] *Ibid.*

[65] *Ibid.*

[66] Archbishop Maréchal to Father Enoch Fenwick, July 7, 1820. Transcript. GUA, 31.7. The archbishop noted that "there was, they say, some eloquence in it. What pleased me most, it was a very short one."

He contended that it was a sacrifice which the archbishop could not possibly refuse to make "without exposing the most important of their establishments to a certain ruin."[67] At the close of the scholastic year of 1820[68] Father Kenney appointed Father Fenwick as the new president of Georgetown. A new prospectus of the college was published on July 26 and served also to announce the new appointment.[69] The new president would continue to have the assistance of Father Baxter as prefect of schools, a position he had received when Father Kenney rearranged the various classes in the preceding January.[70]

Father Fenwick arrived at the college on August 26 and immediately set to work to prepare for the opening of classes on the 15th of September. He found "much to be done before we can get the college fairly under way and Mr. Baxter and [he] [were] very busily employed."[71] The new prospectus had incorporated the changes recommended for adoption by Father Kenney, and to put as many of these into practice as was immediately possible, required long hours of planning.[72]

The classes, each occupying a year, were to be six: rudiments, three grammar classes, humanities, and rhetoric. Graduation did not come automatically at the end of the course by the mere passage of time: "At the completion of the ordinary studies . . . *if the scholar have made sufficient proficiency,*[73] he

---

[67] Archbishop Maréchal to Enoch Fenwick, July 23, 1820. MS GUA, 4.3.

[68] On November 5 of 1819 Father Kenney had "ordained two months vacation for the higher schools: August and September." McElroy Diary. MS GUA, 256.

[69] Mr. William Grace to James Ryder, November 23, 1820. MS WCA, 205 F 4a. The letter was sent to Father Grassi to be given to Mr. Ryder, an American scholastic at Rome.

[70] McElroy Diary, January 4, 1820.

[71] Enoch Fenwick to Archbishop Maréchal, August 31, 1820. MS BCA, 16 R 6.

[72] The complete system, of course, could not be inaugurated at once. The start was made in the classes of humanities, first and second grammar. *The Classical Journal of the College*, MS GUA, pp. 26-27.

[73] *Georgetown College, District of Columbia. 182.* (Father McElroy's Diary completes the date for us as *1820*, GUA, 62.11. Italics mine.)

may receive the degree of Bachelor of Arts. If he remain longer and study the higher branches of mathematics and philosophy, he may take the degree of *Master of Arts,* if success in his examinations entitle him to it." This, in 1820, is the first mention of postgraduate studies in any prospectus of the college. The beginning of the graduate work at Georgetown, however, must be dated earlier. Although it does not seem that they took the M.A. degree, Charles and George Dinnies, the first graduates of the college, did postgraduate work in mathematics and philosophy in 1817-1818.[74]

A very significant change, made at Father Kenney's suggestion and definitely in accord with his insistence on the importance of composition, was the assigning of the same teacher to the classes of Greek, Latin, French, and English languages. As a further advantage, the same teacher was to advance with his pupils through rhetoric class to graduation. Although examinations were held to determine the student's fitness for the next higher class, it was enjoined that his "rank in his school entirely depend on the aggregate merit of his compositions and the premiums be principally for superior merit in each composition."[75] It is not known whether Father Kenney, in making his suggestions, had the advantage of prolonged study of Carroll's original plan of studies for the college, drawn up at the time of its foundation. It would seem that he did. His proposals more than once repeat the thoughtful and far-visioned blueprint drawn up by Georgetown's founder.[76]

---

[74] *The Classical Journal of Georgetown College,* GUA, pp. 5, 11. A newspaper clipping in the Commencement File, Georgetown Archives, informs us that in the "First Class, comprising Metaphysica, Physica, and Chemistry Charles Dinnies and George Dinnies of New York were of equal merit."

[75] "The Substance of some general principles which were proposed for adoption by Father Visitor. . . . They were adopted nem: Cont." *Classical Journal, loc. cit.,* p. 25.

[76] See *supra,* e.g., p. 72.

Although Father Fenwick entered vigorously into the task of revival, he knew many days of discouragement and very humanly complained to Father Francis Neale of his being taken from Baltimore, and from the work at the cathedral that he liked so well, to take direction of "a College which has one foot in the grave."[77] Gradually the college began to increase, but it was a slow process. As his prefect of studies phrased it some months later, "our college is increasing but it is harder task to reform a college than it was for Hercules to clean the stables."[78]

The emphasis on composition, so evident in Father Kenney's program for the revised studies, had its flowering in the first college newspaper, the *College Minerva*.[79] It lived only for a few numbers as it was transcribed by longhand, and one copy apiece was given to each class. It would seem that writer's cramp could well be ascribed as the cause of the early death of the *College Minerva*.

During these years when a good number of the students came from the States of the deep South, traveling was so expensive and the means of travel so restricted that many of the boys did not return to their homes during the summer vacation. Provision was made for these to spend the holidays at some of the Jesuit parishes and farms such as St. Inigo's, and Newtown in St. Mary's County, Maryland, or at Conewago in Pennsylvania. In 1820, being freed from studies and from the restraints of college discipline, the students seem to have relaxed too vigorously, roaming the countryside and raiding the orchards,

---

[77] Enoch Fenwick to Francis Neale, September 6, 1820. MS WCA, 205 G 8.
[78] Baxter to Grassi (to be sent to Mr. J. Ryder), March 31, 1821. MS WCA, 205 D 13.
[79] *Minerva's* birthday is in doubt. "A Scholar of the Olden Days," writing in the *College Journal*, III, No. 4 (February, 1875), 40, recalls the origin of the paper during his student days—1820—1824—but does not say in what year of his course the paper originated.

gardens, and poultry yards, at least at Newtown. Bills were presented for the depredations and the adjustment of financial liabilities led, as the records show, to diplomatic correspondence between the pastor of Newtown, the treasurer of the college, and the procurator of the mission.[80]

It will be recalled that Father Grassi, shortly after his return to Europe, had expressed the hope that it might be possible to send the "best young men after their novitiate or even after philosophy to finish their studies in Rome."[81] His purpose was evident. The American mission must stand on its own feet. Having learned the spirit of the Society, its tradition and its methods, these young Americans would then return to be the American founders of the Society in America. Father Kenney soon became an ardent advocate of the same plan. He had found that the men, with a few exceptions, who had come from White Russia to assist the newly restored Society, had been old men, men who knew little of the language of the country and who were not quick to acquire that language. They had been, again with a few exceptions, ill-suited to be teachers in a college. The young American students, he had found, were keenly disappointed when they discovered that these fathers from Europe were not such as they had hoped for, and as a result the American boys found it difficult either to hold these teachers in great esteem or to place confidence in them.[82] Consequently, in 1820, Kenney arranged that six scholastics should go to Rome for the

---

[80] On July 28, 1823, Father Francis Neale, superior, wrote to Father Enoch Fenwick that "our secular students are not to visit our farms. They are too destructive." MS WCA. For the mission procurator's claims see WCA 171 P 5. On the other side of the ledger we have the account of one of the scholastics that "about 25 boys with their prefects went to Newtown. They stayed only two weeks because they were starved." Mr. Jerome Mudd, S.J., to Thomas Mulledy and Wm. McSherry, May 2, 1821. MS WCA, 205 C 10.

[81] Grassi to Archbishop Maréchal, July 15, 1819. MS BCA, 17 G 12. *Supra*, p. 208.

[82] Father Kenney's Report to the General Congregation at the Professed House in Rome, October, 1820. Transcript of Rev. E. I. Devitt, S.J. GUA, 289.5.

Dahlgren Chapel

completion of their studies. It was an important decision for the future of the mission and for Georgetown. Father McElroy "engaged passage for Gibraltar, thence to Rome in the ship *America*, Captain Barrett. [The scholastics were] Mulledy, Smith, Pise, McSherry, Ryder, and Fenwick."[83] On June 2 the young men were received "with great kindness" by John Quincy Adams, Secretary of State, when they went for their passports. On June 6, accompanied by Fathers Kohlmann, Baxter, Marshall, and McElroy, they went to Alexandria and there boarded ship for Gibraltar. Father McElroy assures us that they "went off in good spirits."[84] He was to be one of many who would anxiously await their return.

At the exhibition, or commencement, of July 26, 1821, the degree of Doctor of Laws was conferred, for the first time in Georgetown's history, on the Reverend John Tuomy, professor of mathematics in the college; and the Master of Arts was conferred on the Reverend James Fairclough.[85]

The following commencement, that of 1822, which was to be the last under the presidency of Father Enoch Fenwick, saw two changes under his direction. The music was now furnished by a college band,[86] and the speeches and compositions were no longer borrowed from others but were the products of the students. Commencement was still an all-day affair and 1822 saw not one, but two, valedictorians.[87]

---

[83] McElroy Diary, May .., 1820. MS GUA, 256.1. To anticipate, three of the scholastics were to become presidents of Georgetown and one an important prefect of studies. Mr. McSherry was also to be the first provincial of the Maryland Province of the Society of Jesus.

[84] *Ibid.* June 2, 6, 1820. MS *loc. cit.* They arrived at Rome on September 6, just three months from their departure. *Ibid.*

[85] For some unexplained reason, Father Fairclough's name does not appear on the program. It is recorded, however, in the *Classical Journal*, GUA, p. 53.

[86] Henry Rieselman, S.J., to George Fenwick, S.J., May 2, 1821, MS WCA, 205 C 9, tells of the beginning of the band and declares that the "people were much pleased."

[87] Exhibition or Commencement of July 29, 1822. Commencement File. GUA.

CHAPTER X

In the
Classroom—And Out

While the foregoing events were transpiring, and the momentous decisions regarding men and money were being made by the presidents and directors, there was occurring a flow of incident that was much more vital to the "Sons of Georgetown"—the everyday life in the classroom and out of it. Many things they did differently than the students of today; but remove the disguise of particular details, and the college student of the 1950's would still recognize his predecessor of the 1820's.[1]

"The College," the prospectus of 1820 informs us, "is situated on an eminence on the Maryland side of the Potomac, and commands a full view of Georgetown, Washington, the Potomac, and a great part of the District of Columbia. Its situation is peculiarly healthy."[2] The next line offers, it is to be feared, one feature of the disguise that the student of the 1950's would have to penetrate before he would recognize his earlier

---

[1] The treatment of the curriculum section of this chapter owes much to an unpublished paper of Francis X. Gerrity, "Educational Institutions at Georgetown, 1810-1860" (1945).

[2] *Georgetown College, District of Columbia, 1820, Rev. Enoch Fenwick, President.* GUA, 62. 11.

brother: "The distance between the College and the Capitol is *only an ordinary walk,* so that the students are frequently present at the most interesting debates of Congress and pleadings of the Supreme Court."[3]

The greater number of students of this period came from the South. Many indeed came into the strictly disciplined life at Georgetown directly from the rather free life of the plantation. For many, the transition was very difficult; for some, indeed, it seems to have been impossible. Riots and attacks on prefects occurred, and while they were not everyday occurrences, they could scarcely be termed rare. The restless were soon weeded out, it may be chronicled.

During this period of the 1820's, Georgetown College was recognized as one of the outstanding institutions in the country offering a liberal education. The curriculum throughout this period was, as it had been from the beginning, essentially classical. It would be a mistake, however, to endeavor to find minute observance of the *Ratio Studiorum.* Father Roothaan's edition of the *Ratio,* which appeared in 1832, was an attempt to adapt the classic Jesuit plan of studies to changed contemporary conditions. In many quarters of the world, and particularly in America, its arrival was a signal, not to continue —with modifications—a plan already in practice, but to return to traditional Jesuit procedure in the colleges of the Society.[4] The confusion consequent upon the suppression of the Society, and the scanty resources of men and money, had obscured the

---

[3] *Ibid.* (Italics not in the original.) The prospectus of August, 1831, repeats the same feature but with the significant addition: "always, however, attended by their Prefect." GUA, 62.11.

[4] Garraghan, *The Jesuits of the Middle United States,* III, 116-118. At Georgetown Father Mulledy did much after the appearance of Father Roothaan's edition to incorporate as much as possible of the principles of the *Ratio.* In 1859 Father Beckx, the general of the Society, commended Maryland and California for having brought "studies . . . in harmony with the system of the Society." *Ibid.,* p. 119.

Ratio even after the restoration. A systematic plan of studies is not the first consideration when a college is striving stubbornly to keep its doors open. As Father Garraghan points out, "Even in our own day anything like a literal application of the provisions of the *Ratio* is felt by Jesuit educators in the United States to be impracticable."[5]

In 1820, the academic year extended from September 15 to July 31, the first term ending on December 23, and the second on July 22. There were three examinations in the year: at Christmas, Easter, and before the summer vacation. There were also two days of public academic exercises at which the students displayed their proficiency in composition, particularly in Latin and Greek. The minor academic exhibition took place in March, and the major, or annual commencement, at the end of July.

There were at this time six classes. To sketch, even in outline, the syllabus of this period taxes the paper with its weight. If it gives pause to the reader, what must have been the apprehension of the prospective student? The first class, requirement for which was that the student be able to read, was Rudiments. Here the young scholars studied English and French grammar, arithmetic, etc., and at the conclusion of the year, were expected to be able to read and write English correctly.[6] In the following year, Third Grammar, English and French grammar was continued and one of the easier French authors was read. Composition in French was begun in this year, and toward the

---

[5] *Ibid.*, p. 117. As Garraghan points out, a modern general of the Society has declared that the *Ratio* is not so much a program or course of studies as a body of pedagogic and administrative detail. It determines not so much what subjects to teach as how to teach them. As the general (Father Wernz) wrote: ". . . as the early Jesuits did not invent new methods of teaching but adopted the best method of their age, so will the Jesuits now employ the best methods of our own time." *Ibid.* See Carroll's advice to Grassi. See *supra*, p. 175.

[6] *Prospectus of 1820.* GUA, 62.11.

close of the year the students began the study of Latin grammar.
Second Grammar concentrated on the addition of Latin to
the curriculum. (The English and French studies continued
throughout the six years.) Latin exercises were done, and the
students read "several books of the easy Latin and French
authors, as Caesar, Bossuet's Universal History, etc." A course
in Geography also occupied a part of the year. By the time a
student reached First Grammar he was reading portions of
Cornelius Nepos, Sallust, Livy, Cicero's minor works, and some
of Ovid's *Elegies*. In this year, besides Latin and French, he
was introduced to the study of Greek, and before the end of the
year was reading portions of the Scripture in Greek, the *Dialogues* of the satirist, Lucian, and Xenophon's history. History
and algebra also took up some of his "leisure" hours. In
Humanities, normally the fifth year, Cicero's minor works and
orations were read, as well as Virgil, Horace, Homer and Livy.
History, algebra, and geometry were continued and "a treatise
of mythology learned." The final year, or Rhetoric, busied the
scholars with the rules of rhetoric, Cicero's orations, Homer,
Virgil, Horace, history, and mathematics. Always the emphasis
was on composition. In 1820 it was announced that there would
"also be a class of bookkeeping, for the convenience of those
who wish to learn it."[7]

Impressive as this syllabus of 1820 is, it seems but an
introduction when placed alongside that of 1835. One can
summon courage enough to read through the course of studies
at this time, only by realizing that the college student of 1835
not only read but followed this syllabus. The first class, Rudiments, was launched immediately into Latin and Greek
grammar, was exercised in Latin and English composition and
read the selected letters of Cicero. Other subjects studied in

---

[7] *Ibid.*

the first year were English grammar, reading, spelling, history of the Old Testament, and the elements of geography, although these were assigned fewer hours than the classics.[8]

In the second class, Third Humanities,[9] the students read the letters of Cicero, *Graeca Minora,* and were given exercises in Greek, Latin, and English composition. English grammar, history of the Old and New Testaments, and the geography of North America offered some diversion from the classics.

Without omitting the customary exercises in languages, the students in Second Humanities read the Roman historians Nepos and Caesar, Ovid's *Metamorphoses* and *Elegies,* and finished *Graeca Minora.* Ancient history and the geography of South America and Europe were the "minors" of this year.

In the fourth class, First Humanities, the number of authors read was again increased. The historian Sallust, Cicero's minor works, Virgil's *Eclogues* and a portion of the Aeneid, Lucian's *Dialogues* and Xenophon were read. Latin prosody was studied, and compositions were exacted in Latin, Greek, and English. Mythology, history of Greece, and the geography of Asia and Africa assisted in limiting the time devoted to the playing field.

The class of Poetry, the fifth year, was by this time considered proficient and a remarkable number of authors was studied. In that year, the select orations of Cicero, a part of Livy, Virgil's *Aeneid,* select portions of the Roman poets Catullus, Tibullus, and Propertius, the *Odes* of Horace, and the *Ars Poetica* were read. Xenophon's history was continued and Thucydides, Theocritus, and Homer were also read. Exercised

---

[8] *Prospectus of Georgetown College, August, 1835.* GUA, 62.11.

[9] The 1835 curriculum extended through a seven-year course. It will be noted that the titles of the courses or years have been changed, e.g., the third class of grammar of 1820 is now the third class of humanities in the 1835 prospectus. The change was made in 1825. *Classical Journal of Georgetown College,* MS GUA, p. 88.

in the composition of Greek, Latin, and English prose and
verse, the students of this year pursued, also, a course of ancient
geography and a history of Rome.

With no stinting of the time given to composition, both prose
and verse, and with the history of the United States now
assigned, the students of Rhetoric or sixth year continued the
assault on the classics. Quintilian, Cicero's *De Oratore, De
Inventione,* and some of his orations, Juvenal, Persius, Horace's
Satires and *Epistles,* Livy, Demosthenes, Homer and Sophocles
were studied.

Neither the student of the time, nor the reader of his
history, could rest with the completion of the sixth year. The
1835 curriculum consisted of seven classes instead of six, with
philosophy again assuming a place in the undergraduate program. In the seventh year, the philosophers grappled with logic,
metaphysics, ethics, and a course in natural and experimental
philosophy: "As the students in this class are supposed to be
good Latin scholars," the prospectus read, "the Lectures on
Logic, Metaphysics, and Ethics are delivered in the Latin
language."[10] The prospectus of 1831 repeats, too, the earlier
note that there would always be "a class of Book-keeping for
the convenience of those who wish to learn it."[11] It further
announced that "the Italian, Spanish, and German Languages
[French was already included in the curriculum] will also be
taught if required; but together with Music, Drawing, Dancing,
etc., they will form additional charges."[12]

The general division into the seven classes of 1835, or the
six of 1820, was not transferred to the departments of mathematics and French. In these, the class of the student was
determined by his proficiency; thus a member of the class of

---

[10] *Prospectus of Georgetown College, August, 1835.* GUA, 62.11.
[11] *Prospectus of Georgetown College, August, 1831.* GUA, 62.11.
[12] *Ibid.*

Poetry might have been, in the third class of mathematics or French, while a boy from Third Humanities might have been in the first class. Although the system allowed for such discrepancies, the prefect of studies was not harassed too often with schedule making.

In 1826, the following class schedule was adopted, and with minor exceptions it would seem to have been followed throughout the period. Classes began at 8:15 with the first period, 8:15 to 10:00, devoted to Latin. Arithmetic or geometry followed from 10:00 to 10:30. 10:30 to 11:15 was devoted to writing or composition.[13] In the afternoon session, 2:30 to 3:30 was given to French and the last hour, 3:30 to 4:30, to "Greek, etc." It would seem that the students of bookkeeping or of the arts of drawing, music, or dancing were forced to pursue these more refined phases of education at the off-hours. On Saturdays, the schedule called for "Catechism at four for all schools."[14]

As noted, at the suggestion of the Visitor, Father Kenney, in the separate schools each instructor taught all the languages. Moreover, the same instructor guided the class through from the first day of Rudiments to the last day of Rhetoric. As the class was promoted, so was its instructor, all completing the scholastic cycle together. While the demands on the teacher were great, the advantages were evidently numerous, particularly in the teaching of languages. Obviously, too, the professor was teaching not a list of names in a class but his pupils. This, desirable in any age, was imperative at this period of non-organized elementary schooling. The students who entered Georgetown, as those of any academy or college of the period,

---

[13] "Class Schedule adopted September 16, 1826," in *Classical Journal of the College* (hereafter CJC), p. 98. GUA. The rhetoricians did not attend the writing class, continuing at geometry until 11:15. On Mondays and Thursdays the students of the poetry and rhetoric classes had "lessons on the Globes" during this period.

[14] *Ibid.*

came from a variety of educational backgrounds. The college
register on October 16, 1827, for example, lists a new student
from Georgetown, D.C. "aged 8 . . . could read words of two
syllables,"[15] and on January 19, 1829, another "aged 19 was
received and placed in the Second class of Rudiments"![16]
Individual problems received individual attention. A student
from Brazil, "age 9 . . . entered the college and not knowing
sufficient to be admitted into the class of Rudiments was put
under the care of Brother Clarke until he should have learned
to read."[17]

The method employed to measure the progress of the students was a general composition and examination. Originally, a
general composition and examination was held at the end of
each term, that is, towards the end of December and of July.
By 1822, however, it was decided that the "distance between
the two was too great."[18] Three were then decreed, to be held at
Christmas, Easter, and Pentecost.[19] The examinations and the
compositions determined the right of the student to advance
to a higher class but the compositions alone determined his
rank in the class.[20] Compositions were written in each of the
languages taught in the college. The topics were chosen, not by
each instructor in his own class, but by each instructor for the
class immediately above his, the instructor of the highest class
selecting the topic for the lowest. The topics selected, a time—
usually two and one-half hours—was prescribed during which
the students would write their compositions in the presence of
their instructors.[21] Examination by the prefect of studies and

---

15 *CJC*, p. 108.
16 *Ibid.*
17 *CJC*, p. 111.
18 Entry dated September 1, 1822, *CJC*, p. 64.
19 *Ibid.*
20 "Some General Principles Proposed by Father Kenney, 1820," in *CJC*, pp. 24-25.
21 Entry dated June 18, 1820, in *CJC*, p. 29.

two assistants followed, and their decision was based on the aggregate merit of the compositions of each student. Premiums, however, were awarded for superior merit in each composition.[22] The judging for premiums, moreover, was not a matter that was taken lightly, as the following entry in the record of the prefect of studies testifies:

> The examination began and was conducted as last year. In consequence of two scholars being equal in Greek in first Grammar and two in Latin in Humanities, those two schools composed again, and only the themes of the four competitors were judged. All the scholars composed, to prevent the scholars from knowing who the competitors were.[23]

In 1826 a new system of grading was introduced. Every instructor gave his students a certain number of points according to the merit of their lessons, memory skill, themes, explanations, and conduct. The student with the greatest number of points for each month was given a "Ticket of Eminence." The scholar, in the respective classes, who had succeeded in amassing the greatest number of tickets at the end of the year, was awarded a premium.[24] Although the system suffered changes through the years, the "Ticket of Eminence," forerunner of the "Dean's list," became a standard feature at Georgetown for many years.

After the composition, the students were tested on the matter of their courses. Examinations were given in everything

---

[22] "General Principles. . . . Father Kenney," in *CJC*, pp. 24-25.

[23] Entry for July 8, 1820, in CJC, p. 46. No reason is assigned for withholding the names of the competitors nor, does it seem, was any consideration given to the "non-contestants" who had nothing to gain but the practice. The emphasis on composition is a recurring theme. Father Enoch Fenwick, then in Baltimore, wrote to his brother George, a student at the college, on March 16, 1814. "Thank you for your note . . . disappointed it was not in a language other than English. Let the next one be in Latin, Greek, or French." MS WCA, 204 R 18.

[24] "Prefect of Studies Report, January 8, 1826," in *CJC*, p. 91.

taught in the college, except writing and arithmetic.[25] The scope of these probings was quite large, e.g., in the class of rhetoric, 1822, (the year the three examinations were begun) the following was the matter for the examinations:

First Examination: This class must explain Cicero's 3 Catalines, the 2nd, 3rd, 4th books of Horace's Odes, the 2nd Book of Homer (omitting the Catalogue of the Ships), the Eclogues of Virgil and learn part of a Treatise on Rhetoric. They must be able to give a synopsis of their orations and explain the Figures of Speech. In French they must make themes on the Prepos. from p. 379-431 Wan [French Grammar—Wanostrocht] and explain Massillon's Sermons on the Incarnation and Passion Sunday. In Mathematics they must learn Geom. of Plains [sic] and Solids and Logarithms.

Second Examination: They must read the Orations for Milo, Marcellus and Ligarius, Horace's Epodes, 1st Book of Georgics, Ars Poetica, and continue the treatise on Rhetoric. They must also read the 3rd Book of Homer. In French, themes on the Gallic Idiom (p. 433-455) and explain Massillon's Sermons on Palm Sunday and Good Friday. In Mathematics, Plane and Spherical Trigonometry.

Third Examination: They must read Pro Lege Manila, Pro Archia, All Horaces Satires, the 2nd Book of Georgics, and the 4th of Homer. They must repeat and be examined on the whole treatise of Rhetoric. In French they must translate some original Book for Themes, and explain Massilon's Sermons on Easter Sunday and Vice and Virtue. In Mathematics, Conic Sections and repetition of the matter of the preceding terms.[26]

These tests, which the general tenor of the records of the prefect of studies indicates were oral, were conducted by the prefect and two others. The instructor whose class was being submitted to the academic ordeal, could not be one of the prefect's assistants on the examining board. That the examina-

---

25 Some General Principles. . . . Father Kenney," in *CJC*, pp. 24-25.
26 Entry in *CJC*, August, 1823, pp. 72 et seq.

tions were thorough, is evidenced by the fact that they lasted generally through several days.[27] That they were not mere routine performances, is witnessed by this entry in a contemporary diary: "July 28, 1819. This day the students were examined in mathematics. The archbishop of Baltimore present. The students answered very well."[28]

As is usual in Jesuit schools—and, in this, Georgetown was in complete harmony with the *Ratio Studiorum*—a system of emulation stimulated the students to apply themselves diligently to their tasks. For those who did superior work there were very tangible rewards. After each general composition and examination the "three first in each class and those who were particularly distinguished in the examen before the Great Academy" were guests at a banquet, and "according to custom indulged with a whole recreation day."[29] Rank in the class was a coveted position. Father Benedict Fenwick strongly urged his brother George in 1815 to be "*imperator primus* in studies."[30] "Tickets of Eminence," as noted previously, were awarded each month and the awarding was no surreptitious affair. Before the assembled faculty and student body, no less a personage than the president of the college bestowed with profuse praise the documents of merit on the favored few.

---

[27] Entry dated July 10, 1820, *CJC*, p. 30. At this time, too, it must be remembered the classes were small in number. The enrollment in 1820 numbered but forty-six students.

[28] McElroy Diary, July 28, 1819. MS GUA, 256.

[29] Entry dated November 20, 1820, in *CJC*, p. 37. On this occasion the prefect of studies strayed from his role of mere chronicler and editorialized a bit. He writes: ". . . and a dinner which *ought to have been a good one* and on the feast of St. Cecily the choristers had the same privilege and *a good dinner*." (Italics not in original.)

[30] Father Benedict Fenwick to George Fenwick, July 18, 1815. MS WCA, 204 G 1. The classes were graded in Roman fashion. *Imperator primus*, of course, being first in rank. He was followed by the lesser lights of tribunes, senators, etc. See *Pro Renovatione Magistratuum Renuntiati Sunt in Literaria Concertatione*. MS GUA, 149.2.

Unfortunately, there were always some to be found wanting
in diligence. The system of emulation did not merely neglect
these nor leave them pining for lost prizes. As the diligent were
rewarded, so the laggards were punished. Public strictures
were heaped on the heads of the indolent, while they were compelled, also, to surrender to study part of their recreation time.
Those who were most remiss in their obligations to the life of
learning were sentenced to a refinement of this last penalty.
At the turn of the stairway leading to the president's room in
the Old North Building, stood a clock important to the life
of every student at Georgetown. Here the "repeaters" were
sentenced to stand and study while their fellow students were at
play. The prefect of studies on one occasion, for example, with
biting irony noted that there was no lower class than that of
Rudiments and hence those "condemned" in that year could not
go lower; so he proposed to "allow them to ascend to a higher
station." They would therefore "ascend the stairs and spend an
hour each day until further notice at the clock."[31] He wished
it further to be understood that those "sent to the clock" were
not to be seen "playing marbles or conversing with one another"
as he had repeatedly observed in the past. Rather, they were to
carry with them "those books which they so much hated and
neglected . . . and try to retrieve the reputation which they
forfeited and the time which they so culpably misspent."[32] The
clock in Old North carried memories for many an alumnus.

Corporal punishment for infractions of the rules in class
was not unknown. Father Benedict Fenwick, then in New York,
placed himself in danger of receiving no news from his brother
George, a student at Georgetown, because he had expressed the
opinion that "the more they whip you, the better I will like
them, at least until you can show me a good premium, honorably

[31] Entry of March 7, 1832 by Father William Grace, in *CJC*, p. 136.
[32] *Ibid.*

acquired."[33] In justifying his observation, the good father declared that it proceeded:

> ... from the great conviction in my mind of the virtue of a rod, a conviction founded on the best of authority, I mean the book of Proverbs, Chap. 13th—24 verse: *He that spareth the rod hateth his son: but he that loveth him correcteth him betimes.* It has a preserving power from all contagion of idleness. It imparts a zest for study and close application, and in the course of time gives a polish to the character and heightens it to a degree which it could never attain without it. Sooner than be without so advantageous a stimulus, you should even go of yourself occasionally to your Master with that vivifying instrument in your hand and politely request him as a particular favour to administer to you some of its rare and surprising qualities. If he be a man of charity, as he undoubtedly is, he will not fail to profit by the opportunity afforded him of testifying his regard for you as well as sincere desire of your improvement.[34]

It is not of record that this encomium to the rod had such an effect on young George that he ran to his master to test his regard for him. It was prescribed that "leather ferulae straps were to be used and that the punishment was to be inflicted by the Prefects," the masters in each school ordering the quality and quantity.[35] The reminder was given that "all should know that corporal punishment is merely the last resource and it is to be avoided at all ages, as much as possible, and ever given with great moderation."[36]

---

[33] Father Benedict Fenwick to George Fenwick, August 9, 1814. MS WCA (not numbered). He enclosed five dollars for pocket money during the vacation.

[34] Father Benedict Fenwick to George Fenwick, June 26, 1815. MS WCA, 204 H 18.

[35] *CJC*, p. 28. "Ferulae" to the contrary notwithstanding, an English visitor to America found on his visit to Georgetown that the students or "nearly all of them seem to part and meet with their preceptors here as with kind and indulgent parents." Reuben Gold Thwaites (ed.), *Early Western Travels* (Clark Co., 1905), Part I. Reprinted in the *College Journal*, LIX, No. 6 (April, 1931), 472.

[36] *CJC*, p. 29.

A reading of some of the censures pronounced on the offenders, however, would indicate that often the students might have been well content to have settled for the "strap" had the choice been given them. A student of a later period describes the reading of the "Black List," as the roll of the miscreants was then called. His description is valid also for the period treated in this chapter:

> Up to this point the Rector had been congratulating and complimenting the honor students and he kept the Black List well out of sight, but now he would bring it forward and look at it for a moment and then his whole expression would change. At this moment the traditional pin drop would have been heard in that breathless silence for we all knew perfectly well the storm that was coming and wondered who were the ones that the bolt would fall upon. There was first a nervous crumpling of the paper and then the torrent burst forth. It is useless to attempt a description.[37]

No description certainly could portray the atmosphere. One can but project himself into the same hall where a short time before words of praise abounded, and wonder as he listened whether the prefect were addressing him as he said:

> One scholar . . . seems to be constantly actuated by a retrograde motion . . . for he has already been a member of every class in the College. He grows more inert as he approaches the lowest point. If he does not improve, his indolence will soon become proverbial. You all know I mean [N.N.][38]

Two students who had been exhorted to greater things at the last report were summoned to the bar on July 25, 1821:

---

[37] *Reminiscences of the Reverend Francis Barnum, S.J.*, p. 31, GUA, 222.4.

[38] "Report of the Prefect of Studies, December 22, 1821," in *CJC*, p. 59. The oratory was also employed in praise but even then sometimes served a double purpose, v.g., "There are two splendid exceptions to the above censures, and their merit shines with increased lustre, because they are surrounded so much by darkness," "Report of Father Roger Baxter, December 21, 1820," in *CJC*, p. 40.

They have not done it [reformed] and besides spending a year in idleness and convincing all their examiners that their minds were dead to everything like finer feelings and ingenuous emulation they have had the bad merit of associating to themselves a third.[39]

Sometimes it was an entire class that fell beneath the scathing sword:

I have nothing to say of the first class of Grammar, except that they have in general maintained the character which they have always supported. But if I must mention any one individual, who has been particularly fortunate in maintaining this character, it is [N.N.]. Unhappily for this class, the character to which I allude is that of indolent insensibility to everything like classical feeling.[40]

The question whether the fear of punishment was greater than the desire for reward was apparently left for academic disputes. Both were used to impel the students to greater scholastic endeavors. While recreation (everyone had to play at least an hour and a half each day) was given its proper and unstinted place. learning at Georgetown College in the first half of the nineteenth century was not a sometime, sideline thing. The graduates knew the "arts" referred to in their degrees.

In the curriculum[41] at Georgetown College, emphasis was placed on certain subjects that are so generally considered to have been neglected at this period that even a minor stressing of them would be noteworthy. Besides the emphasis on the

---

[39] "Report of the Prefect of Studies, July 25, 1821," *CJC*, p. 59.

[40] "Report of Father Roger Baxter, S.J., Christmas, 1823," *CJC*, p. 76. Father Barnum gives a startling example of one audience's reaction. He recalled a boy who was on the Black List to slide down from his chair and huddle up on the floor beneath the seats. "We all knew him," says Father Barnum, "to be a thick skinned lazy fellow, but his skin was not thick enough to endure the scathing structures that poured from the lips of Father Maguire." *Loc. cit.*

[41] Curriculum is here used to include extra-classroom activities which were closely allied with the course of studies. It was the classroom day, not the education day which ended at 4:30.

classics and philosophy that was to be expected in a college that followed the spirit—if not the letter—of the *Ratio Studiorum,* several other subjects were stressed, the most important of which was English. Actually, English was considered to be of more value than Latin or Greek. "Cultivate the vernacular language" is a constant refrain in the reports of the prefect of studies. "Be not content with literal translations" but "grammatical and pure English." "Read good books" and acquire "the harmonious language of Addison, the numbers of Pope, the majesty of Milton."[42] In his report a year earlier, in 1820, Father Baxter had told the students:

> It surely cannot be doubted that the vernacular language is always of the most importance. Without this knowledge every other branch of education would be almost useless.[43]

Closely related to this stress on English composition, was emphasis on public speaking. The earliest non-religious society[44] on the campus was the Philodemic Society, organized on February 22, 1830. The object of this society was "the cultivation of Eloquence, the promotion of knowledge, and the preservation of Liberty."[45] Originally the society held two public meetings annually—one on Washington's birthday, when the Farewell Address was read and commented upon by one of the members, and the second on Independence Day, when the Declaration of Independence was read with appropriate comments by another of the members.

After each public meeting a banquet, attended by members and their "respectable" guests, was held. At these banquets the members, who had reluctantly, it would seem, but dutifully been

---

[42] "Report of Father Roger Baxter, S.J., December 22, 1821," in *CJC,* pp. 56-60.
[43] "Report of Father Roger Baxter, S.J., December 21, 1820," in *CJC,* pp. 37-41.
[44] The Sodality of the Blessed Virgin Mary was founded, as noted earlier, in 1810.
[45] *A Catalogue of the Officers and Students of Georgetown College, 1851-1852* (Baltimore: John Murphy, 1852), p. 16.

the listeners, now were given free rein. The result was a torrent of eloquent toasts. In the same spirit as the public meeting, these toasts were of a patriotic nature. The seventh regular toast of the banquet of February 22, 1832, was to the "Heroes of the Revolution—may the treasures won by their valour, integrity and patriotism be hoarded up with filial affection by their descendants," and the thirteenth regular toast went to "Union—Union—Union. Union of Charity in heaven. Union of affection in Matrimony—Union of patriotism in the Republic—a triple bond by which the three great governments, Celestial, Domestic and Political are preserved." These are but two of the regular toasts. The combined number, regular and volunteer (these seemed never to be wanting) rose to forty.[46]

The annual Philodemic address was for many years a feature of the Society. An outstanding orator, generally an alumnus of the college, was invited to deliver the address and nothing was spared to make the occasion a gala one. Later the address was printed and copies were distributed to all the members.

Toasts, panegyrics, and addresses, however, were the celebrations of the year. The real work of the debating society was done in the regular meetings. The seriousness with which they debated such topics as "A Comparison between Cyrus the Elder, King of Persia and Philip of Macedon," or "Who is the greatest Orator, Cicero or Patrick Henry?" can only be imagined. It is easy to visualize the debate held in 1831, possibly between a youthful northern protectionist and a young southern advocate of free trade, on the question, "Is the Tariff beneficial to the U.S.?"[47]

The Philodemic Society was limited to members of the senior classes, but their younger brothers were determined to take the rostrum, and on January 8, 1839, the Philonomosian

---

[46] *Anniversary Celebration of the Philodemic Society 1832.* GUA, 80.11.
[47] *Minute Book of the Philodemic Society, 1831.* GUA, 17.1.

Society, consisting of students in the lower schools, was organized "with an object similar to that of the Philodemic."[48]

The emphasis on composition and public speaking was given full rein in the various literary exhibitions, academies, commencement exercises, and refectory recitations or "refectories," as they came to be known.

At the exhibitions and academies, open to the public,[49] the students delivered speeches, dialogues, explanations of the classical authors, and poems, which had been prepared in their free time. The titles of a few afford the best description: "A discussion on the relative utility of an ordinary and a classical education (original);"[50] "Soliloquy of Titus over the Ruins of Jerusalem";[51] "A Soliloquy of a School Boy at the College Gate, on the point of eloping, paraphrased from Hamlet's."[52]

The recitations in the refectory consisted of explanations of the classical authors done in English. To many this was a harrowing ordeal, at least in the beginning, and blessed was the relief when it was over. The prefect complained more than once of the frightened orators speaking "too low and too fast" in their haste to descend from the gallows.[53] To others it was just too much to bear, and numerous instances are recorded of

---

[48] *Catalogue. . . . 1851-1852*, p. 17. Other societies later organized included the Reading Room Association, October 23, 1850; The Dramatic Association, December, 1853; the Greek Academy, 1856; the Philistorian Society, January 11, 1857; The Dramatic Reading Association, 1868. The Philharmonic Society was formally organized in 1856 but had existed for many years before that date.

[49] In 1821, e.g., an academy was fixed for the 27th of February, "to accomodate the Members of Congress who might wish to be present as the session ends on the 3rd of March, 1821." "Entry for February 4, 1821," in *CJC*, p. 42.

[50] "Minor Literary Exhibition, March, 1820," in *CJC*, pp. 27-28.

[51] Academy, August 27, 1820," in *CJC*, p. 31.

[52] "Exhibition of February 27, 1821," in *CJC*, p. 43. The term "eloping," as explained earlier, meant running away from school.

[53] "Report of the Prefect of Studies, December 21, 1820," *CJC*, p. 39. On March 25, 1827, this exercise was abandoned in favor of a Sunday evening academy. *Loc. cit.*

the refectories being cancelled due to the appointed speaker "absconding."[54]

If any doubt were to linger as to the importance assigned to public speaking, a rapid survey of the commencement file in the university archives would dispel it. At the early commencements, which began at 9:00 or 9:30 a.m. and continued until 3:30 or 4:00 o'clock in the afternoon, it was not unusual for twenty-five or thirty speakers to deliver orations. As noted earlier, during the exercises of the 1817 commencement the students reenacted, as but a part of the program, a debate in Congress. By 1853, the number of speakers began to decline, although we still find sixteen student speakers, ably supported, however, by a graduate who delivered the annual address of the Philodemic Society.[55]

These literary and oratorical exercises were subjected to the criticism of the faculty. The notes of one professor reveal the attention paid to the speakers:

> 2. On biography—wandered too much—some good sentiments in it—stile [sic] rather stiff and laboured.
> 4. The world—or universal hypocrisy—Both connected—Style not good—careless.
> 6. Continuation of the life of a preacher—Hudibrastic—too many improbabilities in it.[56]

The modern reader or listener would doubtless find these rhetorical productions of the students laugh-provoking. They were grandiloquent, bombastic, and lacking completely in that crispness needed for a present day audience. If a newspaper account of the reception given to one address is indicative of the demands of the contemporary audience, the work was, however, of high calibre:

---

[54] See for example *CJC*, p. 28.

[55] *Catalogue. . . . 1852-1853*, Washington, Goggin and Coombs, 1853, p. 21.

[56] Academy of the School, November 18, 1838, GUA, 12.7.

... of the recitations which we had the pleasure of hearing, that of Mr. P. Pemberton Morris *on the Progress of Literature* struck us, as being an excellent piece of composition, and very gracefully delivered. . . . The talent evinced by Mr. Morris in the delivery of his address and in its composition, drew from the audience very warm plaudits. We presume to add, that so far as we have been able to ascertain the opinions of literary gentlemen, who are best able to appreciate intellectual merit, the rhetorical exercise of Mr. Morris has made an impression most decidedly favorable to that young gentleman.[57]

Pronounced as the emphasis was on composition, public speaking, etc., it did not crowd out of the curriculum at George-town the world of science. The facts of the universe were faced and analyzed in the courses on physical science. The theory of physical science, or natural philosophy as it was termed, was easily fitted into the curriculum. What may be a surprise, is the fact that physical science was taught at this early date by the experimental method.

Certainly as early as 1813, during Father Grassi's time at the college, as noted earlier, chemical experiments were performed at the college,[58] and the prospectus for 1818 lists, in addition to chemistry, courses in physics and astronomy.[59] For the pre-Christmas examination of 1821, the students were required to explain and demonstrate fifty propositions from physics. Thirty years later, the graduating class publicly performed experiments in electro-magnetism, together with experiments in physiology and chemistry.[60] By then, too, the astronomical observatory had been built, an addition to the college that would have given joy to Father Wallace in 1814 had he had the advantage of it while composing his *On the Use of Globes and Practi-*

---

[57] *National Intelligencer*, August 25, 1835.
[58] McElroy Diary, August 12, 1813. MS GUA, 256.
[59] *Prospectus of 1818*. GUA, 62.11.
[60] "Catalogue, 1850-51," in *Catalogues, Georgetown University*, Vol. I, GUA.

cal Astronomy.[61] In 1833, on a visit to the college, Henry Barnard, later principal of St. John's College, Annapolis, inspected the museum which he found, to his great surprise, contained "the largest electrical machine" he had ever seen.[62] Father Mulledy, his guide on the tour, must have been in the tradition of Father Grassi, for Barnard relates "the jolly old President tried an experiment with me—by putting into my hand a vessel charged with gas, and then exploding it by communicating with the machine."[63] Important as the role of science was, it never allowed to sweep all before it—a common enough danger in a later day. The prefect of studies cautioned the students in 1826 ". . . to let the modesty of virtue neutralize the arrogance of Science—for what is science when associated with irregularity: A poniard sheathed with roses."[64]

Any survey of the curriculum at Georgetown during the period 1820-1840, as for many years afterward, would be incomplete if it did not give some attention to the development of memory. The works of Latin authors, e.g., were committed to memory ten lines at a time. After the students gained some experience, it was not unusual for them to commit ten lines to memory in less than ten minutes.[65] For examinations the students were required to know "by heart" extensive sections of the classical authors, Latin and Greek syntax, as well as treatises on history and geography.

Although a survey of the curriculum could understandably lead one to think otherwise, the "men of Georgetown" were not always in the classroom. The routine of an ordinary class-day went something like this: The young collegian would rise in

---

[61] See *supra*, p. 167.
[62] Henry Barnard, "The South Atlantic States in 1833, As Seen by a New Englander," *The Maryland Historical Magazine*, XIII (1918), 289-290.
[63] *Ibid.*
[64] "Report of the Prefect of Studies, March 20, 1826," in *CJC*, p. 93.
[65] Barnum, *op. cit.*, p. 10.

summer at 5 a.m., in winter at 5:30 a.m. "No one," the rules
of 1829 prescribe, "shall rise before the appointed time without
express leave from the Prefect."[66] The day began "with a run
out to the pump for a wash. . . . A long line of roller towels
was hung between two locust trees nearly opposite the college
door. In the winter of 1822-1823 luxuries began to creep in and
we had a wash-room extemporized in the small boys play room
—but in summer we still went to the old pump."[67] Lest the
luxuries of 1822-1823 create the impression that the Spartan
vigor of the men of Georgetown had disappeared, one of the
students of the time recalled in later years that the wash room
was suited to contribute in no small measure to early morning
alertness:

> Then to the wash-room. My recollection of that famous lavatory is
> particularly vivid and feelingly intensified, *even now,* as winter
> approaches. A large room on the ground floor with jets of water
> running into a wooden trough, its sides garnished with tin wash-
> basins. . . . With the thermometer at zero the inducements were
> wonderfully great for a quick bath and rapid transit. Little time was
> lost in seeking the more comfortable shelter of the study-room to
> complete the toilet and prepare for prayers, and many a morning
> have I crossed the "yard" with the stars burning brightly above and
> the frost nipping my shins below, a skeptic anent the good old
> proverb of the "early bird."[68]

With such details to fill in the picture, it would seem that it
must have been comparatively easy to observe the rule that strict
silence be maintained "during the time devoted to washing and

---

[66] *Regulations for the Students of George-Town College, 1829.* GUA, 1.3. An
undated record of "Dormitory Rules," probably c. 1830-40, notes that the
rising hour "is now 5:55 and that a penalty of 20-50 lines to be committed
to memory could be assessed for rising without permission before the bell
rings." GUA, 28.11.
[67] J.W.J., "Recollection of Georgetown in 1820," *The College Journal,* XIII, 104.
[68] W. F. Quicksall to the Editor of the *Journal,* November 23, 1877. *The College
Journal,* XVI (1888), 44.

combing."[69] At 5:45 a.m. all were to be present for morning prayers, which were followed by Mass at 6:00 a.m. Breakfast was still an hour and three quarters away, the time after Mass being devoted to study until 7:45. Classes began at 8:15, continuing until 11:15, when the students, after forming their line in the corridor of Old North, walked in single file to dinner.[70] In the beginning, places in the refectory were assigned according to height, the larger students having the first places. When arranging the various classes at his visitation in 1820, Father Kenney changed this order, so that the first places were henceforth given "by merit."[71] Dinner in the earlier years was followed by recreation of an hour and a half, during which the "study hall was locked and no one was allowed to have a book."[72] Father Kenney again made the change so that a study period from 1:15 to 2:15 followed the curtailed recreation period. Afternoon classes were held from 2:15 to 4:45, and were followed by a half-hour's recreation. The rosary of the Blessed Virgin Mary was recited in common at 5:15, with study again the order until 7:00, when the students again filed into the dining room. Night prayers in common were held at 8 o'clock, and at 8:30, and it seems no insistence was needed, all retired to the dormitories.[73]

There were, of course, variations in the daily order of time. Although the school year was much longer than today, there were frequent holidays, spent most often in walking excursions outside the college. On these forays the collegians went in a

---

69 *Regulations of 1829.* GUA, 1.3.
70 *Ibid.*
71 McElroy Diary, January 4, 1820. MS GUA, 256.
72 J.W.J., "Recollections of Georgetown in 1820," *The College Journal*, XIII, 104. He adds that it was a "useless precaution."
73 Order of Time for Georgetown Students, 1831. MS GUA, 1.5. This order of time "to commence from January 1, 1831," was prescribed by Father Kenney at the time of his second visitation of the mission. See, House Diary, January 1, 1831. GUA, 57.1; Kenney to Mulledy, January 16, 1831. MS GUA, 185.4.

body, attended, of course, by the ubiquitous prefect.[74] Two students were appointed to lead the flock. These excursions were not as dull as they may sound to modern ears. They seem to have been enjoyed by prefect and students alike. Father Kohlmann, when president of the college, received the following request:

Georgetown, Oct. 13, 1818.

Reverend Father:

I take the pleasure to spend a few moments in writing some lines in order to know whether this evening will not be spent as a time of recreation, as Tuesday is commonly spent so.

Our tutor desired us to request it, on account of the good behaviour of the boys, with whom he was so well pleased that he desired them to walk out with him; expecting them to behave as well in every respect; as they do in school.

I hope you will not think us idle by this request, but, as my professor says, it is good for our health I can say truly that I do not wish to be idle but,

To remain your humble student,
ALEX. L. JONCHEREZ.[75]

On certain occasions the walks were far from dull. The editor of the *College Journal* in 1874, bemoaned the fact that he had not been attending school when there had occurred such episodes as the "march of the small boys to Villa under heavy fire of stones from their enemies the townies," when the boys displayed such "steadiness" and countered with "heroic charges."[76] We read, too, of a military engagement between some Georgetown students and a group from Columbian College (now George Washington University). On the occasion of

---

[74] "During their whole stay in the College the strictest attention will be paid to the morals of the students, and they are always under the eye of one or more of the Prefects—even in their ordinary walks and recreations." *Georgetown College, in the District of Columbia, August, 1831.* GUA, 62.11.

[75] Alex. L. Joncherez to Father Kohlmann, October 13, 1818. MS GUA, 203.1.

[76] *The College Journal,* Georgetown College, II (August, 1874), 102.

Lafayette's visit to Washington in 1824, the Columbian boys had captured a Georgetown banner. Later, on the occasion of Lafayette's visit to Georgetown, some Georgetown stalwarts were returning from a meeting with the General at the Rock Creek bridge and spied their lost flag "floating on a little two-story frame building." They rushed to the building and after a brief scuffle regained their proud banner.[77] They were "led," one old diary records, "by their prefect."[78] He was certainly near, and no record is extant of any restraining influence being exerted by him, nor any penalty exacted of the walkers.

Pocket money was kept at a minimum. Father Grassi's prospectus of 1814 declared:

> As long experience has convinced the directors that a profusion of pocket money is very prejudicial, not only to good order, but even to study and application, they therefore request that parents will not be too indulgent to their children, in allowing more than one dollar per month at most and whatever is allowed must be deposited in the hands of the procurator of the house.[79]

Later requests to the parents were that "little should be granted," etc. In his prospectus of 1829, Father Mulledy established that in order that equality in the matter be preserved, the spending money was, in the future, not to exceed twelve and a half cents a week.[80]

It was a rare occasion when the student could leave the

---

[77] "Reminiscences of Dr. DeLoughery, A.B. 1826," *The College Journal*, XIV, No. 5 (February, 1886), 50-51. He recalls that "in commemoration of these events we had a banner painted by an artist named Simpson, representing on one side an eagle holding in its beak a streamer on which was inscribed the motto, "Nemini cedimus"; on the reverse side the coat of arms of the college was placed. What trophies we had carried off from our opponents were afterwards restored." *Ibid.*

[78] John R. Friant, Thomas A. Rover, Edwin M. Dahill, Jr., *Glimpses of Old Georgetown* (Washington, D.C.: Privately published, 1939), p. 13.

[79] Prospectus of May 1, 1814. GUA, 62.11.

[80] Prospectus of 1829. GUA, 62.11.

college unattended by a professor. During a short period, there seemed to have been some laxness in this regard, but it was soon remedied. Father Francis Dzierozynski, the superior of the mission, in his note to the rector of Georgetown, appealed to a long-standing rule that no student be permitted to go out on Sundays and holydays unless the parents or guardians requested it by a note addressed to the president of the college. Those who had "acquaintances only" in the town were not permitted to visit them, for, noted the superior, "these very acquaintances have been the cause of many disorders." The students were to be informed that "no other motive, than their honour and advantage has prompted these measures."[81]

On special occasions the usual walking expeditions were forgotten in favor of trips down the Potomac on board a packet ship. One of the favorite destinations was Mount Vernon, where the students and professors were "kindly received by Col. Washington."[82] On their first picnic to Mason's Island, they were "very politely received by Genl. Mason and Lady, who invited"[83] the students to visit the island whenever they pleased,

---

[81] Father Francis Dzierozynski to Father Vice-Rector, Georgetown College, May 8, 1826. MS GUA, 1.5. There is a significant note in the diary for March 30, 1825. The decision had been made at first not to hold the Holy Week Services at the College that year but Father Rector changed his mind upon realizing that some might take this opportunity to wander, unattended, about the town. GUA, 57.1. The college officials were more successful in this move than they were in substituting, about the same time, milk for coffee at breakfast. The change lasted but three days. The resulting clamor was successful. The "Americans" regained their coffee. *House Diary*, May 30, June 2, *loc. cit.* The coffee had a good reputation. While most other things received nicknames, the "coffee was too good to have a nickname." "Recollections of George-Town in 1820 by J.W.J.," *The College Journal*, XIII (June, 1885), 104.

[82] McElroy Diary, August 25, 1813, MS GUA, 257. The packet, he notes, cost $5.00. The same trip, one year later, cost $10.00.

[83] *Ibid.*, May 19, 1814. "General Mason" was John Mason, son of George Mason, author of the Virginia Bill of Rights and the Constitution of Virginia. Mason's Island, or Analostan Island, had come into the possession of the Mason family by transfer of a patent originally granted by Lord Baltimore.

an invitation they were glad to accept. On one occasion, the training they had received on the "ordinary walks" from the Capitol to the college was called upon. The students and professors, about 50 in number engaged "the Packet . . . and sailed . . . to a Mr. Marshall's place nearly opposite Mt. Vernon." They decided to return to the college about two o'clock in the afternoon, but "the wind and tide being contrary" they were detained on the water all night and reached home only "after walking a great part of the way."[84]

Another somewhat puzzling variation from the ordinary walk schedule occurs more than once in the records and diaries.[85] No less a serious page than that of the *Classical Journal* records that on October 22, 1821: "Recreation was given this afternoon in consequence of the scholars being refused permission *to go to the races,* as had been usually granted and because it was the first day of refectories."[86] We may be sure that on these occasions the first prefect went along.

For some, of course, recreation time was given over to other pursuits than walking. Handball seems to have been the most popular game for the athletically inclined.[87] Fencing and boxing also had their devotees. Others, as early as 1836, organized, for purposes of more regimented recreation, a company known as the College Cadets. The ordinary college dress was adopted as the basic uniform. The trimming of the pantaloons with red braid, the addition of a red sash and a star gave the proper distinction. Spears, we are told, were carried in place of guns and, as an indication of the diversity of ages at Georgetown in

---

[84] *Ibid.* August 8, 1814.

[85] See for example, Grassi Diario, *passim.*

[86] "Entry for October 22, 1821," in *CJC*, p. 56. Italics added.

[87] Father McElroy records that a new handball court was erected in May of 1814. It must have been promised frequent use for, at a time when the college could ill spare it, five hundred dollars was appropriated for the construction. *Notes of Father John McElroy, S.J.* MS GUA, 246.4.

this period, the captain was one of the boys who had left school the year before to fight the Indians in Florida, and had but recently returned to the college.[88] Perhaps, too, they had made part of their armament the two small brass cannon which had been discharged some years before in honor of Vice President Thompkins on the occasion of the latter's visit to the college, and which were used, along with much beating of drums, to celebrate George Washington's birthday in 1819.[89] Others, doubtless after much parental urging, spent their recreation hours, at least "from twelve to two every holy-day," at their dancing and music lessons.[90]

Naturally, there were always some to be found who were not deterred by fear of sanctions from falling into the meshes of college discipline. One young student informed his father of one such tragedy, which occurred on one of the ordinary walks. Robert Aylmer wrote to his father:

> . . . I am about to inform you of a little circumstance which has taken place here, since our last interview. [N.N.] and [N.N.] have been expelled from here, on account of their bad conduct. Mac did not expect they would expell him for he was often heard to say, that they loved money too dearly. . . . [The party went] with the Prefect to Congress. Accordingly the hour arrived they departed. When opposite one of the principal hotels, in Washington City they met a young lad—who invited them to take a glass of good old apple

---

[88] Robert Aylmer to Mr. Henry Aylmer, November 4, 1836. MS GUA, 93.9.

[89] McElroy Diary, March 26, 1818; February 22, 1819. MS GUA, 256. According to Michael Delaney, an alumnus of 1832, the cannon were the work of Andre Joseph Villard who had been commissioned in the Gard de Ville by Lafayette and had later come to America. Delaney possessed two small cannon precisely similar, made by Villard when stationed at the United States Arsenal, Washington, D.C., prior to the war of 1812. Unless there were two sets of cannon at the college, which seems unlikely, Delaney was wrong, however, in declaring that the cannon were presented to the college by Lafayette on the occasion of his visit in 1824. Michael Delaney to the Rev. J. Havens Richards, S.J., February 27, 1894. *The College Journal*, XXII (April, 1894), 130.

[90] R. Aylmer to Mr. H. Aylmer, November 4, 1836. MS GUA, 93.9.

jack and to a game at. . . . In this many hours rolled away, nay, even days and neither James or Mac returned to College.[91]

The duty of "writing home," then as now, must have cut in on the recreation period at times.[92] But, then as now, duty was recalled by necessity. "You seem to think," wrote the same Robert Aylmer, "that I should not write for more money, stating that I might have three or four dollars about me which would suffice. This is very true, but I spent it all for things which are indispensably [sic] necessary. I hope this may be a sufficient cause for my seemingly unreasonable demands." Perhaps he was protesting too much to his indulgent father when he added: "You know too, that I am an economical fellow."[93] In contrast to the telegraphic style of today, the collegian's letters would sometimes "soar" in a manner that does not seem inconsistent with the manners and customs of the age. Parent Henry Aylmer, we may surmise, felt no jar in receiving the following epistle from his son at Georgetown:

> . . . but a few days ago I was very unwell oweing [sic] to the sudden changes of the climate, which is sometimes very cold and at other times very warm, but now the weather is very fair and Spring has once more returned. Spring one of the grandest seasons for the beauty of its scenes represents to mankind the favored garden of another Paradise. On whatever side we cast our eyes nature seems to smile with a magnificence truly astonishing. There we may view green fields which will bestow on the labourer a golden crown. Elsewhere the budding trees and sweet smelling flowers have a tendency to excite the feelings of deepest admiration. It is a new man beginning to feel his heart expanding, while he gazes on every-

---

[91] *Ibid.*, February 16, 1837. *Loc. cit.*

[92] As Robert informed Mr. Aylmer: "This being letterwriting day, a day, the definition of which I have given you in one of my former letters—I did not intend writing today but as it is a kind of obligation put upon us or in other words a Rule of the College I embrace this favorable opportunity of writing to you." October 10, 1839. MS GUA, 93.9.

[93] R. Aylmer to Mr. Henry Aylmer, July 23, 1840. *Loc. cit.*

thing around him. Winter having ceased to chain his towering thoughts, causes now no fear; like a soaring eagle treads beneath him care, and with the electricity of thought riding on the beauteous wings of fancy he is happy only in dwelling near the roaring cataract or mountainous cliff.[94]

No account of college life outside the classroom would be complete without a glance into the dining room. It loomed too large in the students' eyes to be neglected. Robert Aylmer's letters contain no complaints about the menus of his college days. A few samples will indicate the reason. The Lenten season, always a poser for any cook, opened in 1813 with the typical Lenten fare of the period: "Codfish and potatoes, parsnips (fried), fish (fried), and eggs. Rice with milk, some days; other days apple pyes [sic]."[95] The menus on festival days, of course, were much more elaborate: "On Christmas day the Students had for dinner: first dish, Corn'd pork and Cabbage; 2nd (dish), Smoaked [sic] Beef and Turnips; 3rd, Spare Ribs Roasted and 4th Roast Geese, Toddy, Apples, Cakes and Crackers."[96] The mysterious note in the Christmas menu is wrapped within an enigma by a recurring notation: "The students had nothing extraordinary for dinner except *Toddy*."[97] Occasionally, too, "the Students had each a glass of wine after dinner, and crackers."[98] On New Year's Day, 1831, the order of time decided upon by Father Kenney was promulgated. As a fortification, perhaps, in the face of stricter legislation, a special treat

---

[94] R. Aylmer to his father, May 15, 1836. MS GUA, 93.9.
[95] McElroy Diary, March 3, 1813. GUA, 256.
[96] *Ibid.* January 1, 1813. The menu, he notes, is that of Christmas Day, 1812.
[97] *Ibid.*, e.g., February 2 and March 1, 1813. An interesting note of November 26, 1819, informs us that "A French cook [was] hired by the month to instruct Brother D." *Ibid.* (Italics added.)
[98] *Ibid.* Easter Monday, March 23, 1818. He does not record whether a practice in vogue a few years later prevailed at this time. The diary of the Father Minister of the college for Easter Sunday, April 3, 1825, notes that the wine was "mixed with water and sugar." GUA, 57.1.

was given to the students: "after breakfast egg nog [was served] to [the] students seated at their tables, according to the distinction of large and small, that of the large boys being something stronger."[99]

Student life, it would seem, given the changes in manners and customs proper to the period, remains much the same, whatever the year. College administrators, teachers, or prefects at one moment are buoyed up with enthusiasm over a brilliant composition, academic excellence, or a manifestation of generous spirit. But the student can also bring them almost to the depths of despair. Father Dubuisson came close to the brink in 1827 when he declared that "it was plain that the want of piety among the boys, the love of dressing, the rage of going out, the ruinous habit of visiting confectioners shops, and the great liberty in reading, have had a large share in producing the evil."[100]

There were, of course, always some who, the college judged, would be better educated at home. An abortive riot of 1833 resulted in some forty or fifty being separated from the rolls of Georgetown.[101] In general, however, allowing even for Robert Aylmer's wings of fancy, he was close to the sentiment of most of the students when he wrote in his final letter to his father: ". . . and now for the last time I bid adieu to my own 'Alma Mater'— my cherished home."[102]

[99] *Diary of the Father Minister, Georgetown College,* January 1, 1831. MS GUA, 57.1.
[100] Father Stephen Dubuisson, S.J., to Father A. Young, S.J., March 3, 1827. MS WCA, 208 Z 12a.
[101] Father Felix Grivel to Mr. Samuel Barber, S.J., June 22, 1834. MS WCA, 211 W 13.
[102] Robert Aylmer to Mr. Henry Aylmer, July 23, 1840. MS GUA, 93.9.

CHAPTER XI

New Blood
and Wider Horizons

When classes resumed in September, 1822, Father Benedict Fenwick, succeeding his brother Enoch, again assumed the presidency of Georgetown. President of Georgetown, at this period, was not a long term position. Between the departure of Father Grassi in 1817, and the appointment of Father Mulledy in 1829, Georgetown was to see six presidents, and one of them —Benedict Fenwick—served twice.

Father Fenwick had been recalled by Father Kenney from his arduous and delicate labors in Charleston, and had served as the vice president of the college just the year before.[1] Archbishop Maréchal had been in Rome, and finding on his return to the United States that Father Fenwick was now president of Georgetown, he wrote to him "hinting" at another post he desired him to take. In his reply Father Fenwick stated that it did not depend on him to choose his own situation, but that that choice belonged exclusively to his superior. It was, he declared, the "Superior who has to appoint—it is my province to obey." "I do not think," he continued, "that in the present situation of affairs he will willingly consent that I shall quit Georgetown.

---

[1] Hughes, *History of the Society of Jesus, Documents*, Vol 1, Part II, p. 896.

The college is in a much worse condition than when I left for Charleston. It wants fostering. He has appointed me to look after its concerns and to ameliorate it if possible."[2] His personal wish, besides, was that he be permitted to remain at Georgetown. Charleston had been a difficult assignment. He needed "repose."[3] He had "battled enough in the world [and] must now by retirement endeavor to repair the damages . . . sustained."[4] "At least," he wrote, "I prefer solitude to an active life. I here enjoy it in great measure—after encountering many hardships, it feels like a calm after a violent blow at sea."[5]

Father Fenwick had performed a valuable service for the Church in America by his zealous work in Charleston, and was understandably anxious for "retirement and repose." But Georgetown's condition called for a fresh, vigorous, president —one who would, like Grassi, revive Georgetown. Unfortunately, the man was not available. No wonder the ancients of the mission eagerly awaited the return of the young Jesuits from Rome. No wonder, too, that one of the students of the 1820's could recall that "it was not until the return of Fathers Mulledy, Fenwick [George], and Ryder and Young that the College lifted up its head again."[6] The newly restored Society was still in its infancy and the members of the old Society were passing on.[7] The Society in America in 1822 consisted of "twenty-six Fathers, ten scholastics in theology, seventeen scholastics in

---

[2] Father Benedict Fenwick to Archbishop Maréchal, November 30, 1822. MS BCA, 16 P 34.

[3] *Ibid.*

[4] *Ibid.*

[5] *Ibid.*

[6] J.W.J., "Recollections of Georgetown College in 1820," *op. cit.*

[7] In April of 1823 Father Charles Neale, the superior of the mission, died. He had appointed his brother Francis as his successor. Before Francis could make the announcement to Archbishop Maréchal he was seized with an attack of apoplexy and Father Benedict Fenwick had to make the announcement. Benedict Fenwick to Archbishop Maréchal, April 30, 1823. MS BCA, 16 P 38.

Philosophy, Rhetoric and Belles-Lettres, fourteen scholastics in the novitiate, twenty-two lay brothers out of and four lay brothers in the novitiate."[8] Of this number thirteen were engaged as "President and professors in the college of Georgetown."[9] There was great promise for the future, but those who were guiding the present fortunes of Georgetown seemed to be tired. A student of the time observed with keen judgment that Father Fenwick "was a just man in his treatment of the boys, and was much loved. But the management of the college *appeared to be placed entirely under the control of others.* From that time until the close of my collegiate career everything seemed to be gradually declining."[10]

Father Roger Baxter, prefect of studies at the college,[11] writing to the Reverend George Fenwick, one of the Georgetown theologians at Rome, lamented the fact that at the close of the school year 1822-23, there were not forty students in the college, while down in the city the Washington seminary at this time numbered nearly one hundred on its rolls. Father Baxter reflected the discouragement that must have seized others besides himself. He was, he revealed, thinking of requesting a return to his native Lancashire in England.[12]

During Father Fenwick's presidency occurred the visit of Lafayette to the college, an event already referred to in connection with the battle of the banners. The general was escorted to

---

[8] *The Laity's Directory to the Church Service for the Year of Our Lord M.D.C.C.C.XXII*, Revised and corrected by the Rev. John Power (New York: William H. Creagh, 1822), p. 126.

[9] *Ibid.*

[10] Dr. Edward de Loughery, A.B. '26, "Reminiscences," *The College Journal*, XIV (1886), p. 50. Italics not in the original.

[11] Judah Delano (ed.), "The Georgetown College," *The Washington Directory* (Washington: William Duncan, 1822), p. 132. Among others on the faculty were the "Rev. Thomas Levins [as] Professor of Mathematics and Natural Philosophy and Rev. M. [sic] Dzierozynski [as] Professor of Moral Philosophy." *Ibid.*

[12] Father Roger Baxter to George Fenwick, August 17, 1823. MS WCA, 206 R 10.

the college by a troop of light horse cavalry and was received in the parlor by Father Dzierozynski, who had succeeded Father Neale as superior of the mission. Father Thomas Levins, who was dismissed from the Society a few months later, and who could hardly at this time be considered favorable to Father Dzierozynski, records in his diary that the superior "made a frightfully bungling speech."[13] The accuracy of Father Levins' reporting cannot be established with certainty, but his report might well be true. Father Dzierozynski had every reason to be embarrassed, and his embarrassment might well have been reflected in his speech of welcome. Father John William Beschter, who apparently had kept a close eye on the American tour of Lafayette, had reported from Baltimore to Father Dzierozynski but a month before that the general, when invited in Boston by the Reverend Taylor to assist at Mass "[had] thanked him, saying that he was to go to the Presbyterian Church."[14] And, but four days before the visit to Georgetown, Father Beschter had written that Lafayette had received the highest honors at the Masonic lodge in Baltimore and had scandalized the people at the cathedral by refusing to kneel during the consecration of the Mass, insisting on remaining standing although "Old Mr. Carroll . . . spoke aloud—'either kneel or sit down.' "[15] Father Dzierozynski, doubtless, was just as well pleased that "the stay [of Lafayette at Georgetown] was very short."[16] Whatever embarrassment Father Dzierozynski may have felt, it apparently did not communicate itself to General Lafayette. His reception

---

[13] Diary of Father Thomas C. Levins, October 14, 1824. GUA Shea Transcripts. See Diary of Brother Joseph Mobberly, October 14, 1824, V, 64. MS GUA, 4.5. Mobberly was violently opposed to the Lafayette welcome. He attached one of the Lafayette badges to a page of his diary "as a lasting memorial of American folly and Lafayetteian vanity." *Ibid.*
[14] Father John William Beschter, S.J., to Father Francis Dzierozynski, S.J., September 14, 1824. MS WCA, 206 K 12.
[15] Beschter to Dzierozynski, October 10, 1824. MS WCA, 206 K 17.
[16] Diary of Father Thomas C. Levins, October 14, 1824.

is said to have made such an impression on him that he included a mention of it in his remarks to the National Assembly on his return to France.[17]

The college continued to decline, and once again in its history the question of Georgetown's closing arose.[18] When Father Fenwick retired from the presidency in 1825 to become the second bishop of Boston, the school numbered scarcely thirty students. His successor, the Reverend Stephen Larigaudelle Dubuisson,[19] was unable to improve the situation. Father Dubuisson did not complete the year as president, resigning on the 7th of July, 1826. Father William Feiner, who had been professor of theology and German, and prefect of studies under Father Dubuisson, succeeded to the direction of the college. When classes opened in September, he found that the rolls of the institution numbered thirty-three students, of whom six were day scholars.[20]

It is difficult to assign any cause or series of causes for the steady decline of Georgetown during the years between the presidency of Father Grassi and that of Father Mulledy. There were lean times for the country generally for a few years after the financial panic of 1819, but the later years could not be so described. One cause of Georgetown's retrogression is at least hinted at in some of the correspondence of the period: there was some measure of internal dissension at the college. Father

[17] Shea, *History of Georgetown University*, p. 65.
[18] In 1823 there was no commencement at the college. The Bachelor of Arts was conferred on one student.
[19] Father Dubuisson was born in Santo Domingo, October 21, 1786. He had been on the personal staff of Napoleon but when the Emperor attacked and imprisoned Pope Pius VII, Father Dubuisson resigned his commission and came to the United States. In December of 1815 he entered the Society of Jesus at Whitemarsh. He was ordained in 1822 and after his year as president of Georgetown he was called to Rome, only to return with the Americans in 1828.
[20] Entry of September 14, 1826. *CJC*, p. 97.

Francis Neale, the Nestor of the mission, complained to Father Dzierozynski that he had received a "dreadful description of the state of the college. . . . There must be authority over and union among the professors;"[21] and Father Beschter found it hard to hear people talk of the downfall of the college, especially when they reported to him that the character of the professors had been publicly impeached, and the report had not been contradicted.[22] Father McSherry, sending news of the college to some of the theologians still in Italy, presumed that Father Ryder would know "why the college is so low. . . . Private dissensions tend always to destroy good order, and when that is destroyed you know nothing can thrive."[23]

"Close the College" apparently became a louder and more often repeated solution. Father Beschter would seem to be expressing more than his own opinion when he suggested to the superior that the Washington Seminary be removed to Georgetown, and the seminary building be used to house the novices. The difficulties at the college were intensified, he felt, by the attitude of hopelessness taken by some of the members of the Society throughout the mission.[24] They had, he judged, by their attitude of despair, hurt, if not destroyed, the reputation of the college. Even the archbishop, he felt, would like to see the college closed.[25] This, it would seem, was a true analysis. The closing of the college, of course, would free men to serve in the congregations of the diocese, and we have seen that the archbishop on more than one occasion expressed his displeasure

[21] Father Francis Neale to Father Francis Dzierozynski, October 27, 1824. MS WCA, 206 K 20. "Basil Spaulding," he added, "says that his son learns nothing." *Ibid.*

[22] Beschter to Dzierozynski, September 8, 1826. MS WCA, 207 G 2.

[23] Father William E. McSherry, S.J., to Father James Ryder, S.J., December 26, 1828. Transcript by Martin I. J. Griffin. GUA, 143.11.

[24] Beschter to Dzierozynski, August 31, 1827. MS WCA, 208 T 4.

[25] *Ibid.*

that the superior of the mission would assign to the college, priests of the Order whom the archbishop desired for the parishes. There, he felt, their talents would be put to better use than if they remained at the college.

If any one cause of the college's ill fortunes might then be assigned, perhaps it was the general one that the enthusiasm, the energy, and the vision of a Carroll or a Grassi were not at hand to give new life to the weakened, run-down institution. Relief was in sight if the young theologians, alumni of the college, should be sent from Rome, and other stations in Italy, to impart the spark of youth. The name of Mulledy would take its place in the history of Georgetown next to Carroll and Grassi, but the college was to see darker and darker days until its owner arrived. Meanwhile, the Washington Seminary, (due in part to the rapid strides the city was making while the Georgetown area declined),[26] St. Mary's in Baltimore, and Mt. St. Mary's in Emmitsburg, were all enjoying prosperity. The last-mentioned college was at about this very time offered to the Society. Father John Dubois, upon learning that he had been appointed bishop of New York, made the proposal through Father John McElroy.[27] Father McElroy was "to sound out" the superior. Father Dzierozynski expressed his appreciation for the love of the Society which prompted Father Dubois' offer, but, in prudence, had to decline for lack of members to staff the institution. He feared, too, he declared, to incur the enmity of the archbishop and the Sulpician fathers who might feel slighted. He hoped that the college would pass to the Sulpicians lest it fall into the hands of non-Catholics.[28]

---

[26] Father Dubuisson to Father A. Young, S.J., March 3, 1827. MS WCA, 208 Z 12a. Father Dubuisson at this time was in Rome.

[27] Father John Dubois to Father John McElroy, S.J., July 5, 1826. MS WCA, 207 H 3. Father Dubois added: ". . . if I were not to go to New York yet I would give this establishment to you because I love the Society."

[28] Father Dzierozynski to Father McElroy, July 25, 1826. MS WCA, 207 H 3.

As Shea has remarked, this was, at the college, a period of change from which the institution did not benefit. "The changes," he remarked, "were doubtless unavoidable, but the students and parents who would have gladly placed their sons at Georgetown seemed to look for a more permanent and stable administration."[29] Father Dubuisson was reverenced for his virtue, but he lacked the energy and impulse to revive the college. Discipline, as noted in a previous chapter, was not his strong point. He had, during his short tenure, laid down very rigid rules, but lacked the skill to see that they were enforced.[30] He later declared that the explanation for the decline of the college would require him to narrate a long tale, and that (unfortunately) would be impossible. His own investigation of the discipline problem had resulted merely in a statement, as we have seen, deploring the want of piety among the boys. This defect he had attributed to "a love of dressing, a ruinous habit of visiting confectioners shops, and a great liberty in their reading."[31] The efforts of the officers of the college, he admitted, had not met with any success in "bringing up youths to such principles and moral habits as become a Jesuits' College."[32] It would seem that Father Dubuisson was in the same tradition as the Fathers Neale. A holy and devoted missionary and director of souls, he lacked that understanding of the American boy that would be so bright a part of the equipment of a Father Mulledy or Father George Fenwick.

Father William Feiner, successor to Dubuisson, was a native of Poland, a man of learning and ability, but of very poor health. He died at Georgetown on June 9, 1829, at the early age of thirty-seven. His remarks to the students on the occasion

---

[29] Shea, *History of Georgetown University*, p. 73.
[30] *Ibid.*, p. 72.
[31] Dubuisson to Father A. Young, March 3, 1827. MS WCA, 208 Z 12a.
[32] *Ibid.*

of examination reports, and other occasions, reflect his great desire to improve the college, but his health did not permit him to give that energetic and farseeing direction which the situation demanded.[33] For a short while before becoming president, he had acted as treasurer of the institution, and, "finding large payments coming due, and being no financier, saw no other way to raise funds than to economize, and this was the cause of the complaints of the boys."[34]

Difficult as the times were, attempts were made to add periodically to the library that had been remembered so generously in the will of the founder of the college. When Mrs. Anne Royall visited the school in 1826, she noted that it had a library containing nine thousand volumes.[35] By the time of the publication of the prospectus of 1831, this number had been increased to twelve thousand, and when Father Joseph Finotti drew up his *Manual to the Library of Georgetown College* in 1847, he counted thirteen thousand, four hundred and thirty-seven books in the various libraries of the institution.[36]

In connection with the visit of Mrs. Royall, the college, it would seem, had its share in correcting some false impressions the good lady had formed. In concluding her remarks about her visit to the town, she wrote:

> How much have I heard about these Roman Catholics! I have heard them stigmatized by every harsh name and accounted little better than heretics. But I must confess, I never was amongst people more liberal, more affable, condescending, or courteous, than the citizens of Georgetown. I could have spent my days with this endearing people.[37]

---

[33] V.g., Report of the Easter Examinations, 1826. GUA, 12.16.
[34] Dr. Edward De Loughrey, "Reminiscences," *The College Journal*, XIV (1886), 50.
[35] Anne Royall, *Sketches of History, Life and Manners in the United States. By a Traveller.* (New Haven: Printed for the author, 1826), p. 178.
[36] Father Francis Barnum, S.J., "Stray Notes," II, 23. MS GUA, 444.3.
[37] Royall, *op. cit.*, p. 182.

When Father Feiner's failing health made it evident that he could no longer carry out the duties of the office, Father John William Beschter succeeded to the presidency. He assumed the office at the end of March, 1829, and completed the year, when he was replaced by Father Thomas Mulledy.

Father Beschter had left the charge of St. John's Church, Baltimore, to take the post of minister of the community at Georgetown the year before, and he had the happiness of receiving into the Catholic Church, Mrs. Susan Decatur, widow of the great naval hero.[38] At that time Mrs. Decatur resided in a cottage near the college grounds.[39]

While the college was declining due to a lack of sufficient and capable educators, it was natural that the thoughts of many should turn toward the promising young scholastics who had been sent to Rome in 1820. They had been ordained and were anxiously awaited back in America. Father McElroy, as noted earlier, was among the loudest in his pleas that they be permitted to return, for they would "with those that are left . . . be the germ of the Society in this country."[40] He persuaded the venerable Father Kohlmann to intercede with the Father General of the Order. Their return passage money had been sent to defray their expenses, but apparently Father General did not feel that the time for their departure was yet at hand.[41] By the late months of 1827 rumors of the return began to gain cre-

---

[38] Entries of November 25, 1828, and December 31, 1828, in the *House Diary* record the baptism and First Communion of Mrs. Decatur. GUA, 57.1; Father McSherry to Father Ryder, December 26, 1828. Griffin Transcript, GUA, 143.11.

[39] "The Decatur Cottage," *The College Journal*, V (1877), 73f. The site is now, of course, part of the college grounds, forming part of the location of the present White-Gravenor building. Mrs. Decatur died June 21, 1861, and was buried in the old parish cemetery on the college grounds. In the Spring of 1953 the remains were removed to Holy Rood Cemetery in Georgetown.

[40] McElroy to Dzierozynski, September 29, 1827. MS WCA, 208 T 14.

[41] Kohlmann to McElroy, December 1, 1826. MS WCA, 207 F 2.

dence. To Father Kohlmann it seemed that the Father General was about "to do something very great for the American mission."[42] Kohlmann was convinced that divine providence had retarded the return of the young American Jesuits "with no other view than that of rendering it more useful in the execution of his holy designs."[43] From this same letter it appears that the delay had been caused from a desire on the part of the general that the young men be fully imbued with the spirit of the Society and its traditional procedures. Father Dubuisson, after completing his final year of the course in the Society, was sent to the Roman College to "spend with us about three months and as many at the Gesu to become acquainted with everything" before his return to America.[44]

Meanwhile, the young priests, too, anxiously awaited the order to sail for America. Rumors buoyed up their hopes, but there was nothing certain yet about their going to America, wrote Dubuisson on October 21, 1827, to Father George Fenwick, then at Reggio.[45] Father Thomas Mulledy, in the following July, wrote from Genoa to Father Dzierozynski at Georgetown that the Father General seemed determined to send three or four, it would seem, including Father Dubuisson, to America in the fall. Mulledy, himself, had been told—it would seem—unofficially, that he would be setting out for America. At

---

[42] Kohlmann to Father Thomas Mulledy (at Turin), October 11, 1827. MS GUA, 35.10.

[43] *Ibid.* Father Ryder was professor of theology in the Papal College of Spoleto. Father McSherry was for two or three years in the College of St. Francis of Paula in Turin as Minister. Father Young was prefect of schools and professor of theology at Tivoli College. Father Fenwick was assigned to Reggio di Modena, teaching everything from natural theology to grammar. Father Mulledy filled many important offices in Italy. *The Woodstock Letters*, XLIV (1915), 325. The writer in the *Letters* suggested that the Americans were employed in these duties "probably as an equitable payment of the expense of their studies." *Ibid.*

[44] *Ibid.*

[45] Dubuisson to Father George Fenwick, October 21, 1827. MS WCA, 208 S 1.

least on this occasion, he was a doubting Thomas. The same story had been repeated to him for three years successively. "You will pardon me," he wrote, "when I tell you that I hesitate a little to give implicit confidence to everything that is said with respect to our departure."[46]

Mulledy, to his great satisfaction, was wrong in refusing to believe the report. At last the "avant garde" of Fathers Mulledy, McSherry, and Young sailed from Leghorn on the good ship *Eugene* on October 3, 1828.[47] Father Kohlmann, whose interest in the American mission was always very great, was deeply disappointed that he was unable to see them off for America. He realized that they were "destined for a great work: the restoration of the Society in America."[48] The Father General of the Society also expressed his awareness of the hopes that were being placed in the young American Jesuits. Solemnly he declared that a great task was being given them, and that the eyes of many would be upon them.[49] The original foundation of the college is easily recalled as one reads the correspondence of this period. The realization that seized Carroll and his companions that they were inaugurating a great, important, and pioneer work is reflected forty years later in the consciousness of the young American Jesuits that they were to put new and badly needed energies into that great project. They were under no illusions regarding the expectations held out for them and they were equally anxious to begin the task.

---

[46] Father Thomas Mulledy to Father Francis Dzierozynski, July 8, 1828. MS GUA, 185.2.

[47] *House Diary*, entry for December 11, 1828. MS GUA, 56.1. Father Beschter, minister of the community at the time, mistakenly wrote October 30 as the day of departure.

[48] Kohlmann to Father William McSherry, S.J., September 13, 1828. MS WCA, 208 H 4b. On the same day he wrote to Father Dzierozynski, at Georgetown to announce the glad tidings. MS WCA, 208 H 4.

[49] Father General Aloysius Fortis, S.J., to Father Mulledy and Companions. September 20, 1828. MS WCA, 208 H 6a.

Father James Ryder, who was to return the next year, although as yet he did not know it, sent a familiar "bon voyage" letter to one of the fortunate ones, Father William McSherry. Ryder, "though with heavy heart," sincerely congratulated McSherry. His wish was that "the guardian angel of America" would waft him safely to his destiny, and so guide his conduct in the land of the future that the country might hold him as revered and the Society proudly boast of him as a worthy offspring. "Great hopes," he informed McSherry, "are entertained by all our friends regarding you and your companions."[50] He predicted that McSherry would be elevated to positions of authority[51] and presumed as a friend to offer "Mac" some advice:

> You know better than I, that the spirit of novelty is odious ever to the most sanctified American, and that far more good is to be done in America by reason and good example than by authority and force. Accordingly, all the true spirit of the Society you have imbibed in Italy, infuse into Ours, without letting it appear that it is imported from Italy, and be "to their virtues ever kind, and to their faults a little blind."[52]

He urged him vigorously "to endeavor to animate the studies of the scholastics by frequent academical exercises," and "for God's sake, banish the limping, half-formed courses, that here in Italy are so frequent from choice, and perhaps in America may have hitherto arisen from necessity."[53] In America, the feelings of Father Dzierozynski were the feelings of many.

---

[50] Father James Ryder, S.J., to Father William McSherry (from Spoleto), September 16, 1828. *The Woodstock Letters*, XLIV (1915), 323-325.

[51] His prediction was accurate. Father McSherry, after his return, was appointed minister of Georgetown College, socius to the visitor (Father Kenney) in 1830, first provincial of Maryland in 1833—then rector of Georgetown and again provincial.

[52] *The Woodstock Letters*, XLIV (1915), 324.

[53] *Ibid.* "You perhaps may smile," he added, "at my simplicity in supposing you immediately to be made chief of cooks and bottle-washers in America. Perhaps you may soon have to repent that my supposition is too true." *Ibid.*

"After so many perplexed years," he wrote, "hope begins to unfold."[54]

Years before Carroll had looked to Europe, to Liége and to Stonyhurst for the young, active replacements, the new blood he needed for the college. Liége and Stonyhurst, then engaged in their own rebuilding, could not supply the need. Georgetown had, through the years, to raise up its own. Again the college looked to Europe, awaiting their return.

It was, then, an important day in Georgetown's history when Father Dzierozynski received the following letter from New York:

> I write in a hurry to inform your Reverence that Fr. McSherry, Father Young and myself arrived last night in this port after a tedious passage of seventy-one days from Leghorn. We will be on as soon as the Brig arrives which has our things on board—for you must know that we left her thirty miles off Sandy Hook and fifty from this city where we were boarded by a news schooner and as the wind was dead ahead and we on a short allowance for some time the Captain advised us to embrace the occasion to go on board of her to the City where we arrived in ten days after we left the Brig.
>
> THOS. F. MULLEDY, S.J.[55]

On the night of December 22, 1828, they arrived at the college.[56] In the following year they were to be joined by three others who would add their names to Georgetown's history. In September, 1829, Fathers Ryder, Fenwick, and Dubuisson left Italy for New York. On the feast of the Immaculate Conception, December 8, 1829, they arrived at Georgetown, having sailed from Le Havre in late October.[57] Many echoed Father Nicholas

---

[54] Dzierozynski to McElroy, December 17, 1828. MS WCA, 208 G 8a.

[55] Mulledy to Dzierozynski, December 13, 1828. MS GUA, 185.2.

[56] Dzierozynski to McElroy, December 23, 1828. MS WCA, 208 G 8a.

[57] Dzierozynski to McElroy, December 9, 1829. MS WCA, 209 P 5a; Father Nicholas Sewall (in England) to Archbishop Whitfield, October 21, 1829. MS BCA, 23 A N1.

264 Georgetown University

Sewall's wish: "These," he wrote, "with those who went last year will, I hope, reestablish Georgetown."[58]

The long desired[59] replacements were soon appointed to important positions in the college. In January of 1829, Father Mulledy became prefect of studies and professor of philosophy, Father Young was given the class of rhetoric, and Father McSherry that of poetry.[60] On February 20, 1829, Father Beschter, since there was no hope of Father Feiner's recovery, was appointed vice rector and acting president.[61] On June 9, Father Feiner died and Father Beschter was named to head the college. He completed the year in this position, but before classes resumed in September of 1829 Father Mulledy was named president. When the second contingent of returning Americans arrived at the college, then, they found a former companion as rector and president of the college. They were being called to the task sooner than anticipated.

---

[58] Sewall to Whitfield, October 21, 1829. MS BCA, 23 A N1. Charles Constantine Pise, who had been a member of the scholastic band that sailed for Italy in 1820, left the Society of Jesus and returned to America. Ordained in 1825, he taught rhetoric at Mt. St. Mary's College. Later he was stationed at St. Patrick's, Washington, and while there was elected on December 11, 1832, Chaplain to the United States Senate—the only priest to hold that post. It would seem that his departure from the Society was due to financial reasons. He later sought reappointment to the post of chaplain to the Senate in order to assist him in supporting his mother and sister. Father Charles Constantine Pise to Archbishop Whitfield, November 25, 1833. MS BCA, 23 p. 11. He remained a devoted friend of his former companions. In 1845 when he published his *St. Ignatius and His First Companions* (New York: Edward Dunigan), he dedicated it to "The College of Georgetown, D.C. — My venerable Alma Mater—the Nurse of Letters, Science and Virtue, ever animated by the Spirit of Loyola, and the First Nine, this volume a trifling but very sincere token of gratitude is most respectfully and affectionately inscribed." The degree of Master of Arts was conferred on him at the commencement of 1830.

[59] See for example. Entry of December 22, 1828. *House Diary*, Georgetown College, MS GUA, 56.1.

[60] Entry of January 22, 1829. *Ibid.*

[61] Entry of February 20, 1829. *Ibid.*

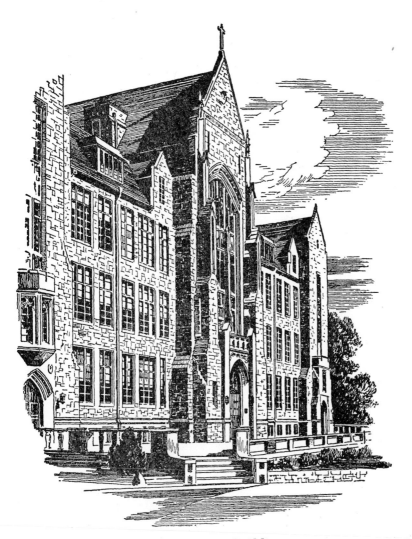

White-Gravenor Building

Shortly after taking office Father Mulledy issued a new prospectus of the college, which announced that day scholars would be admitted into the college upon payment of a fee of five dollars for fuel and servants.[62] In accordance with the decision given by the Reverend Father General in connection with the Washington Seminary, "no charge," it declared, "is made for tuition."[63] The president declared that it had been found necessary to establish certain regulations which would be strictly adhered to. The students must "be able to read and spell correctly." They must be "dressed genteelly in every respect," and "must come provided with the usual books belonging to the class."[64]

On November 9, 1829, the rector's entrance book recorded the admission into the college of Andrew Jackson Hutchings, grandnephew and ward of President Andrew Jackson.[65] The lad had been quite unruly and "Old Hickory" thought to tame him with the rather strict discipline of Georgetown.[66] His account was itemized according to the prospectus and, although he came furnished with a bed, he "brought no spoon."[67]

Father Mulledy began at once to improve the college with the aid of his companions from Italy. The course of studies was organized, and every opportunity was seized to make the

---

[62] Prospectus of October 1829. GUA, 62.11. The policy of accepting day students on such terms had been adopted also by Father Feiner but Father Mulledy furthered the plan more energetically and used it as well, apparently, to make the college better known. See *CJC*, p. 111.

[63] Prospectus of October, 1829. GUA, 62.11.

[64] *Ibid.*

[65] *Entrance Book of the Rector, Georgetown College, 1809-1858*, November 9, 1829. GUA, p. 46. *The Treasurer's Journal*—E records for April 1, 1830, an interesting juxtaposition: "Candy—12 cents. . . . Soda powders—37½ cents." GUA, p. 336.

[66] Marquis James, *The Life of Andrew Jackson* (New York: Garden City, 1938), p. 545. Young Andrew's college career at Georgetown, as at three other institutions, "was interrupted at the request of the faculty." *Ibid.*, pp. 577-597.

[67] Entry for November 9, 1829. *Rector's Entrance Book, 1809-1858.* GUA.

college known.[68] To the great satisfaction of the veteran priests of the mission, the college grew steadily in numbers and reputation. From England Father Nicholas Sewall wrote to the archbishop of Baltimore, James Whitfield, that it gave him great pleasure to hear of the revival of the college. With great accuracy he predicted that it was but the beginning of a greater era which would see not only the Atlantic provinces supplied with good preachers, but in time the Society would be sending "some zealous missioners to the Indians in your back country to form reductions among them as our Spanish Fathers did formerly in Paraguay."[69] And Father Dzierozynski proudly wrote to Father McElroy, then busily engaged himself in furthering St. John's Literary Institute in Frederick, Maryland, that the College of Georgetown numbered in July of 1830 one hundred and forty students, half of them boarders.[70]

At the beginning of his term Father Mulledy filled the office of prefect of studies as well as that of president, but with the increase in numbers he soon found it necessary to divide the functions.[71] Father William Grace, some of whose reports to the students we have seen, became prefect of studies. A very able faculty made his task an easier one. Besides the young Americans returned from Rome, he had the able assistance of Father Joseph Lopez as professor of Spanish, and Father Beschter as

---

[68] Father William F. Clarke, S.J., recalled that "the following September [1829] schools opened with 60 scholars, Father Tom Mulledy having been made Prest and drummed up scholars during vacations." J. Fairfax McLaughlin, *College Days at Georgetown* (Philadelphia: Lippincott, 1899), p. 144. Father Clark's reminiscences are contained in a letter to the author.

[69] Father Nicholas Sewall to Archbishop Whitfield, June 15, 1830. MS BCA, 23A, N2.

[70] Dzierozynski to McElroy, July 18, 1830. MS WCA, 209 M 6. Two other Georgetown names of the past expressed their gratification: Father John Grassi, S.J., and Bishop Benedict Fenwick, S.J. See Grassi, S.J., to McElroy, July 29, 1830. MS WCA, 209 M 9; Bishop Fenwick to Father George Fenwick, October 31, 1830. MS WCA, 209 K 22.

[71] Entry for September 14, 1829. *CJC*. GUA.

professor of German. Father Dzierozynski served on the theology faculty, and Father James Callaghan taught mathematics. Father James Gartland, with the assistance of the scholastics, James Deary and Thomas Lilly, taught humanities and Fathers James Van de Velde and James Lucas taught French.

The increase in the student body made possible the organization of extra-curricular activities. Father James Ryder, an eloquent preacher, initiated in 1830 the foremost of these, the Philodemic Society, already referred to. Patriotism was its keynote, the two principal occasions celebrated being Washington's Birthday and Independence Day. At the fourth meeting of the Society, when its name was chosen, a badge was likewise adopted. This emblem is a shield, the upper edge being in two curves. On one side is the American eagle, the shield of the Republic displayed upon its body, with a trident in one claw and the other resting upon a globe. Above the eagle is a harp surrounded by rays. On the reverse, Mercury—the god of eloquence—clasps the hand of the goddess Liberty, who holds in her left hand the rod surmounted by the cap. An inscription extending around the rim of both sides proclaims that the members of the Philodemic Society pledge the eloquence they hope to acquire to the service of freedom.[72]

On November 12, 1830, Father Peter Kenney announced his arrival in the United States as Visitor of the Mission of North America for the second time.[73] His previous visit in 1820 had been abruptly terminated because, among other reasons, he feared that he might be named bishop. Bishop DuBourg, then in St. Louis, had petitioned Rome that Father Kenney be named to the See of New York, and had requested Bishop Plessis of

[72] "Colit Societas Philodemica E Collegio Georgiopolitano—Eloquentiam Libertati Devinctam." *Minutes of the Philodemic Meetings*, September 25, 1830; January 18, 1831. GUA, 80.1. "The Philodemic Society," *The College Journal*, I (April, 1873), 50.

[73] Kenney to McElroy, November 12, 1830. MS WCA, 209 H 6.

Quebec to support the request. In Ireland, petitions had been made to have Father Kenney appointed to the coadjutorship of Kerry and the See of Dromore. After Bishop DuBourg had sent his petition, Archbishop Maréchal, it was reported, was making efforts to secure Father Kenney for the See of Philadelphia.[74] At the time of his departure, the Jesuits were likewise disappointed, for Father Kohlmann and his consultors had asked that Father Kenney be allowed to remain as superior of the mission of Maryland.[75] Had this request been granted, it is more than likely that Georgetown's history for the period 1820-1830 would have been vastly different. The problem of manpower would have vexed any superior, but Peter Kenney would have taken vigorous steps to provide some remedy for the situation.

On this second visit, Father Kenney's patent was that of Visitor with power of superior.[76] At first there was doubt whether he actually was superior, since Father Dzierozynski had not been informed that he was being superseded. Meeting with his consultors, Father Dzierozynski convinced them that this was the meaning of the patent and the appointment was so announced. Father Kenney was accordingly formally installed in his new charge at the community dinner of the college on November 14.[77]

By the time the Visitor had arrived at the college, the restoration under Father Mulledy had progressed very rapidly, and Father Kenney found little to change.[78] A new order of time, as noted earlier, for both the community and the students was introduced, and a definite schedule of holidays was drawn up. That Father Kenney was a man for detail, however, may be seen

[74] Garraghan, *Jesuits of the Middle United States*, Vol. 1, p. 313.
[75] *Ibid.*
[76] "Visitor cum potestate superioris." Kenney to McElroy, November 12, 1830. MS WCA, 209 H 6.
[77] Garraghan, *Jesuits of the Middle United States*, Vol 1, p. 313.
[78] Kenney to Mulledy, January 16, 1831. MS GUA, 185.4.

from the following letter written from Frederick a short time
after the visitation of Georgetown:

> I am quite pleased that you got an Italian cook; and if he be active,
> clever and economical he will be well worth what you promised
> him. If the smoke be kept out of the kitchen—Father Ryder will
> have every help to make the refectory rival the best that can be
> found in Italy. How does the new distribution of time work?[79]

It will be recalled that on the occasion of his former visitation in 1820, Father Kenney had rearranged the classes and
organized the curriculum with a view to "individual attention."
The teacher was to teach pupils and not classes. In 1831 Kenney
had not changed his opinion. Due to the great increase in the
student body, Father Mulledy had sought his advice on how
best to provide for the classes. Apparently the rector had proposed two plans, one of which seems to have involved an increase in the number of classes, while the other called for the
engaging of more teachers. Despite the financial difficulties of
the college, Father Kenney advised the latter course.[80]

Besides attracting students in large numbers to the college,
Father Mulledy and his more than able assistants maintained
rigorous academic standards. Composition continued to hold its
preferred position. There were weekly compositions in English,
weekly translations from Greek or Latin into English, and exercises or themes daily in Latin, Greek, and French. An hour and
a quarter each day was devoted to mathematics, and a total of
five hours of study was exacted as preparation for the recitations. The note in the prospectus of 1820 to the effect that mere
passing of time was not sufficient for advancement, was studiously put into practice. The rejection of several students for

---

[79] "I am happy to hear that the College is in such good order it can't be reformed,
and that there are 103 boarders." Father Beschter to Father George Fenwick,
February 21, 1831. MS WCA, 210 Z 8.

[80] Kenney to Mulledy, April 9, 1831. MS GUA, 185.1.

graduation served notice that this was not a mere catalogue threat. Each candidate for a diploma, besides completing successfully the prerequisite classical course, was required to pass an examination in moral and natural philosophy and the full course of mathematics.[81]

A present day feature of Catholic college life was introduced into the United States at Georgetown about this time. Father Fenwick had been deeply impressed by the devotions held in honor of the Blessed Virgin Mary at the Roman college during the month of May. He resolved, when appointed director of the sodality at Georgetown, to introduce this beautiful custom. May, 1830, marked the beginning of the Month of Mary in the United States.[82]

The uniforms which had attracted the attention of George Washington, were once again placed before the bar of presidential approval. On January 6, 1831, attired in full uniform, the students marched to the president's house. Andrew Jackson, we are told, in a brief speech praised their modesty, discipline, and studious character, and urged them to make their future lives worthy of their training.[83]

The new popularity of the college and the rapid increase in student enrollment soon necessitated the erection of additional buildings. This question, it will be recalled, had not arisen since the erection of the Old North building over thirty years earlier. At the close of the school year, 1831, Father Mulledy met with his consultors to consider the possibility of a new building to be joined to the east end of Old South.[84] The new structure was to contain the refectory, chapel, study hall, and living quarters for the boarders. A passage would connect the infirmary with

---

[81] Shea, *History of Georgetown University*, pp. 93-94. Shea is here quoting from an unidentified "paper of the day." *Ibid.*, p. 93.

[82] *Ibid.*, p. 94.

[83] *Ibid.*, p. 96.

[84] *Minutes of the Consultors' Meeting*, June 20, 1831.

the new building.[85] Any possible doubt about the need for the new building was removed on Christmas Day, 1831. A fire broke out in the clothes room near the students' dormitory and caused considerable damage before it was brought under control. The resulting cramped quarters emphasized the fact that the new building must be made the first consideration of college business.[86]

The project was delayed by a perennial problem of non-founded colleges. The new building was badly needed to house the increased enrollment, and the fees to be received for board and lodging would maintain the building; but what to do until the financial balance should be acquired? The building was needed for the students; but the students were needed for the building. Father Kenney summed up the situation for many when he wrote: "I feel greatly inclined to sanction the immediate erection of the new Building, but it is necessary to proceed with caution when there is question of $12,000."[87]

There was no question that twelve thousand dollars was little enough to pay for what they were going to receive. Much was due to the college in back fees—some nine thousand dollars; and Father Kenney felt that it would be very useful to consider how much of that nine thousand dollars had been collected since it was due in the preceding September.[88] He was more than a little inclined to have the ground-breaking as soon as possible. He was aware of the need; in fact, he offered to Father Mulledy for the use of the students the rooms at Georgetown set aside for himself and Father McSherry. Rather than deprive the students of suitable living quarters, Fathers Kenney

[85] Father Kenney wrote from St. Louis, December 11, 1831, that he was "very glad that the much wanted infirmary is covered in. I trust that it is strongly built." Kenney to Mulledy, December 11, 1831. MS GUA, 185.1.
[86] Shea, *History of Georgetown University*, p. 101.
[87] Kenney to Mulledy, February 29, 1832. MS GUA, 185.1.
[88] *Ibid.*

and McSherry would move to one of the farms.[89] The Visitor, however, was determined, prudently, not to act against the advice of the consultors, both his own and Father Mulledy's. He declared that if more than one of the consultors were to dissent, then the plan should be suspended until it could be judged whether their reasons would induce the permanent abandoning of the plan.[90]

After frequent exchanges of letters, by late June or early July of 1832 the decision was made that Mulledy might proceed with the building.[91] The original plan to build to the east of the old building was abandoned in favor of a site at the western end of the same building.[92] Now that the decision had been reached, Kenney was quite enthusiastic. The digging of the foundation was begun on July 9, and on the 13th he wrote to a fellow Jesuit in Dublin in glowing terms of Mulledy's achievement. There had been built in the last year, Kenney wrote, "a noble infirmary, four stories counting the basement which gives a fine kitchen."[93] The new building just begun would give "noble cellars on the basement, a refectory on the second, a study in the third, and a chapel with covered ceiling on the fourth story."[94] The over-all length of the building "including hall with the common staircase and the walls will be more than ninety feet long and this will leave the great apartments above seventy long in the clear."[95] The construction was expected to take a year, but by the following June Father

[89] Kenney to Mulledy, April 27, 1832. MS GUA, 185.1.
[90] Kenney to Mulledy, March 15, 1832. MS GUA, 185.4.
[91] To Father McElroy Kenney wrote that the "debt of the college of every description is $13,979.14. The Students in the house owed $10,200 and we have in the bank (in stock) $5,000 adding up to very cogent reasons for new building."
[92] Kenney to Mulledy, March 15, 1832. MS GUA, 185.4.
[93] Kenney to Rev. R. Haly, July 13, 1832. MS WCA, 210 P 4a.
[94] *Ibid.*
[95] *Ibid.*

Kenney was able to offer his congratulations to the president on "entering the new house a month ahead of what I expected."[96]

Father Mulledy's financial difficulties were relieved somewhat in 1834 by the presentation by Mrs. Susan Decatur of seven thousand dollars, prize money due to Admiral Decatur from the Tripolitan war, and which Congress had at last paid to his widow. Mrs. Decatur did not make an outright gift to the college. The stipulation was made that the college should pay her an annuity, while she lived, of six hundred and thirty dollars, or nine per cent. Mrs. Decatur did not die until 1860, so that she received from the college much more than double the original amount. The college was satisfied, however, for the money came at a time when it was desperately needed.[97] Its actual value to the college more than exceeded its face value.

In announcing his arrival in the United States to begin the visitation, Father Kenney had also informed Father McElroy that the mission would soon be erected into the status of a province. The year 1833, an important year in Georgetown's history, saw the fulfillment of this prediction. On August 28, 1832, the consultors of the college, as well as of the mission, met at Georgetown and agreed to petition the Father General that Maryland be erected into a province.[98] On June 4, 1833, Kenney wrote to Dzierozynski and his consultors that Father General had elevated the mission to the dignity of a province,

---

[96] Kenney to Mulledy, June 22, 1833. MS GUA, 185.4. The builders, Marden and Duffey, under the superintendence of Thomas Faye, appointed by the college, agreed to begin the work on July 3, 1832, and to complete it by June 15, 1833. They were faithful to their contract, almost to the day. MS GUA, 226.4.

[97] "The Decatur Cottage," *The College Journal*, V (April, 1877), 74. The college, it would seem, did not actually receive the money from Mrs. Decatur until 1837. The gift is the one apparently referred to in a letter of Father McSherry to Father McElroy of November 23, 1837, in which he writes: "Mrs. Decatur was to be here today to give the money to me." MS WCA, 212 T 7.

[98] Garraghan, *Jesuits of the Middle United States*, Vol. 1, p. 327. There had been a possibility that the mission would be erected into a vice province.

to be known as the Province of Maryland. Father William McSherry, who had not long before taken his solemn vows in Rome in the presence of the Very Reverend Father General Roothaan, was appointed the first provincial of the new province. Father McSherry was but thirty-four years of age. On July 8, 1833, the Georgetown community was ordered to assemble in the ascetory for the official announcement.[99] With thoughtful and touching consideration, Father Kenney sent the first notice of the actual day of appointment to Father Francis Neale, "the only survivor of . . . Liége in the Society."[100] "To you," wrote Kenney, "before any of the other members of the new province is due the intimation that at six o'clock this evening Father McSherry becomes its first provincial."[101] The joy of this made the years since 1773 seem few.

It was a tribute to Neale and it was Kenney's hope that the former might live long "to witness the fruits of a mission commenced two hundred years ago and of that zealous solicitude which [Neale] contributed to its survival and to the preservation of its property."[102] The honor to the mission followed close upon another conferred upon Georgetown. The Sacred Congregation *De Propaganda Fide* by a decree of March 30, 1833, conferred upon the college the power to grant degrees in philosophy and theology.[103] The mission and its college had come of age.

---

[99] *House Diary*, July 8, 1833. MS GUA, 86. See *Woodstock Letters*, LXII, 117; 309-348.

[100] Father Fidele de Grivel, S.J., to Father Nicholas Sewall, S.J., May 30, 1832. *Woodstock Letters*, X (1882), 247.

[101] Kenney to Francis Neale, July 8, 1833. MS WCA, 210 F 2.

[102] *Ibid.*

[103] In congratulating Fathers McSherry and Mulledy on "receiving the diploma for conferring degrees in theology," Kenney hoped that "no one will ever blame the College for facility in getting these degrees." He regretted that at one university they "issue B.A. and M.A.'s to people who can't conjugate *amo*." Kenney to McSherry, July 24, 1833. MS WCA, 210 F 8.

Georgetown in 1833 presented a prosperous picture. The new building added to the older ones formed a very respectable campus grouping. Henry Barnard on his visit found the "situation of the college . . . delightful." He could imagine nothing finer; and he added, rather unfortunately, "were it not for its Catholicism [the college] would be a very eligible situation for a youth from 12 to 17."[104]

---

[104] "The South Atlantic States in 1833, as Seen by a New Englander [Henry Barnard]," *Maryland Historical Magazine*, XIII (1918), 289-290.

CHAPTER XII

Georgetown:
Set for the Future

In the summer of 1833 when the opening of the new building, later to be called Mulledy Building, was fittingly celebrated by a "feast of green turtle served up in soup, besides chicken and steak, etc.,"[1] Georgetown presented a different picture than that which used to meet the eye of John Carroll. It was different but, though it would have delighted him, it would not have surprised him. He had exulted over the need to erect the north building, and had been ever confident that his beloved "academy" would continue to grow. One may well conjecture that at least he dreamed of the Georgetown campus as it exists today, dominated by the Healy Building. The statue of the founder which stands before it would not have entered the dream.

To the original modest structure of "sixty-three or sixty-four feet by fifty" had been added the "noble one" to the north. To these now had been added an infirmary building, and the "New Building" completed in that summer of 1833. On the western side of the pathway, between the south and north buildings, about where the Dahlgren Chapel now stands, had been erected

[1] Michael Delaney to Rev. J. Havens Richards, S.J., February 27, 1894. *The College Journal*, XXII (April, 1894) 130.

a small one-story building, used at various times as an infirmary for the Jesuit brothers, a house for lay workmen, and store-rooms, etc.[2] The grounds around the college had been beautified through the labors and beneficence of Brother Joseph West, S.J., to whom the college is indebted for the once famous walks.[3] Before recent building and improvements necessitated a change, "the Walks" extended for nearly a mile through the woods behind the college buildings.

Meantime, the school continued to prosper under the direction of Father Mulledy and the prosperity gave every indication of being permanent. The cholera epidemic which threatened so much of the United States in 1832, spared the college and the town had relatively few severe cases.[4] The town had but four hundred cases in all. In Washington there were two thousand people stricken with the dread disease.[5] Although no student at Georgetown was stricken, when the scholastic year of 1833 opened, many parents hesitated to enroll their sons for a year at college. Only fifty students appeared on the opening day, though the number was more than doubled by the first week in October

---

[2] Delaney to Father Richards, February 27, 1894, *op. cit.* This building stood in the midst of the grove of locust trees whose lowest branches served as racks for the roller towels used in the morning ablutions described earlier. See *supra*, p. 240.

[3] Shea, *History of Georgetown University*, pp. 98 ff. About this time, too, some consideration had been given to a possible purchase of the home of "Mr. Key" for a college villa. Presumably this was the Francis Scott Key house which stood on the present M Street near the aqueduct bridge. The prospect, though inviting, had to be abandoned due to the uncomfortable size of the college debt. Evans, *op. cit.*, p. 60; Kenney to Mulledy, October 23, 1832. MS GUA, 185.1.

[4] Shea, *History of Georgetown University*, p. 104. Special prayers were recited at Trinity Church, Visitation Convent, and at the college "to obtain a total preservation from the disease or a mitigation of its violence." Kenney to Archbishop Whitfield, August 20, 1832. MS BCA, 23A H3.

[5] Father Fidelis Grivel, S.J., to Father Nicholas Sewall, S.J., July 9, 1833. *The Woodstock Letters*, X (1882), 253. There were at this time an estimated two thousand, five hundred Catholics in George Town and four or five thousand in Washington. *Ibid.*

and continued to grow through the fall of 1833. By November, the total was one hundred and seventy.[6] The college had closed in the preceding summer with an enrollment of one hundred and forty-eight boarders and twelve half-boarders.[7]

The prosperity of the school and its sound organization were due in no small part to the labors of Father Peter Kenney who had twice come to America in the role of Visitor of the Maryland and Missouri missions. Georgetown's role in the future of the Society and of the Church in America, was appreciated fully by the Irish Jesuit, and he gave freely of advice and encouragement. To him in great part was due the decision to grant province status to the mission and that decision is a measure of the success and security attained by the province and its principal work, Georgetown College. In 1833, there were ninety members in the province of Maryland: thirty-eight priests, twenty scholastics and thirty-two coadjutor brothers. Of these, forty or almost half, were stationed at Georgetown.[8] With genuine sorrow and deep appreciation, the community at Georgetown bade farewell to Father Kenney on July 11, 1833. "Never," says the diary of the house, "has a man lived among us whom all without exception so loved and reverenced."[9] He had appreciated Georgetown and Georgetown had every reason to appreciate him. That Georgetown in 1833 could face the future more calmly was in no small part due to Father Kenney.

---

[6] Shea, *History of Georgetown University*, p. 104.

[7] Grivel to Sewall, July 9, 1833, *op. cit.* Bishop Fenwick, S.J., to Rev. G. Fenwick, S.J., August 1, 1833, MS WCA, 210 F 10.

[8] "The Jubilee of the Province," *The Woodstock Letters*, XII (1883), 205.

[9] *Ibid.* Father Peter Kenney, a native of Dublin entered the Society in 1804 at the age of twenty-five. He revived the ancient Irish Mission and was its first superior until he was appointed visitor of the American mission in 1819. On his return to Ireland in 1822 he was again appointed superior and in 1829 when the mission became a vice province, was appointed its first vice provincial. On his return to Ireland after his second visit to America he resumed the post of vice provincial, retaining the office until 1836. He died in Rome at the Gesu in 1841. *Ibid.*, p. 207.

In 1833, the financial situation was relieved somewhat by a generous grant from the Federal Government. As Congress had in 1832 made a grant of land to Columbian College,[10] in the District of Columbia, friends of Georgetown felt that the same liberality might well be accorded to the college. An act was introduced into the House granting twenty-five thousand dollars in city lots to Georgetown College. House Bill 651 was then reported back to the House by Mr. Thomas McKennan of Pennsylvania on January 2, 1833.[11] After being referred to the committee of the whole it was passed on February 26 by a vote of 97 to 84.[12] In the Senate it was to have more difficulty. Senator King of Alabama, who had two young relatives among the students at the college, voted against the bill. Senator Daniel Webster, although he was not present at the voting, spoke in favor of it as did John Tyler, of Virginia.[13] The bill passed the Senate by the narrow margin of fourteen to thirteen, and was sent to the president for his signature on March 2, 1833.[14] The deed for the property, however, was not finally executed by William Noland, Commissioner of Public Buildings, until February 20, 1837.[15]

A more important and more secure protection from financial difficulties came in the same year of 1833. When Father Mc-Sherry arrived from Rome with the decree naming the Mary-

---

[10] Now George Washington University.
[11] Shea, *History of Georgetown University*, p. 106.
[12] Entry, February 26, 1833. *House Diary, 1825-1872.* MS GUA, 57.1.
[13] Entry of March 1, 1833. *Ibid.*
[14] 22nd Congress Sess. II, Ch. 86, 1833. Statute II, March 2, 1833 (6 Stat. 538, 1833); *Journal of the Senate of the United States of America, December 3, 1832-March 2, 1833.* (Washington: Duff Green, 1832), pp. 228, 248. Those who voted in the affirmative were: "Messrs. Benton, Bibb, Chambers, Clay, Clayton, Didley, Ewing, Mangum, Poindexter, Robbins, Robinson, Seymour, Silsbee, Tyler." On the negative side were: "Messrs. Bell, Foot, Grundy, Hendricks, King, Moore, Naudain, Prentiss, Smith, Tipton, Tomlinson, White, Wright." *Ibid.*, p. 228.
[15] "Washington Lots" File, *Property File.* GUA.

land mission a province of the Society of Jesus, he brought also an ordination of the Father General permitting the colleges of the Society to receive tuition for scholars.[16] This problem of tuition for the day scholars, it will be recalled, had been acute since the days of the opening of the Washington Seminary. Father Kohlmann had been particularly vigorous in his representations to Rome, but repeated requests were of no avail. The general, Father Fortis, was not convinced that the situation was serious enough to warrant the request of such a broad dispensation from the rule. The Washington Seminary, as a result, had been forced to close in September of 1827. Three years later, when Father Kenney came to America on his visitation, he was instructed to see that the regulations of Father Fortis were strictly enforced. He reported that one of the arguments used by those in favor of a dispensation, namely that there was a prejudice in America against free-schools, did not exist, or, if it had ever existed, had vanished. He expressed his opinion that the existing legislation should not be changed.[17]

On his visit to St. Louis, Father Kenney found the Jesuits charging the day-scholars five dollars a year, "which," he wrote, "though a mere pittance is still real tuition-money."[18] He found (the year was 1832!) that this amount was in excess of the expenses incurred on the scholars' behalf if the teachers were left out of account.[19] The custom of charging five dollars for fuel, etc., as has been noted, had been adopted likewise at

---

[16] Kenney to Beschter, May 3, 1833. MS GUA, 62.12; Kenney to McElroy, April 14, 1833. The "Ordinatio de Minervali" is dated February 1, 1833. The document is preserved in the office of the Provincial of the Maryland Province, Baltimore, Md.

[17] Kenney to Roothaan, July 3, 1830. Archives of the Society of Jesus, Rome. Cited from Garraghan, *Jesuits of the Middle United States*, Vol. 1, p. 304.

[18] Kenney to Roothaan, April 25, 1832. *Ibid.* Kenney advised Father Roothaan, however, not to forbid the arrangement until he could study the situation more closely.

[19] *Ibid.*

Georgetown, particularly, for example, during the years of Father Feiner's presidency, when the number of boarders was extremely low. Father Mulledy's first prospectus of October, 1829, had contained the same provision.[20] The prospectus for 1831 did not mention day scholars, the decision having been made on August 19, "that in the future there shall be no day-scholars."[21] At this time, of course, it would have been next to impossible to receive them into the college, as the number of boarders was even then necessitating the construction of the "New Building."

The movement toward a relaxation of the Jesuit regulations with regard to pupils' fees, was initiated from outside the Society, and from St. Louis rather than from Washington which had been the first source of discussion over the matter. Bishop Rosati of St. Louis was eager to see a flourishing Catholic college grow up in his diocese, and it could hardly do so when the tuitions of five hundred students were necessary to pay the annual salary of a single professor. And, while the evidence had not been clear to Father Kenney, it was obvious to others that "Catholic parents were not rare who preferred to send their sons even to non-Catholic institutions rather than have them attend a free school with its alleged note of social inferiority."[22] Bishop Rosati, then, and not the members of the order, petitioned the Holy See for a dispensation from that point of the Jesuit rule which forbade them to receive money, or be in any other way recompensed for instructing the students. Early in January, 1833, the secretary of the Propaganda, Monsignor Castracane, requested an opinion from Father Roothaan, the Jesuit general, with respect to the petition. Father Roothaan's reply was to send to the secretary a copy of the letter he had

---

[20] *Prospectus, Georgetown College,* October, 1829. GUA, 62.11.
[21] Notation of August 19, 1831. *House Diary, 1825-1872.* MS GUA, 57.1.
[22] Garraghan, *Jesuits of the Middle United States,* Vol. 1, p. 306.

received from Bishop Rosati, containing a fuller explanation of the situation, and to request that his Holiness, Gregory XVI, declare what course, under the circumstances, the Society should follow.[23] The answer of the Holy Father was decisive. He granted the dispensation as being absolutely necessary in view of the circumstances, and he commissioned Father Roothaan to set down the terms under which it was to be applied. The grounds for the dispensation were those that had been originally alleged: inability of the Jesuit schools to support themselves without the tuition fees, and the prejudice, at least among some parents, against free schools.[24] Father General complied with his commission and drew up the practical directives for putting the concession into effect.

Father Roothaan's *Ordinatio de Minervali* which Father McSherry brought from Rome, contained the conditions under which the concession was to be used. It declared that the dispensation had been reluctantly accepted, and regretted that necessity had made it imperative. It enjoined that the tuition rates were to be fixed according to the norm of other such schools in the country by the provincial of the province, after the latter official had heard his consultors and the rector of the college; that poor boys were not to be turned away or in any way neglected through inability to pay; that lawsuits were not to be instituted in order to recover unpaid tuition fees; and that the income from the tuition fees was to be expended on the support of the Jesuit teachers, and on school equipment, including furniture and libraries. In the event that support for the Jesuit teachers was forthcoming from some other source, that source alone must be used, and the tuition fees wholly applied to the

---

[23] *Ibid.* Father Roothaan did not wish to ask directly for a dispensation, nor could he, "as he expressly declared, in virtue of the special vow taken by all professed members of the Society of Jesus according to which they are not to permit any mitigation of the rule in matters of poverty." *Ibid.,* pp. 306-307.

[24] *Ibid.*

school and its improvement.[25] Since the *Ordinatio* of 1833 the prejudice against free schools, except perhaps in rare cases, has disappeared from the American scene; but the financial position of Jesuit schools, not enjoying large endowments, still makes the tuition fee necessary as the ordinary means of support. The endowed or founded school, however, still continues to be the Jesuit ideal.[26]

Father Kenney's further study of the situation seems to have changed his opinion. He saw clearly the need for the dispensation and the arrival of the *Ordinatio*, he declared, would facilitate the progress of the Society "here [Philadelphia] and in all the great cities of the Union."[27]

While the dispensation made Georgetown's future more secure, it had very little immediate effect. The large number of boarders—in 1833, one hundred and forty-eight with twelve half-boarders—taxed the accomodations of the college to the full. In Washington, however, the project was begun in earnest to set up again the Washington Seminary, "in the same and very proper place, without any harm for Georgetown College."[28] The project succeeded, although the site was changed. The Washington Seminary became Gonzaga College, and later moved to its present location near the Capitol.

The rapid increase in enrollment during the presidency of Father Mulledy gave a new turn to the familiar pattern of expansion and consolidation. Applicants for admission were not too carefully screened, with the result that many were found whose presence outside the walls would have been more advan-

---

[25] R. P. Joannes Roothaan, S.J., "Ordinatio de Admittendo Minervali pro America Foederata," Romae, 1 Febr. 1833. Records of the Provincial, Maryland Province, Baltimore, Md.

[26] Garraghan, *History of the Society of Jesus*, Vol. 1, p. 308.

[27] Kenney to Beschter, May 3, 1833. MS GUA, 62.12.

[28] Father Grivel to Father N. Sewall, July 9, 1833. *The Woodstock Letters*, X (1882), 253.

tageous to the college than their being numbered among its elect. Father Stonestreet, himself a student and later president of Georgetown, was perhaps too severe in his judgment; but even if allowances were made for broad strokes of rhetoric, the picture remains one in which the need for discipline is very clear. "Even if we compare the present condition of Catholic youth," he wrote in 1854, "with what it was—say, fifteen or twenty years ago—those who have been in our college during this time, feel how much their manners and morals have improved."[29] Maternal education, he felt, had been almost entirely neglected in those days and as a result "little bears and fierce young tigers were sent down from the North and up from the South" to our college. Particularly in the case of the latter, they had "run wild to their college term among the slaves upon their fathers' farms."[30]

A more than unusual incident in 1833 highlighted the disciplinary problem. This was the so-called "great rebellion" of November, 1833, remembered in later years by one student, as being in the estimation of the students "as important as the great English one of 1641."[31] A party of the students in charge of Mr. Charles Lancaster had been taken to Washington to hear the debates in Congress. On the return walk, a student from Norfolk slipped from the entourage on more than one occasion to make hasty purchases at various taverns along the route.[32] Eventually these expeditions left their tell-tale mark and Mr. Lancaster reported the culprit to the president.[33] After a meeting of the consultors, the young man was expelled.[34] The student had been very popular among his classmates, and they resolved

---

[29] Stonestreet, "Georgetown College," op. cit., p. 1.
[30] Ibid.
[31] Reminiscences of John T. Doyle." The College Journal, XXIV (July, 1896), 116.
[32] Shea, History of Georgetown University, p. 105.
[33] Entry of November 2, 1833. House Diary 1825-1872. MS GUA, 57.1.
[34] Ibid.

to express their indignation in his behalf in violent fashion. Their odium was fastened on the young prefect, Mr. Lancaster, who had reported the infraction of the rules.

The conspirators arranged that when the students went to the recreation hall after dinner, the younger students should extinguish the lights, and the seniors, armed with sticks and stones, would rush Mr. Lancaster and punish him for degrading their hero. The conspiracy, unfortunately for the plotters, was not airtight. The president was informed and precautions were taken. At the appointed hour the juniors carried out their part of the scheme and extinguished the lights. The seniors rushed— not upon the young prefect as they had hoped—but into the brawny defence of a cordon of Jesuit brothers who had locked and guarded the door leading from the senior section of the recreation hall.[35] A second consultation resulted in the expulsion of twelve or thirteen more students.

This action was met by the students with a war of attrition. Some, we are told, attempted to burn down the house, others broke windows, smashed furniture, and ran riot in the dormitories and study hall.[36] The college authorities met the challenge and appeared ready to clear the college if necessary. Father Grivel, who believed that the "insurrection" had been caused because in the preceding year the college had "received every scoundrel," totaled the casualties at fifty boarders, forty of whom had been expelled, while the others decided to resign.[37] The college, he declared, lost no credit by its action[38] and the house diary gratefully noted that "amid all these dangers none

[35] *Ibid.*

[36] Entries of November 3, 4, 5, 1833. *Ibid.*

[37] Father Grivel, S.J., to Mr. Samuel Barber, S.J., June 22, 1834. MS WCA, 211 W 13. Mr. Barbelin's estimate of 80 is too high. Felix Barbelin, S.J., to Samuel Mulledy, S.J., April 22, 1834. MS WCA, 211 W 6.

[38] Father Grivel, S.J., to Father Wm. McSherry, S.J., January 21, 1834. MS WCA, 211 Z 4.

of the community suffered the slightest wound."[39] In the return
to normalcy the influence of Father George Fenwick was paramount. One of the young professors at the college at the time
termed him "the firmest pillar of study in Georgetown [and]
. . . more than ever a friend of all our boys."[40] New prefects
were named and peace again reigned. Among the new prefects
was Father James Ryder, future president of the college, whom
Bishop Fenwick, not long before, had described as a "right
down nice little fellow."[41]

While loud in his praise of Father Mulledy's learning and
executive ability, John Gilmary Shea has judged that the disciplinary problems would have been lessened had Father Mulledy
ruled the college with a sterner hand. The lack of discrimination
in taking into the school students who were unfitted for collegiate studies, undoubtedly was the main reason for problems
such as the ill-starred "insurrection," but Father Mulledy's
easy-going nature may have led some to believe that his good-
humored familiarity with them would preclude any use of
strict disciplinary sanction. Father Mulledy was a big, powerful, jovial man, and to Shea it seemed that "to him the respect
of the students seemed rather a matter to be gained by physical
strength, than the deference due to superiors, arising from
higher motives."[42] At least on one occasion, Father Kenney felt
called upon to exhort Mulledy to support and assist the professors with his authority.[43] That Father Mulledy did not distain
the physical is illustrated in the following anecdote:

> A story is told of President Mulledy while still a scholastic—a Jesuit
> is so known previous to ordination—which marks the temper of the

---

[39] Entry of November 3, 4, 5, 1833. *House Diary 1825-1872.* MS GUA, 57.1.
[40] Barbelin to S. Mulledy, April 22, 1834, *loc. cit.*
[41] Bishop Fenwick to Father George Fenwick, December 6, 1833. MS WCA, 210 C 4.
[42] Shea, *History of Georgetown University,* p. 117.
[43] Kennedy to Mulledy, November 2, 1832. MS GUA, 257.1.

man and the occasional roughness of the material he had to mould
to ways of peace and gentleness. While teaching class one day, a
burly backwoodsman, renowned for fistic prowess, defied his
authority, and proposed to throw him out of the window if he
insisted on it. It was a crisis, as all present knew and unless the
teacher could command it, his usefulness was gone. Mr. Mulledy,
without stopping the lesson, quietly sent to his President for permission to treat the defiance in his own way, and that obtained, tucked
up his soutane and gave battle to his refractory pupil, polishing him
off artistically, to the delight of his class. It is even said that he
completed the challenger's prescription by pitching him out of the
window, which for the story's sake, as the window was a low one,
one would like to believe. However this may be, it is safe to say that
that teacher's authority was not again questioned, nor was there a
more popular president. Boys do not dislike to see their teacher
abdicate his throne on occasion, and show himself of the same flesh
and blood as themselves.[44]

J. Fairfax McLaughlin, a student at Georgetown in the
1850's, was inclined to believe that in Father Mulledy "the
rough, turbulent element, of which in old times Georgetown
had more than its share, found . . . its master."[45] If Father Mulledy had been lax at other times he had not shown himself to be
so in November of 1833.

During Father Mulledy's term as president two men, whose
names recall Georgetown's pioneer days, passed to their reward.
At the Independence Day celebration of 1832 one of the toasts
offered was to: "Charles Carroll of Carrollton; the glorious
Nestor of American Independence; may his virtues ever shine
as a light to direct our footsteps, and his life be prolonged to be
a witness of their practice."[46] But in November of the same year,
in union with the country, Georgetown mourned the loss of the

[44] D. A. Casserly, "Georgetown College," *Scribner's Monthly*, XX (May, 1880-
October, 1880), 669.

[45] J. Fairfax McLaughlin, *College Days at Georgetown and Other Papers* (Philadelphia: J. B. Lippincott Company, 1899), p. 125.

[46] Shea, *History of Georgetown University*, p. 103.

cousin and schoolboy companion of its founder, and the last of
the signers of the Declaration of Independence. And in 1836 the
Father General of the Society of Jesus, John Roothaan, sent to
Father McElroy a letter, not completed, found among the papers of Father Anthony Kohlmann, S.J. He had died April 10,
1836. Fittingly, Father Roothaan added: "To him, beyond a
doubt, your America stands in debt."[47]

At the close of the school year, 1835, Father Mulledy whom
Father Grivel had described a year earlier as "worn out,"[48]
asked to be relieved of the presidency. Fathers Young, Ryder,
and Fenwick were considered for the post but eventually Father
Mulledy was asked to continue his very successful term as president.[49] In 1837 Father Mulledy's request was granted but not
in the way he desired. Father William McSherry, S.J., the first
provincial of the Maryland province, was named to succeed him
and Father Mulledy was appointed to the office vacated by
Father McSherry.

Father Mulledy had "given credit to the college."[50] A visitor
in 1832 had found that he and the other officers of the college
had devoted themselves "to the improvement and to the extension of the course of the collegiate studies"[51] in order to make
the instruction "as ample and various as it was in the most
celebrated Catholic colleges in Europe."[52] The increase in enrollment, as well as the rapid advancement of the students
evidenced at the recent commencement, "gave unequivocal testimony of their unwearied exertions and of their triumphant suc-

---

[47] Kohlmann to McElroy, February 1, 1836. MS WCA, 211 K 6. Father Roothaan's
notation: "Ipsi utique vestra America aliquid debet," is undated.

[48] Grivel to McSherry, January 21, 1834. MS WCA, 211 Z 4.

[49] McSherry to Dzierozynski, August 8, 1835. MS WCA, 211 N 4.

[50] Grivel to McSherry, January 21, 1834. MS WCA, 211 Z 4.

[51] "Sketch of the Jesuit Fathers of Georgetown College, D.C.," in the *Irish Shield*,
reprinted in *United States Catholic Intelligencer*, III (1832), 38.

[52] *Ibid.*

cess."[53] The older members of the province had anxiously awaited the return of the "young Americans" to restore the college and the province. The "young Americans," with Fathers McSherry and Mulledy in the lead had not disappointed them.

On Christmas Day, 1837, Father McSherry became the seventeenth president of Georgetown. In ill health at the time, his term was to be a short one. Towards the end of 1839, he was relieved of his office because of serious illness. He died on December 18, 1839.[54] One of his first acts as president had been to arrange for a fitting memorial service for one to whom Georgtown and the new province owed so much. On December 20, 1837, Father Francis Neale had died at St. Thomas Manor, Charles County, Maryland. Beginning in January, 1792, he had for many years been a professor in the college, often its vice president, and had held the office of president from December, 1810, to the end of September, 1812. On January 16, 1838, the students and faculty of the college attended a solemn requiem Mass offered for the repose of his soul by the Rt. Rev. Benedict Fenwick, Bishop of Boston, who had been a student at the college in Father Neale's time as professor.[55] The Mass was celebrated in Trinity Church, Georgetown, where Father Neale had been pastor for twenty years.

Although many years of fruitful endeavor still lay before him, no account of this period would be complete without some mention of Father George Fenwick, S.J. To him, in no small part, was due much of the success Georgetown enjoyed as it neared its fiftieth year. He must be numbered in any list of the

---

[53] *Ibid.*

[54] Father McSherry was born July 19, 1799, about six miles from Charlestown, West Virginia. He entered Georgetown College on November 6, 1813, and in 1815 joined the Society of Jesus. He had been one of the band of Americans sent to Rome for further training and had become the first provincial of the Maryland province on February 7, 1833.

[55] *House Diary, 1825-1872.* MS GUA, 57.1.

Copley Hall

most successful and beloved teachers at the college. With Father
Fenwick the story of the Maryland mission and Georgetown
seems to turn full cycle. Descended from one of the most prominent of the founders of Maryland, he was born in a house whose
site now forms part of the college grounds.[56] He was a student
in the college, which later was directed by two of his brothers.
Father Benedict Fenwick served as ninth and twelfth presidents
of Georgetown; Father Enoch Fenwick as its eleventh president. George followed them into the Society of Jesus and was,
as noted earlier, one of the "young Americans" sent to Rome.
On his return he was assigned to Georgetown, and until his
death in 1857 Father Fenwick was to hundreds of students
"Father Georgetown."[57]

Father Fenwick was ever aware of his own splendid heritage, which was that of Georgetown. He considered the example
of the New England Puritans in commemorating the settlement
at Plymouth to be a constant reproach to the sons of Catholic
Maryland, who allowed the anniversary of their own historic
beginning to pass unnoticed. He accordingly determined to
remedy the neglect. Using the Philodemic Society of the college
as a means of arousing enthusiasm, he eventually succeeded in

---

[56] Father Fenwick was a descendant of Cuthbert Fenwick, of Fenwick Manor on
the Patuxent River. Cuthbert Fenwick was in turn descended from the
Catholic Fenwicks of Fenwick Tower in Northumberland, England. Father
Fenwick was the youngest of four boys—three of whom entered the Society
of Jesus. Most Rev. M. J. Spalding, Archbishop of Baltimore; Rt. Rev.
Edward D. Fenwick, Bishop of Cincinnati; and Robert J. Brent, Attorney-
General of Maryland, were his cousins. See J. Fairfax McLaughlin, "Father
George Fenwick, S.J.," *The United States Catholic Historical Magazine*,
I (October, 1887), 4-5.

[57] "His character was that of the old Maryland and Virginia planter—solid,
hearty, frank and lovable; of easy and dignified manner among strangers,
he unbent with the playfulness of a boy among intimates." *Ibid.*, p. 4. He was
a thorough classical scholar, possessed a fine taste, and was widely acquainted
with English literature, besides being a thorough teacher and a wise director
of studies. *Ibid., passim.*

inaugurating an annual celebration of the landing of the Catholic Pilgrims. No pains were spared to make the first celebration a success. On May 9, 1842, the faculty and student body of the college, and a great number of guests, in all about two hundred persons, embarked on the steamboat *Columbia*.[58] A procession had been formed in the college yard, and with the band in front, the parade proceeded to the dock, "exciting," we are told, "the admiration of the citizens" of Georgetown.[59] The following morning the boat reached St. Inigoes, Maryland. A procession was formed to proceed to the old church of St. Inigoes, and high Mass was celebrated by the Most Reverend Archbishop of Baltimore, Samuel Eccleston. After Mass the procession formed again and the pilgrims marched to the *Columbia* "with banners floating."[60] They navigated up the river about three miles to the spot where the founders of Maryland "first planted the standard of civil and religious liberty."[61] A large crowd, estimated in the thousands, had assembled to join the college pilgrims. The principal address was delivered by William George Read of Baltimore, the Philodemic orator of the day.

The high spot of the ceremony came, however, with the singing of an ode composed for the occasion by George Washington Parke Custis, the adopted son of George Washington. Father Fenwick joined Mr. Custis in the singing of the ode to the air of "The Star Spangled Banner."[62] When the crowd insisted on an encore, Miss Carroll, a granddaughter of Charles Carroll of Carrollton, joined the singers. The significant coincidence was not lost on Custis. A few days after the celebration, he noted that when Miss Carroll joined the "Protestant citizen" and the "Catholic clergyman," the trio then consisted of "the

---

[58] Entry of May 9, 1842. *House Diary*, May, 1838 to August, 1852. MS GUA, 56.3.
[59] *Ibid.*
[60] *Ibid.*
[61] *Ibid.*
[62] McLaughlin, "Father George Fenwick," *op. cit.*, p. 10.

granddaughter of the venerable Carroll, a most respected ecclesiastic of one of the oldest families of olden days, located near to the interesting scene of the landing of the Pilgrims, and the last male survivor of Washington's domestic family, in the grayhaired person of his adopted son."[63] John Carroll would have been pleased to have been present at this American Catholic celebration of the coming of the *Ark* and the *Dove*.

There was no formal celebration of Georgetown's fiftieth year. The pioneers had labored to keep alive the college on which John Carroll had placed all his "hope of permanency and success to our H. Religion in the United States."[64] The foundation had been laid and it was for the present to build upon the past.

Succeeding decades of the nineteenth century were to see the opening of a Medical School and a Law School. The Graduate School would be expanded. The twentieth century would witness the foundation of a Dental School, a School of Nursing, a world renowned School of Foreign Service, and the shrinking of world distances in a new and modern era would call for an Institute of Languages and Linguistics. Advances in health research would later result in the formation of a more extensive Medical Center.

John Carroll's vision of the future of Georgetown University was clear when he wrote to Father Plowden in 1787 that the president must be a man ". . . experienced in the detail of government for such a place of education, and capable of embracing in his mind a general and indeed universal plan of studies, of which the academical institution is only a part."[65]

---

[63] George Washington Parke Custis to William George Read, May 13, 1842 in *Philodemic Addresses, 1831-1867*, GUA, p. 38.

[64] Carroll to Plowden, March 1, 1788. MS WCA, 202 B 17.

[65] Carroll to Plowden, January 22, 1787. MS WCA, 202 B 13.

1. Archival Material

Baltimore Cathedral Archives. A very rich source, particularly for the Carroll correspondence—to and from—as well as for that of Neale, Maréchal, and Whitfield.

Catholic University of America, Archives of the. The Stonyhurst Transcripts. Copies of Carroll-Plowden letters made for Msgr. Peter Guilday by Rev. J. Hungerford Pollen, S.J.

Georgetown University Archives. Particularly worthy of note are: First *Ledgers* of the College; List of the Students from 1791 to 1915 compiled from original records; Diary of John McElroy, S.J.; *Minutes of the Board of Directors 1797-1815;* Prospecti of the College; Carroll letters; Neale letters, Kenney letters, Grassi letters, originals and transcripts; *The Classical Journal,* a diary of the prefect of studies; the House Diaries.

Hall of Records, Annapolis, Maryland.

Irish Province, S.J., Archives of the. Letters from various members of the Maryland Province to Rev. Peter Kenney, S.J.

Society of Jesus, Rome, Archives of the. Some correspondence, but of particular note is the *Diario* of Rev. John Grassi, S.J.

University of Notre Dame, The Catholic Archives of America of the. The will of Archbishop Carroll; some Neale letters.

Woodstock College Archives. Here are now located the archives of the Maryland Province, S.J., as well as the archives of the college. Valuable for the correspondence of the members of the Society of Jesus. A remarkable number of letters were preserved. The most important collection is the Carroll to Plowden collection obtained from England by Rev. Thomas Hughes, S.J. The contract for the first building at Georgetown is also preserved here.

Decretum Erectionis Provinciae Marylandiae and the *Ordinatio de Minervali* of Very Rev. John Roothaan, S.J. These last two items are preserved in the office of the Father Provincial, Maryland Province, S.J., Baltimore.

2. Printed Sources

American Catholic Historical Society of Philadelphia, Records. Vol. I, 1884.

Annals of the Congress of the United States. Thirteenth Congress. Third Session, September 19, 1814-March 3, 1815. Washington: Gales and Seaton, 1854.

A Catalogue of the Officers and Students of Georgetown College, 1851-1852. Baltimore: John Murphy, 1852.

A Catalogue of the Officers and Students of Georgetown College, 1852-1853. Washington: Goggin and Coombs, 1853.

The College Journal. Vol. I, 1872—

Fish-Devitt Transcripts. *Propaganda Documents, Appointment of the First Bishop of Baltimore.* (From the Fish Transcripts of the originals translated into English by E. I. Devitt, S.J.) Reprint from the *Records of the American Catholic Historical Society of Philadelphia,* December, 1910.

Foley, S.J., Henry. *Records of the English Province of the Society of Jesus.* Vol. 5. London: Burns, Oates, 1883.

Griffin, Martin I. J. (ed.). *The American Catholic Historical Researches.* Vols. I (1884)-XXIX (1913). Philadelphia and Ridley Park, Pennsylvania.

Hughes, S.J., Thomas. *History of the Society of Jesus in North America, Colonial and Federal. Documents,* Vol. 1 Parts I and II. New York: Longmans, Green and Co., 1910.

Journal of the Senate of the United States of America: Being the Second Session of the Twenty-Second Congress, Begun and Held at the City of Washington, December 3, 1832. And in the Fifty-Seventh Year of the Independence of the Said United States. Washington: Duff Green, 1832.

Laity's Directory to the Church Service for the Year of Our Lord, M,DCCC,XXII. Revised and corrected by the Rev. John Power of New York. New York: Wm. H. Creagh, 1822.

Massachusetts Historical Society Proceedings, 1858-1860. Boston: 1860.

Oliver, Rev. Dr. George. *Collections towards Illustrating the Biography of the Scotch, English, and Irish Members of the Society of Jesus.* London: Charles Dolman, 1845.

Reports of Committees of the House of Representatives, at the Second Session of the Twenty-Second Congress, Begun and Held at the City of Washington, December 3, 1832. And in the Fifty-Seventh Year of the Independence of the United States. Washington: Duff Green, 1832.

Sommervogel, S.J., Carlos. *Bibliothèque de la Compagnie de Jésus.* Vols. I-X (1890-1909). Paris: Alphonse Picard, Libraire des Archives des Chartres.

The Woodstock Letters, 1872—. Woodstock College, Woodstock Maryland.

3. Books

Adams, Henry. *The Formative Years.* Condensed and edited by Herbert Agar. Vol. 1. Boston: Houghton Mifflin Co., 1947.

Bayard, Margaret. *The First Forty Years of Washington Society* (portrayed by the letters of Mrs. Samuel Harrison Smith). Edited by Gaillard Hunt. New York: Scribner's Sons, 1906.

Bowler, Sr. Mary Mariella. *A History of Catholic Colleges in the United States of America.* Washington, D.C.: Catholic University of America, 1933.

Brent, Daniel. *Biographical Sketch of the Most Rev. John Carroll.* Edited by John Carroll Brent. Baltimore: John Murphy, 1843.

Brown, Elmer Ellsworth. *The Making of Our Middle Schools.* New York: Longmans, Green and Co., 1903.

Bryan, Wilhelmus. *Bibliography of the District of Columbia.* Washington: Government Printing Office, 1900.

Burns, C.S.C., Rev. J. A. *The Principles, Origin and Establishment of the Catholic School System in the United States.* New York: Benziger, 1912.

——— *A History of Catholic Education in the United States.* New York: Benziger, 1937.

Burton, Edwin H. *The Life and Times of Bishop Challoner, 1691-1781.* London: Longmans, Green and Co., 1909.

Busey, Samuel C. *Pictures of the City of Washington in the Past.* Washington, D.C.: W. Ballantyne & Sons, 1898.

Carroll, John. *Eulogy on George Washington.* Delivered in St. Peter's Church, Baltimore, February 22, 1800, by John Carroll, First Bishop and Archbishop of Baltimore, with a foreword by Peter Guilday, Ph. D. New York: P. J. Kenedy & Sons, 1931.

Cassidy, Francis Patrick. *Catholic College Foundations and Development.* Washington: The Catholic University of America, 1924.

Clarke, R. *Lives of the Deceased Bishops of the Catholic Church in the United States.* New York: P. O'Shea, 1872.

Curti, Merle. *The Social Ideas of American Educators.* Chicago: C. Scribner's Sons, 1935.

De Courcy, Henry, and Shea, John G. *History of the Catholic Church in the United States.* New York: Kenedy Co., 1875.

Delano, Judah. *Washington Directory.* Washington: William Duncan, 1822.

Dexter, Edwin Grant. *A History of Education in the United States.* New York: The Macmillan Co., 1904.

Dignan, Rev. Patrick Joseph. *A History of the Legal Incorporation of Catholic Church Property in the United States, 1784-1932.* New York: P. J. Kenedy and Sons, 1935.

Dilhet, Jean. *État De L'Église Catholique ou Dioceses Des États—Unis de L'Amérique Septentrionale.* Translated by Rev. Patrick William Browne, S.T.D. Washington, D.C.: Catholic University of America, 1922.

Dole, Esther Mohr. *The American Revolution.* Privately printed, 1941.

Dunigan, S.J., David R. *A History of Boston College.* Milwaukee: The Bruce Publishing Co., 1947.

Easby-Smith, James S. *Georgetown University in the District of Columbia, 1789-1907.* 2 vols. New York: The Lewis Publishing Co., 1907.

Ecker, Grace Dunlop. *A Portrait of Old Georgetown.* Richmond: Dietz Press.

Ellis, John Tracy. *A Select Bibliography of the History of the Catholic Church in the United States.* New York: Declan X. McMullen Co., 1947.

Erbacher, O. F. M., Sebastian Anthony. *Catholic Higher Education for Men in the United States, 1850-1866.* Washington: Catholic University of America, 1931.

Eulogies and Funeral Discourses. (A bound volume of pamphlets in Georgetown University Library.)

Evans, Henry Ridgely. *Old Georgetown on the Potomac*. Washington, D.C.: 1933.

Fitzpatrick, John C. (ed.). *The Writings of George Washington*. Vol. 35 (March 30, 1796-July 31, 1797). Washington: Government Printing Office, 1940.

Fell, Sr. Marie Leonore. *The Foundations of Nativism in American Textbooks 1783-1860*. Washington, D.C.: Catholic University of America, 1941.

Finotti, Rev. Joseph M. *Bibliographia Catholica Americana*. New York: The Catholic Publication House, 1872.

Fitzpatrick, John C. (ed.). *The Diaries of George Washington, 1748-1799*. Vol 4, 1789-1799. Boston: Houghton Mifflin, 1925.

Force, Peter. *The National Calendar and Annals of the United States for MDCCCXXXII*. Vol. 10. Washington City: Peter Force, 1832.

Friant, John R., Rover, Thomas A., and Dahill, Jr., Edwin M. *Glimpses of Old Georgetown*. Washington: 1939.

Gahn, Bessie Wilmarth. *Georgetown and Colonial Days, Rock Creek to the Falls*. Silver Spring: Privately published, 1940.

Garraghan, S.J., Gilbert Joseph. *The Jesuits of the Middle United States*. 3 Vols. New York: America Press, 1938.

Geiger, Sr. Mary Virginia. *Daniel Carroll, Framer of the Constitution*. Washington: The Catholic University of America, 1943.

Gemmill, Jane W. *Six Years at the National Capital*. Philadelphia: Claxton and Co., 1884.

Gibson, Sr. Laurita. *Some Anglo-American Converts to Catholicism Prior to 1829*. Washington: The Catholic University of America, 1943.

Gillow, Joseph. *Bibliographical Dictionary of the English Catholics*. Vols. 1 and 2. London: Burns & Oates, 1885.

Godecker, Sr. M. Salena. *Rt. Rev. Simon William Bruté de Rémur*. Part II (Priestly Career in Maryland). Washington: The Catholic University of America, 1929.

Goebel, Rev. Edmund J. *A Study of Catholic Secondary Education During the Colonial Period up to the First Plenary Council of Baltimore, 1852*. New York: Benziger, 1937.

Gorman, Robert. *Catholic Apologetical Literature in United States, 1784-1858*. Washington: The Catholic University of America, 1939.

Greene, Evarts Boutell and Harrington, Virginia D. *American Population Before the Federal Census of 1790*. New York: Columbia University Press, 1932.

Greene, Evarts Boutell. *The Revolutionary Generation, 1763-1790*. New York: The Macmillan Co., 1943.

Griffin, Rev. Joseph A. *The Contribution of Belgium to the Catholic Church in America, 1523-1857*. Washington: The Catholic University of America, 1939.

Gruggen, S.J., George, and Keating, S.J., Joseph. *Stonyhurst, Its Past History and Life in the Present*. London, 1901.

Guilday, Rev. Peter. *The Catholic Church in Virginia, 1815-1822*. New York: The United States Catholic Historical Society, 1924.

—— *A History of the Councils of Baltimore, 1791-1884*. New York: The Macmillan Co., 1932.

—— *John Gilmary Shea, Father of American Catholic History, 1824-1892*. Reprinted from Records and Studies, July, 1926; New York: The United States Catholic Historical Society, 1926.

—— *The Life and Times of John Carroll*. 2 vols. New York: The Encyclopedia Press, 1922.

Hamilton, Stanislaus Murray (ed.). *Letters to Washington and Accompanying Papers*. Vol. 4, 1770-1774. New York: Houghton, Mifflin and Co., 1901.

Hansen, Marcus Lee. *The Atlantic Migration, 1607-1860*. Edited with a foreword by Arthur M. Schlesinger. Cambridge: Harvard University Press, 1940.

Herbermann, Charles G. *The Sulpicians in the United States*. New York: The Encyclopedia Press, 1916.

Hines, Christian. *Early Recollections of Washington City*. Washington: Chronicle Book and Job Print, 1866.

Hurd, Charles. *Washington Cavalcade*. New York: E. P. Dutton and Co., Inc., 1948.

Hughes, S.J., Thomas. *History of the Society of Jesus in North America*. New York: Longmans Green and Co., 1907.

Ives, J. Moss. *The Ark and the Dove*. New York: Longmans, 1936.

Jackson, Richard P. *Chronicles of Georgetown*. Washington: R. O. Polkinhorn, 1878.

Lockwood, Mary S. *Historic Homes in Washington: Its Noted Men and Women*. New York: Belford Co., 1889.

Mackall, Sally Somervell. *Early Days of Washington.* Washington: The Neale Co., 1899.

James, Marquis. *The Life of Andrew Jackson.* New York: Garden City Press, 1938.

Joachim, Jules. *Le Pere Antoine Kohlmann,* S.J. Paris: Editions "Alsatia," 1937.

Kingston, J. *The New American Biographic Dictionary,* or Memoirs of the Most Eminent Persons that have ever Lived in This or Any Other Nation. Baltimore: Warner and Hanna, 1810.

Lathrop, George Parsons and Lathrop, Rose Hawthorne. *A Story of Courage, Annals of the Georgetown Convent of the Visitation of the Blessed Virgin Mary.* Cambridge: Riverside Press, 1895.

Lochemes, Sr. M. Frederick. *Robert Walsh: His Story.* Washington: The Catholic University of America, 1941.

Lossing, Benson J. *Recollections and Private Memoirs of Washington by His Adopted Son, George Washington Parke Custis.* New York: Derby and Jackson, 1860.

Loth, David. *The People's General.* New York: Charles Scribner's Sons, 1951.

Lucey, S.J., William Leo. *Edward Kavanagh.* Francestown, New Hampshire: Marshall Jones Co., 1946.

McCormick, Leo Joseph. *Church-State Relationships in Education in Maryland.* Washington: The Catholic University of America, 1942.

Madden, Richard C. *Joseph Pierre Picot De Limoelan De Cloriviere, 1768-1826.* Washington: The Catholic University of America, 1938.

McDonald, S.S., Lloyd. *Seminary Movement in United States, 1784-1833.* Washington: The Catholic University of America, 1927.

McGucken, S.J., William J. *The Jesuits and Education.* Milwaukee: The Bruce Publishing Co., 1932.

McLaughlin, J. Fairfax. *College Days at Georgetown and Other Papers.* Philadelphia: J. B. Lippincott and Co., 1899.

Monaghan, Frank. *French Travellers in the United States, 1765-1932,* New York: New York Public Library, 1933.

Moore, Joseph West. *Picturesque Washington.* Providence: J. A. and R. A. Reid, 1884.

Morrison, A.D. (ed.). *The District in the XVIIIth Century* (As Described by the Earliest Travellers). Washington: Judd and Detweiler, Inc., 1909.

Nevils, S.J. Coleman. *Miniatures of Georgetown, 1634-1934.* Washington: Georgetown University Press, 1934.

Nielson, Peter Raymond. *Financial History of United States, 1811-1816.* Washington: Catholic University of America, 1926.

Parsons, Wilfrid. *Early Catholic Americana.* New York: Macmillan, 1939.

Pickell, John. *A New Chapter in the Early Life of Washington.* New York: D. Appleton & Co., 1856.

Pious Guide to Prayer and Devotion. Georgetown (Potowmack) : James Doyle, MDCCXCII.

Proctor, John Claggett. *Washington, Past and Present.* New York: Lewis Historical Publishing Co., 1930.

Ray, Sr. Mary Augustina. *American Opinion of Roman Catholicism in the Eighteenth Century.* New York: Columbia University Press, 1936.

Reuss, Francis X. *Biographical Cyclopedia of the Catholic Hierarchy of the United States, 1784-1898.* Milwaukee: M. H. Wiltzuis and Co., 1898.

Riordan, M. J. *Cathedral Records from the Beginning of Catholicity in Baltimore to the Present Time.* Baltimore: The Catholic Mirror Publishing Co., 1906.

Robertson, William Spence. *Iturbide of Mexico.* Durham, North Carolina: Duke University Press, 1952.

Rochefoucauld-Liancourt, Duc de La. *Travels Through The United States, etc., in the Years 1795-1797.* Translated by H. Neuman. Vol. 2, London, 1799.

Roemer, Theodore, O.F.M. Cap. *The Catholic Church in the United States.* St. Louis: Herder, 1950.

Rowland, Kate Mason. *Life and Correspondence of Charles Carroll of Carrollton.* New York: Putnam, 1898.

Royall, Anne. *Sketches of History, Life and Manners in the United States. By a Traveller.* New Haven, 1826.

Ruane, S.S., Joseph William. *The Beginnings of the Society of St. Sulpice in the United States (1791-1829).* Washington: The Catholic University of America, 1935.

Ruskowski, S.S., Leo F. *French Emigré Priests in the United States (1791-1815).* Washington: The Catholic University of America, 1940.

Scharf, J. Thomas. *Chronicles of Baltimore*. Baltimore: Turnbull Brothers, 1874.

Schwickerath, S.J., Robert. *Jesuit Education, Its History and Principles*. St. Louis: B. Herder, 1904.

A Short Account of the Establishment of the New See of Baltimore in Maryland and of the Consecration of the Rt. Revd. John Carroll Bishop Thereof on the Feast of the Assumption, 1790. London: John Coghlan, 1790.

Smith, Ellen Hart. *Charles Carroll of Carrollton*. Cambridge: Harvard University Press, 1942.

Spalding, M. J. *Sketches of the Life, Times, and Character of Rt. Rev. Bishop Joseph Flaget, First Bishop of Louisville*. Louisville: Webb & Levering, 1852.

Schauinger, Joseph Herman. *William Gaston, Carolinian*. Milwaukee: The Bruce Publishing Co., 1949.

Semmes, John E. *John Latrobe and His Times, 1803-1891*. Baltimore: Noonan Remington & Co., 1917.

Shea, John Gilmary. *History of the Catholic Church* (The Life and Times of the Most Rev. John Carroll [1888]), (From the Division of the Diocese of Baltimore, 1808, and Death of Archbishop Carroll, 1815, to the Fifth Provincial Council of Baltimore, 1843 [1890]). New York: J. G. Shea.

——— *History of Georgetown University*. New York: P. F. Collier, 1891.

Shearer, O.F.M., Donald C. *Pontificia Americana, A Documentary History of the Catholic Church in the United States, 1784-1884*. Washington: The Catholic University of America, 1933.

Smith, Margaret Bayard. *The First Forty Years of Washington Society*. Edited by Gaillard Hunt. New York: Charles Scribner's Sons, 1906.

Smith, John T. *The Catholic Church in New York 1808-1905*. 2 vols. New York: 1905.

Sperry, W. L. *Religion in America*. Cambridge: Harvard University Press, 1945.

Stonestreet, S.J., Rev. Charles A. *Discourse on the Rt. Revd. Benedict J. Fenwick, D.D.* Frederick: J. W. Boughman, 1846.

Stratemeier, George Boniface, *Thomas Cornwaleys, Commissioner and Counsellor of Maryland*. Washington: Catholic University Press, 1922.

Taggart, Hugh T. *Old Georgetown* (a reprint from the *Records of the Columbia Historical Society.* XI, 1908). Lancaster: New Era Printing Co., 1908.

The American Almanac and Repository of Useful Knowledge for the Year 1837. Boston: Charles Bowen, 1837.

Torbert, Alice Coyle. *Eleanor Calvert and Her Circle.* William Frederick Press: New York, 1950.

Townsend, Geo. Alfred. *Washington, Outside and Inside.* Hartford, Connecticut: J. Betts & Co., 1873.

Trappes-Lomax, Michael. *Bishop Challoner* (A Biographical Study derived from Dr. Edwin Burton's *The Life and Times of Bishop Challoner*). London: Longmans, Green and Co., 1936.

Treacy, Rev. Wm. P. *Old Catholic Maryland and Its Early Jesuit Missionaries.* Swedesboro, N.J.: published by author, 1889.

Varnum, Joseph B., Jr. *The Seat of Government of the United States.* Washington: R. Farnham, 1854.

Wallace, S.J., James. *A New Treatise on the Use of the Globes and Practical Astonomy.* New York: Smith and Forman, 1812.

Walsh, William Thomas. *Education of the Founding Fathers of the Republic.* New York: Fordham University, 1935.

Warden, D. B. *A Statistical, Political, and Historical Account of the United States of North America.* Edinburgh: Archibald Constable and Co., 1819.

——— *Description of the District of Columbia.* Paris: Smith, 1816.

Watterson, George. *A Picture of Washington.* Washington: William M. Morrison, 1840.

Weis, Frederick Lewis. *The Colonial Clergy of Maryland, Delaware and Georgia.* Lancaster, Mass.: privately published, 1950.

Wharton, Anne Hollingsworth. *Social Life in the Early Republic.* Philadelphia and London: J. B. Lippincott Co., 1903.

Windle, Mary J. *Life in Washington and Life Here and There.* Philadelphia: Lippincott, 1859.

Yeager, Sr. M. Hildegarde. *The Life of James Roosevelt Bayley, 1814-1877.* Washington: Catholic University of America, 1947.

4. Articles

Antony, C.M. "Lulworth Castle: Its History and Memories," *The Catholic Historical Review,* I, 243-257, October, 1915.

"Archbishop Maréchal's Account to Propaganda, October 16, 1818," *The Catholic Historical Review*, I, 439-453, January, 1916.

Barnard, Henry. "The South Atlantic States in 1833, as Seen by a New Englander," *The Maryland Historical Magazine*, XIII, 267-386, 1918.

Becket, John J. A. "Georgetown University," *The Cosmopolitan*. IX, 449-459, February, 1890.

"Biographical Sketches of Early Missionaries," *The Woodstock Letters*, XV, 154-168, 1886.

Brislen, O.S.F., Sr. M. Bernetta. "The Episcopacy of Leonard Neale," *Historical Records and Studies*. XXXIV. New York: The United States Catholic Historical Society, 1945.

Brook, James, "Maryland in 1773," *Maryland Historical Magazine*, II 354-362, December, 1907.

Burns, C.S.C., James A. "Early Jesuit Schools in Maryland," *Catholic University Bulletin*, XIII 361-381, July, 1907.

Campbell, Bernard U. "The Life and Times of Archbishop Carroll," *The United States Catholic Magazine*. V, 595-599; 676-682, November-December, 1846.

——— "Sketches of the Early Missions in Maryland," *United States Catholic Historical Magazine*. VII, 528-535; 580-586, October-November, 1848.

——— "The Most Rev. Leonard Neale," *The United States Catholic Magazine*. III, 505-512, 1844.

Campbell, S.J., Thomas. "The Beginnings of the Hierarchy in the United States," *Historical Records and Studies*, I, 251-277, 1899.

"Carroll's Relatio of March 1, 1785," *Catholic Historical Review*, VI, 244-246, April, 1920.

Casserly, D. A. "Georgetown College," *Scribner's Monthly*. XX, 665-675, September, 1880.

"Catalogus Sociorum Missionis Americae Foederatae, ineunte anno 1807" (reconstructed), *Woodstock Letters*, XVI 169-172, 1887.

"The Catholic Church in the United States," *The Catholic World*. XXIII, 434-452, July, 1876.

"The Catholic Seminary, Washington," *The Woodstock Letters*. XI, 91-93, 1882.

"Charles Carroll of Carrollton," *The Catholic World*. XXIII, 537-550, July, 1876.

Devitt, S.J., Edward I. "Bohemia," *Records of the American Catholic Historical Society*. XXIII, 97-139, June, 1913.

———— "A Dark Chapter in the Catholic History of Maryland," *United States Catholic Historical Magazine*. I, 121-149, April, 1887.

———— "The Suppression and Restoration of the Society in Maryland," *The Woodstock Letters*. XXXIV, 203-235, December, 1905.

Devitt, S.J., Edward I. "Georgetown in the Early Days," *Records of the Columbia Historical Society*, XII, 21-37, 1909.

———— "The Clergy List of 1819, Diocese of Baltimore," *Records of the American Catholic Historical Society of Philadelphia*, XXII, 238-267, December, 1911.

Downing, Margaret B. "Georgetown-on-the-Potowmack," *Historical Records and Studies*, XX, 158-165, 1931.

———— "The Catholic Church in the District of Columbia from Colonial Times until the Present," *Records of the Columbia Historical Society*, XV, 23-53, 1912.

———— "The Royal Road to the Capital," *Historical Records and Studies*, XVI, 54-65, May, 1924.

"Extracts from the Carroll Papers," *Maryland Historical Magazine*. X, 1915.

Fenwick, S.J., Rt. Rev. Benedict J. "Brief Account of the Settlement of Maryland with a Notice of St. Inigoes," *The Woodstock Letters*, IX, 167-180, 1880.

Garraghan, S.J., Gilbert J. "John Anthony Grassi, S.J., 1775-1849," *The Catholic Historical Review*, XXIII, 273-292, October, 1937.

Guilday, Rev. Peter. "The Priesthood of Colonial Maryland," *The Ecclesiastical Review*. Washington. January, 1934 (reprint).

Hicks, S.J., Leo. "The Foundation of the College of St. Omers," *Archivum Historicum* Anno XIX, Fasc. 37-38, 146-180, January-December, 1950.

Hughes, Rev. Thomas. "Educational Convoys to Europe in the Olden Times," *American Ecclesiastical Review*, XXIX, 24-39, 1903.

Hurley, S.J., Philip S. "Father Robert Molyneux, 1738-1808," *The Woodstock Letters*. LXVII, 271-292, 1938.

J.C.J. "Death of Rt. Rev. Dr. Fenwick," *The United States Catholic Magazine*. Edited by Rev. Charles I. White and Very Rev. M. J. Spalding, D.D. V, 506-509, September, 1846.

"Letters of Father Anthony Kohlmann, S.J.," *The Woodstock Letters*, V, 137-150, 1875.

Morgan, James Dudley. "First Mayor of Washington City," *Columbia Historical Society Review*, II, 236-251, 1899.

McElroy, John, S.J. "Reestablishment of the Society in the United States," *The Woodstock Letters*, XVI, 161-168, July, 1887.

McLaughlin, J. Fairfax. "Father George Fenwick, S.J.," *United States Catholic Historical Magazine*. I, 392-406, October, 1887.

———— "The Beginnings of Georgetown College," *The Catholic World*, XLVI, 610-619, February, 1888.

———— "William Gaston, the First Student of Georgetown College," *Records of the American Catholic Historical Society*. VI, 225-251, 1895.

McSweeney, LL.D., Edward F. "Judge William Gaston of North Carolina," *Historical Records and Studies*, XVII, 172-188, 1926.

"Narrative of the Establishment of the Catholic Religion in Maryland and Pennsylvania," *The Woodstock Letters*, IX, 157-167, 1880.

Parsons, S.J., J. Wilfred. "The Catholic Church in America, 1819," *The Catholic Historical Review*. V, 301-310, January, 1920.

———— "Rev. Anthony Kohlmann, S.J.," *The Catholic Historical Review*. IV, 38-51, April, 1918.

Plowden, S.J., Charles. "Account of the Destruction of the English Colleges at Bruges in 1773," *Records of the English Province of the Society of Jesus*. Edited by Henry Foley, S.J. V, 173-183, 1883.

Purcell, Richard J. "The Education of the Carrolls in Maryland," *Catholic Educational Review*, XXX, 586-597, 1932.

———— "Education and Irish Teachers in Maryland," *Catholic Educational Review*, XXXII, 143-153, 1934.

———— "John McElroy," *Dictionary of American Biography*, XII, 36-37, 1936.

———— "Leonard Neale," *Dictionary of American Biography*, XIII, 400-401, 1936.

Reardon, Timothy J. "A Century of Catholic Progress," *Historical Records and Studies*, XVI, 78-86, May, 1924.

"The Rise of Religious Liberty in the United States," *The Catholic World*. XXIII, 721-741, September, 1876.

Scisco, Louis D. "The Archives at Baltimore," *Historical Records and Studies*, XXI, 87-95, 1910.

"Selections from the Correspondence of the Deceased Mathew Carey, Writer, Printer, Publisher," *Records of the American Catholic Historical Society of Philadelphia*. XIII, 237-247, 1902.

Smith, F.S. Key. "A Sketch of Francis Scott Key, with a Glimpse of His Ancestors," *Records of the Columbia Historical Society*, XII, 71-88, 1909.

"Some Quaint Wills of Early Catholic Settlers in Maryland," *Records of the American Catholic Historical Society of Philadelphia*, XIII, 22-44, 1902.

Treacy, Rev. William P. "A Biographical Sketch of Father Robert Molyneux, S.J.," *American Catholic Quarterly Review*, XI, 140-153, 1886.

———— "Some Early Catholic Grammar Schools," *United States Catholic Historical Magazine*, I, 71-73. 1887.

Wheeler, Joseph T. "Reading Interests of Maryland Planters and Merchants, 1700-1776," *The Maryland Historical Magazine*, XXXVII, 26-41; 291-310, March, September, 1942.

"'Voyage of the Very Rev. Fr. John Grassi, S.J., from Russia to America. January, 1805-October, 1810." *The Woodstock Letters*. IV, 115-136, 1875.

Zwinge, S.J., Joseph. "The Novitiate in Maryland," *The Woodstock Letters*, XLIV, 1-14, 1915.

5. Newspapers

The American Gazeteer. Boston.
Centinel of Liberty and Georgetown Advertiser.
Georgetown Weekly Ledger.
The Maryland Journal and Baltimore Advertiser.
The National Gazette and Literary Register. Philadelphia.
National Intelligencer. Washington.
The Philadelphia Catholic Instructor.
United States Catholic Intelligencer. Boston.

6. Unpublished Material

Gerrity, Francis X. "Educational Institutions at Georgetown, 1810-1860." Unpublished paper, Georgetown University, 1945.

Szymczak, Thomas. "Contemporary Ideas on American Education, 1814-1840." Unpublished Master's thesis, Georgetown University, 1951.

INDEX

310 Georgetown University